GREAT CIVILIZATIONS OF ANCIENT AFRICA

◁▷◁▷◁▷◁▷◁▷◁▷◁▷◁▷◁▷◁▷◁▷◁▷◁▷◁▷◁▷◁▷◁▷
◁▷◁▷◁▷◁▷◁▷◁▷◁▷◁▷◁▷◁▷◁▷◁▷◁▷◁▷◁▷◁▷◁▷
◁▷◁▷◁▷◁▷◁▷◁▷◁▷◁▷◁▷◁▷◁▷◁▷◁▷◁▷◁▷◁▷
◁▷◁▷◁▷◁▷◁▷◁▷◁▷◁▷◁▷◁▷◁▷◁▷◁▷◁▷
◁▷◁▷◁▷◁▷◁▷◁▷◁▷◁▷◁▷◁▷◁▷◁▷

LESTER BROOKS

FOUR WINDS PRESS
NEW YORK

FOR REPRINT PERMISSION GRATEFUL ACKNOWLEDGMENT IS MADE TO:

Indiana University Press for "My Africa" by Michael Dei-Anang from POEMS FROM BLACK AFRICA, edited by Langston Hughes. Copyright © 1963 by Langston Hughes.

Oxford University Press for "Utendi wa Inkishafi" by Abdulla ben Nasir from SWAHILI POETRY. Copyright 1962.

Twayne Publishers, Inc. for selection from LIBRETTO FOR THE REPUBLIC OF LIBERIA by Melvin B. Tolson. Copyright 1953 by Melvin B. Tolson.

Walker & Company, Inc. for "Evaluation" and "Song of the Turtle" from ANTS WILL NOT EAT YOUR FINGERS, edited by Leonard Doob. Copyright © 1966 by Leonard Doob.

JACKET:

Ivory Pendant Mask from Benin, Nigeria, probably 16th century. Height, 7½ inches. British Museum.

916
B79

Designed by Lucy Bitzer
Maps by Irmgard Lochner

THANKS ARE DUE:

To the unknown bards who, through countless generations sang the sagas of great men and times in Africa's past;

To those travelers through the ages who visited Africa and set down their wondrous observations;

To the contemporary historians who have quickened interest in Africa with their research and fresh insights;

To those who kindly aided in this book: Mrs. Jean Hutson and her able associates at the Schomburg Collection, New York Public Library (especially for access to the William L. Hansberry papers); the Brooklyn Museum, N.Y.; Metropolitan Museum of Art, N.Y.; Philadelphia Museum of Art; the Museum of African Art, Washington, D.C.; the New Canaan, Conn., library and the Ferguson Library, Stamford, Conn. To Ernest R. Grigg, III, of the United States Mission to the United Nations, for reviewing the manuscript.

◁▷ ◁▷ ◁▷ ◁▷ ◁▷ ◁▷ ◁▷ ◁▷ ◁▷
CONTENTS
◁▷ ◁▷ ◁▷ ◁▷ ◁▷ ◁▷ ◁▷ ◁▷ ◁▷

AFRICA

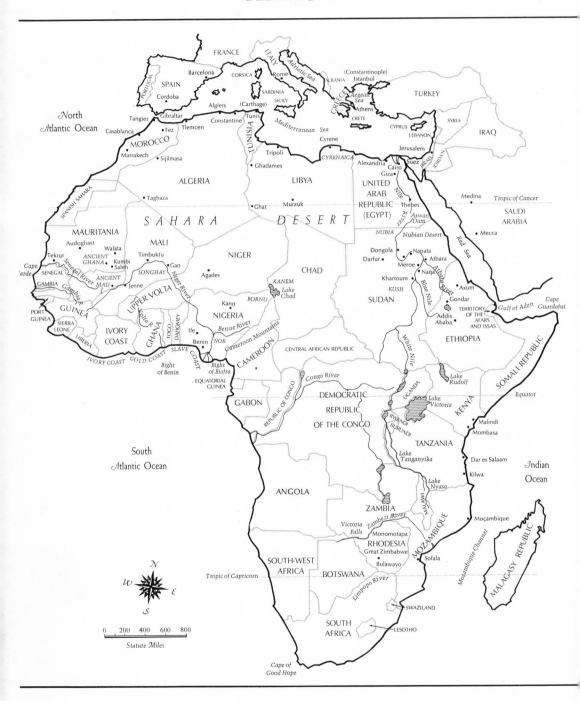

North
Atlantic Ocean

FRANCE
ITALY
SPAIN
PORTUGAL
Barcelona
CORSICA
Rome
Adriatic Sea
(Constantinople)
Istanbul
ALBANIA
GREECE
TURKEY
Cordoba
SARDINIA
Aegean Sea
Athens
SICILY
(Carthage)
CRETE
CYPRUS
SYRIA
IRAQ
Algiers
Tangier
Gibraltar
Constantine
Tunis
LEBANON
Casablanca
Tlemcen
Mediterranean Sea
Cyrene
Jerusalem
Fez
MOROCCO
Tripoli
CYRENAICA
Alexandria
Cairo
Suez
ISRAEL
JORDAN
Marrakech
Sijilmasa
Ghadames
Giza

SPANISH SAHARA
Taghaza
Ghat
Murzuk
ALGERIA
LIBYA
UNITED
ARAB
REPUBLIC
(EGYPT)
Thebes
Aswan
Dam
Medina
Tropic of Cancer
SAUDI
ARABIA

S A H A R A   D E S E R T
NUBIA
Nubian Desert
Mecca
Red Sea
MAURITANIA
Audoghast
Walata
MALI
Timbuktu
NIGER
CHAD
Dongola
Napata
Darfur
Meroe
Atbara
Axum
Nile River
Tekrur
ANCIENT
GHANA
Kumbi
Saleh
Gao
KUSH
Naqa
Khartoum
Gondar
Gulf of Aden
Cape
Guardafui
Cape
Verde
SENEGAL
Senegal River
SONGHAY
Agades
KANEM
Lake
Chad
SUDAN
Blue Nile
Addis
Ababa
TERRITORY
OF THE
AFARS
AND ISSAS
GAMBIA
Gambia R.
ANCIENT
MALI
Jenne
Niger River
BORNU
NIGERIA
White Nile
ETHIOPIA
PORT
GUINEA
GUINEA
UPPER VOLTA
Volta R.
Kano
Benue River
Cameroon Mountains
SIERRA
LEONE
IVORY
COAST
GHANA
TOGO
DAHOMEY
Ife
Benin
NOK
CENTRAL AFRICAN REPUBLIC
LIBERIA
IVORY COAST
GOLD COAST
SLAVE COAST
Bight
of Benin
Bight
of Biafra
CAMEROON
EQUATORIAL
GUINEA
Congo River
GABON
REPUBLIC OF CONGO
DEMOCRATIC
REPUBLIC
OF THE CONGO
UGANDA
Lake
Rudolf
KENYA
SOMALI REPUBLIC
Equator
Lake
Victoria
Malindi
Mombasa
RWANDI
BURUNDI
TANZANIA
Dar es Salaam
South
Atlantic Ocean
Lake
Tanganyika
Kilwa
Indian
Ocean
Lake
Nyasa
MALAWI
ANGOLA
ZAMBIA
Victoria
Falls
Zambezi River
Moçambique
MOZAMBIQUE
Monomotapa
RHODESIA
Great Zimbabwe
Sofala
Mozambique Channel
MALAGASY REPUBLIC
Bulawayo
Tropic of Capricorn
SOUTH-WEST
AFRICA
BOTSWANA
Limpopo River
SWAZILAND
SOUTH
AFRICA
LESOTHO
Cape of
Good Hope

N
W   E
S

0   200   400   600   800
Statute Miles

TRADE ROUTES

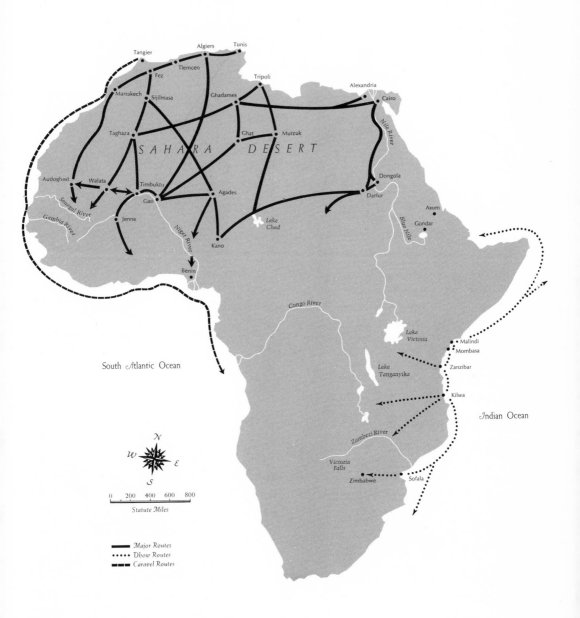

Tangier
Algiers
Tunis
Fez
Tlemcen
Marrakech
Sijilmasa
Ghadames
Tripoli
Alexandria
Cairo
Taghaza
Ghat
Murzuk
SAHARA DESERT
Nile River
Dongola
Audoghast
Walata
Timbuktu
Agades
Darfur
Axum
Gao
Jenne
Senegal River
Gambia River
Kano
Niger River
Lake Chad
Gondar
Blue Nile
Benin
Congo River
South *Atlantic* Ocean
Lake Victoria
Malindi
Mombasa
Lake Tanganyika
Zanzibar
Kilwa
Indian Ocean
Zambezi River
Victoria Falls
Zimbabwe
Sofala

N
W E
S

0 200 400 600 800
Statute Miles

━━━ *Major Routes*
•••• *Dhow Routes*
▬ ▬ ▬ *Caravel Routes*

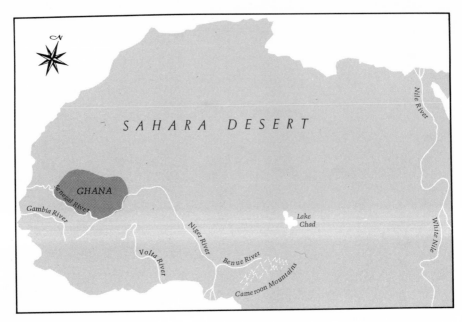

ANCIENT GHANA *(700-1200 A.D.)*

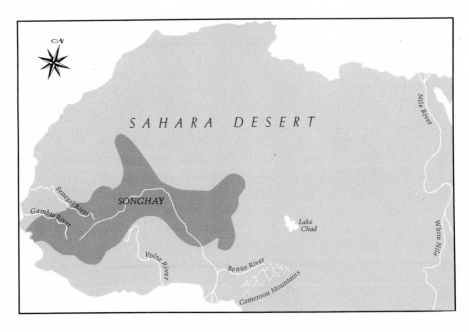

KANEM–BORNU *(800-1800 A.D.)*

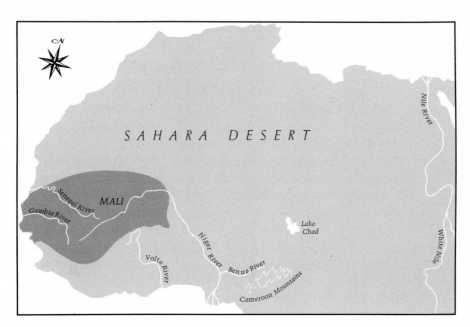

MALI *(1200-1500 A.D.)*

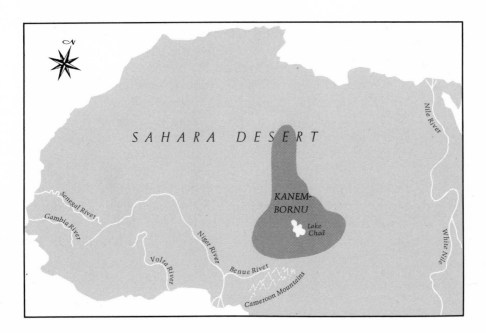

SONGHAY *(1350-1600 A.D.)*

◁▷ ◁▷ ◁▷ ◁▷ ◁▷ ◁▷ ◁▷

PREFACE

◁▷ ◁▷ ◁▷ ◁▷ ◁▷ ◁▷ ◁▷

Recent research for another book has taken me deep into the
literature of whites and blacks in this nation. It has been a
depressing investigation because the needle playing the record
seems to return invariably to the groove of the "inferiority" of
the Negro—as seen by white writers and scholars. The arguments
against ending slavery, the bitter denunciations of Emancipation,
the vilification of blacks and whites who favored Reconstruction
laws that would protect and aid the Negro—all of these are still
in the background, sometimes muted, sometimes leaping into
the present, even in today's supposedly advanced American
society. Almost two centuries of living with the Declaration of
Independence and the Bill of Rights have not yet convinced all
Americans of each citizen's rights and responsibilities.

Similarly, the sciences—sociology, anthropology, biology,
historiography, economics—and the arts (especially the communication arts of journalism and education) have failed to educate
many American citizens to the truth about the achievements of
black men. Because of this, we—each of us individually and

collectively—have suffered from the blight of white racism. In economic terms, this has stunted the growth of the nation and limited the achievements and aspirations of generations of black citizens to the detriment of all of us. In social terms, it has damaged the physical and mental health of millions, and has thwarted their efforts to live and to achieve their potential.

As recently as World War II and the period that followed it, respectable American writers were still speaking about Negroes as "a child race," without any heritage of civilization, accomplishment or understanding of the functions required to organize cities, states, federations, nations, armies and to administer justice, conduct trade, achieve heights of artistic expression and leave their mark on the world. Because such beliefs persist today it is important to pursue the distant past of black accomplishment in Africa. It is necessary to hold these achievements up to public view for the education of both black and white citizens. Thus, blacks will be able to appreciate their long and admirable heritage. And whites can and must learn that Africans achieved extraordinarily over long centuries and that their descendants can and will do so again.

We will rapidly review black achievements in a number of African settings. It should be clear, from the critical state of race relations in our nation today, that there is need for a new velocity and a new magnitude of activity in African studies to illuminate the twilight of Africa's past greatness. It is up to the current generation to dig further—literally and figuratively—to unravel the mysteries of the cultures we will glimpse here as well as others in the fabulous history of Mother Africa.

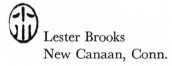 Lester Brooks
New Canaan, Conn.

So Geographers, in Afric maps,
With savage pictures fill their gaps,
And o'er unhabitable downs
Place elephants for want of towns.

JONATHAN SWIFT
On Poetry, a Rhapsody

Spain, France and Africa have moved the dawn of the human race back far beyond Archbishop Ussher's date. In fact, skulls found in Africa in the 1960's and dated by scientifically accurate techniques have carried the date of early man back to primitive beginnings around 1.75 million years ago!

Archbishop Ussher's neatly worked out theory of the Creation of earth and man collapsed as more and more irrefutable facts about the green years of the world and *homo sapiens* became known. A similar, well-deserved fate may be in store for the wide range of mistaken beliefs about Africa and the African peoples held by many of us today.

It is the purpose of this book to present, in survey form, information about *some* of the achievements of *some* of the peoples of Africa. Hopefully, this introduction will stimulate enough interest in the reader to cause him to read more about the fascinating backgrounds of the extraordinary peoples of Africa. Too long we have been enthralled by the clichés and the glib half-truths, some simple-minded and some sly, concerning the vast, ancient, varied and influential African continent. It is a land of extremes, of paradoxes, of grandeur, of staggering accomplishments and abysmal exploitation.

In most people's minds the picture of Africa is a clutter of images: the "dark continent," wall-to-wall jungle full of barking savages, many of them cannibals; "the white man's graveyard," Tarzan's playground; a perfect place to hunt exotic beasts, except for the torrid climate, murderous insects and snakes; a mecca for slow self-immolation by saintly missionaries; a land of witch-doctors, Mau-Maus, diamonds, throbbing drums and witless, naked, paint-daubed blacks always on the verge of battle; the stomping ground of an odd assortment such as Trader Horn, Frank Buck, Albert Schweitzer, Stanley and Livingstone,

Napoleon, Antony and Cleopatra, Moses, Joseph and so many Old Testament people, prophets and Pharaohs.

Few Americans are aware of the achievements of black people in Africa. Quite to the contrary, the prevailing view is that black Africans have been notably lacking in achievement. This concept is untrue. At a time in the United States when Negro Americans are beginning to enter the mainstream and their fellow Americans are conscious of them as never before, the mistaken belief that blacks were rootless savages in Africa has huge—and decidedly dangerous—implications.

It is a simple picture, easily grasped. But it is antiquated and racist, having its roots in the rationale worked out by the slavers and slave-trading nations to justify their terrible, inhuman commerce.

To deliver the "black savages" to the tender mercies of slave-keepers in the Americas was to "improve their lot," in this argument. Existing side by side with this rationale was a convenient alternative simply denying that the blacks were men and considering them members of a subhuman species who had never achieved anything in Africa and were incapable of learning in their new homeland. Bible citations were often (and still are) used to buttress the argument that the sons of Ham were condemned to be "hewers of wood, drawers of water," etc.

Counter-arguments citing African achievements have been relatively few. This is due largely to the fact that most of the history read by Americans has been written by Americans or Europeans, drawing on American or European sources. These histories often present an inadequate view of world history, relegating Africa and Asia to cursory, "roundup" chapters appended to the chronicle of European and American events, which is considered to be all-important.

It was not always so. In antiquity scholars wrote about Africa, and their works were widely circulated. Herodotus wrote of his travels into Egypt and Kush; Pliny the Elder included Africa in his *Natural History;* Diodorus Siculus reported on Ethiopia as well as Egypt in the first century B.C., Stephanus of Byzantium in the fifth century A.D. wrote about Ethiopia—"the earliest established country on earth. . . ." Both Pomponious Mela's and Strabo's geographies included the known lands of Africa. And in literature there were, among many works, the fourth century romance called *Aethiopica* by Heliodorus of Emesa and the later *Fall of Troy* by Quintus of Smyrna, both of which featured black heroes.

Figure 18

Closer to our own time, Charles Rollin in his *Historia Ancienne* (in 1730), James Cowles Prichard in the early nineteenth century, d'Olivet in his great *L'histoire Philosophique du Genere Humain* and Heeren, the eminent Gottingen historian, all studied, wrote and praised black African civilizations. And the explorers and on-site experts Cailliaud (in his *Voyage à Meroe*), the brilliant Champollion in his letters, and Hoskins in his *Travel In Ethiopia* confirmed and endorsed the views that Egyptian civilization stemmed from earlier black achievements and that the Egyptians themselves were Africans, not Asians.

For a good part of the twentieth century, however, interest in the early history and development of Africa has remained dormant, and until recent years there has not been any sizable school of African historians either in or out of Africa that has presented the African picture accurately. Nor, it might be pointed out, was there any considerable degree of enthusiasm for the whole subject by the American public or its school systems. Hopefully, there is a growing interest at this time. There should be, for Africa is both important and fascinating.

AFRICA IN MEN'S MINDS

Mother Africa has always been fabulous in myth, legend and history. It was to the Ethiopian highlands that the Greek gods went when they wished to relax and enjoy themselves. Along the Red Sea and Gulf of Aden was the Land of Punt, rich and exotic, to which one of the most famous expeditions of history was sent by the powerful queen-king of Egypt. Gold and copper came from the hills of Punt, and by 2500 B.C. ships of sixty oars were built here—a feat the Romans mastered some twenty-five hundred years later—for use in the Red Sea trade.

Meanwhile, south of Egypt grew a civilization called Kush or Meroe. Centered at a place called Napata, then moved to Meroe (both of them on or near the Nile), Kush rose to world prominence when it took over Egypt. The Kushites developed ironworking to a high art, and after the glory of Egypt was but a memory, Kush carried on, only to fall under the pressure of a competing culture, Axum. The Bible mentions Kush, referring to Bathsheba, David's wife, as a Kushite. And the Bible tells the story of the eunuch, a servant of Candace, queen of Kush (actually, "Candace" was the Kushite word for "queen") who was converted to Christianity.

Axum has evolved over the centuries into present-day Ethiopia, whose ruler is rich in storied titles. One of his honorifics is *Negusa Nagast*, which was the title of ancient Axum's ruler and was used by the king of the Habashan (from which word the corruption "Abyssinia" comes) people. Ethiopians believe him to be the direct descendant of the Queen of Sheba and her famous lover, King Solomon.

In the Dark Ages Europeans quivered to the legends of Prester John, the "priest-king" of a mighty African empire.

Prester John was expected to attack the pagan Moslems from the south as the Crusaders struck them with frontal assaults. The legend persisted into the sixteenth century and the Portuguese who explored the African coast thought several times that they had all but located the elusive but unfortunately mythical king.

One ruler who was thought to be a myth but who turned out to be real was the Monomotapa. Word of a "Benametapa" seeped out of Africa in the reports of Portuguese explorers. He did exist and ruled a large East African empire.

Another extraordinary person from Africa's past was the great Mansa Musa, ruler of medieval Mali. It was his spectacular trip to Mecca that made "Melle" and him famous, and made both names synonymous with gold.

Some places in Africa became renowned: Timbuktu was one; Nub—Nubia—the land of gold and slaves, was another. The "Mountains of the Moon" were cited in sagas and thought to be imaginary (apparently they are the slopes of the Ruwenzori Range, between Uganda and Congo, where flowering plants twenty feet tall grow on high moorlands).

Some secrets Africa kept. The Benin arts and culture in what is now Nigeria were discovered only in the nineteenth century although the traders and slavers had visited Benin for some two hundred years. Its cast bronze treasures were originally attributed (by Europeans unwilling to credit black men with such extraordinary achievements) to refugees from the Lost Continent of Atlantis or to European wanderers.

Nearby in antiquity was a culture called Nok, whose vigorous art was found only in this century, two to three thousand years after it was made.

And in Zimbabwe, inland in modern-day Rhodesia, the secrets of the Mashona died with them. Further north in East Africa were the Azanians, who terraced the mountains and fortified the hilltops and who have now vanished.

Some secrets are only now being dug out of the African past: In the caves and rock hills of the Sahara anthropologists have, within the last twenty-five years, begun serious study of the paintings and carvings left by the people who lived there when the desert was a fertile place. They are found along definite routes from Morocco to Timbuktu and in the area south of modern Libya to the Niger River. Herodotus in 500 B.C. wrote that the Guaramantes (Berbers) raided the "Ethiopians" (the Greek word for blacks) in the desert using horse-drawn chariots. Sure enough, pictures of the chariots are found in the cave-drawings of the Sahara. Further study of these will tell us much about conditions and commerce among these peoples.

Another enticing secret is that of the Iron Age town of Engaruka in East Africa—thousands of deserted, unexplained stone houses in the Rift Valley near the Kenya-Tanzania border.

And there are others. Secrets unexplained, sites unexplored, mysteries unsolved—Africa has them all. The major challenges include finding more historical, archeological and anthropological evidence about the great Sudanese cultures, about Meroe (Kush), Zimbabwe, Azania and the Nok to round out what is known and replace conjecture with fact. There are almost unlimited opportunities for solid research in Mother Africa's past, a past which she often does not reveal easily. Though the problems are, in some cases, formidable, the great potential is a stimulating, rather than overwhelming, challenge.

The body perishes, the heart stays young.
The platter wears away with serving food.
No log keeps its bark when it ages,
No lover sleeps while his rival weeps.

SONG OF THOSE GROWING OLD
Traditional Zulu verse

◁▷ ◁▷ ◁▷ ◁▷ ◁▷ ◁▷ ◁▷ ◁▷ ◁▷ ◁▷ ◁▷ ◁▷ ◁▷ ◁▷

MOTHER AFRICA

◁▷ ◁▷ ◁▷ ◁▷ ◁▷ ◁▷ ◁▷ ◁▷ ◁▷ ◁▷ ◁▷ ◁▷ ◁▷ ◁▷

I

THE EARLIEST HUMANS LIVED IN EAST AFRICA
about two million years ago. Two-legged, upright-walking creatures, of which man is one species, abounded in this region for
millions of years. In fact, fragments of one such relative of man
have been discovered on an island in Lake Victoria and found
to date back twenty-five million years!

The evidence turned up by the archeologists and anthropologists tends to confirm the broad framework of the Bible

story of the Garden of Eden: There was a fertile area with a benign climate in the region now known as Kenya, Uganda and Tanzania where man and many types of apes flourished and from which man migrated to Europe and Asia. The outward differences—color, hair, bone structure, musculature—evidently developed through the process of natural selection after that original emigration. Apparently, therefore, Africa was "the mother of us all," and so it seems that we are all "cousins," if not brothers.

The early men mentioned above were brought to world attention by the famous Kenyan archeologist Dr. L. S. B. Leakey who has made the study of man in Africa his life work. It was he who discovered the "ape" fragments on an island in Lake Victoria and named the creature *Proconsul*. He considers it an ancestor of man. The oldest known true ape remains come from Egypt, however, and are some forty million years old.

The Leakeys (professor, wife and son) have made many finds in this area. In the lowest layer of soil in Olduvai Gorge in Tanzania (which looks like a slightly smaller version of our Grand Canyon) they discovered the skull and remains of the oldest creatures who qualify as men, according to the definition "animals who make tools." Leakey named these creatures *Zinjanthropus*—the men of Zanj, the land of African legend. Another find has been assessed by scientific dating techniques as even older, and this creature Leakey calls pre-*Zinjanthropus* or *homo habilis*. He is known to be more than 1.75 million years old.

Figure 2

The Leakeys cleared some of the places where these men lived, and they deduced that these Early Stone Age beings used chipped-rock hand axes as tools, ate fruit, nuts, plants and occasional small animals. *Zinjanthropus* is known as "nutcracker man" because of his enormous teeth—especially his molars—

with their heavy coating of enamel, ideal for grinding vegetable matter to swallowable pulp.

Descendants of *Zinjanthropus* have been found in South Africa. At the southern tip of the continent in a crushed lime-stone cave, Australian Professor Raymond Dart discovered the remains of an 800,000–year-old man. He dubbed him *Australopithecus Africanus*, meaning "African southern ape," but *Figure 3* he is truly a man. He stood about four feet tall, his brain was slightly larger than his Olduvai great-grandfather's and he weighed about seventy pounds. His arms were shorter than apes' arms, his feet were flat, and instead of a tail he had a big rear end with a network of muscles allowing him to use his body in ways apes cannot. He was definitely earthbound and not a tree-dweller.

From more than six hundred found so far it is apparent that *Australopithecus* had developed into a meat eater—he no longer had the huge teeth of his nut-and-vegetable-chewing ancestor. And with him were found heavy bones probably used as clubs, plus the toothy jaws of other animals which he used as knives or saws.

Other ancient men have been found in parts of the world far removed from Africa. However, the oldest European man is a mere 360,000 years old; the Peking or Java man, *Pithecanthropus*, is about 400,000 years old. Anthropologists theorize that these may have been descendants of *Zinjanthropus*, and that East Africa may have been a passageway for migrants to Europe and Asia who followed the retreating glaciers as the Ice Age dwindled and released habitable lands from its frigid grip. During such periods hippopotami and crocodiles frolicked as far north as England's Thames River.

Throughout time there has been incessant moving about

of the peoples of Africa. Because of changes in climate, or floods, earthquakes and other natural occurrences, movement of game or discovery of new foods, or invasions, wars or pressure of other tribes, men in Africa have shifted about all over the continent. There was even a time when many tribes lived in what is now the Sahara. Before 1500 B.C. when it really dried up, the Sahara desert was laced with rivers, covered with grassland and alive with animals large and small. Men lived there and left their records in hundreds of caves, where they painted *Figure 1* and carved pictures in the rock—pictures of the giraffes, antelopes, elephants and other animals of the region.

Sometime before history began — pre-4000 B.C. — the major types of man found in Africa narrowed down to two: the so-called Negroid peoples (that is, the Bushmen and Hottentots), and the Hamites.

Scientists believe that today's Bushmen and Hottentots are the closest decendants of *Zinjanthropus* and *Australopithecus*. They have found remains of early Bushmen as far north as Tanzania and as far south as the Cape area. They argue, however, about whether the Bushmen originated in the north and moved south or vice versa. Physically, these people are generally short—about five feet tall, plus or minus an inch or two—have round, prominent foreheads, pointed chins, "peppercorn" hair, eye folds and light brown skin.

Where these Negroes came from is unclear. One theory says that they came to Africa from Asia; another has them originating in Africa. In any case, the oldest known skeletons with so-called Negroid characteristics come from near Khartoum in present-day Sudan and north of Timbuktu in Mali and date back to the Middle Stone Age.

MAN IN AFRICA

The next landmark in the evolution of man was the taming of
the food supply, the "discovery" of crops and the beginning of
agriculture. This was the New Stone Age and the people of the
Nile delta were among the world's first to plant and reap and
domesticate animals. Perhaps somewhat later the people of West
Africa, south of the Sahara, took to raising food crops, and those
of the East African highlands began developing animal-raising
agriculture.

The "taming" or regularization of the food supply was
truly a revolution in man's development. Among other things,
it made specialization possible. Some families were released from
the food hunt and could develop other needed specialties: tool-
making, shelter-building, potting, organizing the tribe, "medicine" and/or religion—the very fundamentals of civilization.

In the benign valley of the Nile men settled early,
developed fast, and matured a civilization that achieved monumental heights almost overnight, as the time of man is reckoned.
With the Egyptians comes the historic period, when the written
word tells us how the people lived.

South of the Sahara barrier, cultures also were developing.
There was contact with the peoples north of the desert via
overland trips by brave men raiding and trading in both directions. This was a period—up to 1000 B.C.—when sub-Sahara
Africa was, if anything, more advanced than Europe in cultural
development. Tribes were expanding, beginning to start nations.
Many tribes were nomads and destined to remain so. Most, if
not all, developed codes of ethics and discipline; many charted
complicated religions and philosophies of nature, life, and man's
fate. They set up both schemes of law and tribal, national

organization. They investigated the medicinal qualities of plants which, with magical accompaniment by their doctors, served as cures—or killers. And, so far as we know today, the phenomenon of metal mining and working originated among these Africans.

Anthropologists who study languages estimate that some verbal communication—beyond basic grunts—developed in Africa some five thousand years ago at the same time that agriculture and a settled, rather than nomadic, life became established. Today there are two thousand dialects and some six hundred languages in Africa. Were there more five thousand years ago? Probably. Today there are four main groups: the West and East Sudanic, the throat-clicking talk of the Boskops and Hottentots, and the Hamitic-Semitic in the north and northeast. Of course in the last thousand years Arabic has been absorbed into much of African speech. In East Africa, for example, ki-Swahili, a Bantu derivation of Arabic, is the most important tongue.

About the time of Christ, two technological advances occurred in this huge continent that changed the history of Africa and its people. One was the introduction of foods from India and/or Indonesia, especially the yam and banana, which made it possible to feed many more people much more easily. Thus the stage was set for the population explosion which took place in East Africa.

Second, the knowledge of how to produce iron tools and weapons came into this area, presumably from the north. With increased food and the means to plant and harvest it came the superior weapons with which conquest was simplified. As a result, the Bantu-speaking peoples dominated the entire east and southeast African region within a short time.

There were other factors that determined where and

how Africans lived. Perhaps the most important of these factors were those that were determined by the land itself. Mother Africa was not even-handed in her dealings with her children.

The Land

In a continent so vast, with practically every conceivable kind of terrain and climate except arctic, it is not surprising that some groups of men found extremely favorable living conditions, others managed to survive under extreme difficulties, and most settled for something between the two extremes. It could not be otherwise on this gargantuan land mass, three times the size of the United States and more, a continent so huge that even its minor features stagger our imaginations. All of Ireland could be dropped into Lake Victoria. The rainforests of the Congo alone are larger than France or Germany. The Great Rift Valley in East Africa—a jagged crack in the earth's crust similar to California's San Andreas Fault—stretches more than three thousand miles, from the Red Sea to the Zambezi River, and is generally about forty miles wide and some fifteen hundred feet below the ground level of the country it cuts through. Africa totals 11.5 million square miles and of these, 4.5 million are desert (the area of the U.S.A. is 3.5 million square miles).

The coastal portions of present-day Morocco, Algeria, Tunisia, eastern Libya and the very tip of South Africa have climates similar to those of Spain, Lebanon and other countries bordering the Mediterranean. But south of the narrow strip of green in North Africa there is a vast sea of sand stretching from the Atlantic to the Red Sea and extending some thirteen hundred miles north-south. From the southern edge of this desert barrier there is a wide belt of semi-desert grass land and savanna woodland, also from coast to coast. However, it also extends south along all of eastern, central and eastern South Africa. It is this area that used to be called the "bush"—"small bush"—as opposed to "big bush," which is dense tropical rain forest along the Guinea coast and the equator as far as the Great Rift Valley in East Africa.

The Mediterranean coast of Africa has always been hospitable to men, and here the Phoenicians, Greeks and Romans settled. The Sahara has become inhospitable to human life in the past four thousand years, turning from a green woodland teeming with game and fish to its present rocky, sandy bleakness. The Nile's waters are a narrow, leafy ribbon of exception to the severe sterility of the brown desert.

The sweeping steppe and savanna, or small bush land, below the Sahara ranges from slightly watered to heavy rainfall and from coarse grass to scattered short trees and light forests among which live the wild game for which Africa is so famous. In the big bush along the equator the rainfall is torrential, the humidity oppressive, the rain forests dense and nearly impenetrable and the soil has much of its plant food washed out. The animal life includes many birds, reptiles, insects, bacteria and worms and few mammals.

One of the major hazards to human settlement in large parts of Africa has been disease. In the tropical big bush area and in the savanna at low altitudes flourish insects that are carriers of such man- and beast-killers as malaria, yellow fever and sleeping sickness. The water so necessary for drinking also is commonly contaminated or contains worms. Even the soil itself contains parasites that maim or kill men and animals. This factor of disease and parasites has had important effects on African history. One insect alone, the tse-tse fly, has prevented agriculture from developing in much of the land between the latitudes ten degrees above and below the equator. Where the tse-tse lives, sleeping sickness kills large animals, including men, and makes impossible stock-raising or using animals to till the soil.

To generalize about climate, geography or indeed almost any condition in Africa is dangerous if not downright foolish. On the equator, within sight of its hottest, most humid jungles, are its tallest mountains, the Kilimanjaro, with year-round snow-covered peaks. And in one country, Kenya, the climate ranges from the mountain slopes to semi-desert to cool highlands and down to the sweating tropical coast of the Indian Ocean. Dry, almost desert stretches exist almost alongside the tropical rain forest in Ghana; the Nile valley is really a narrow oasis hundreds of miles long, squirming through desert sand.

In spite of vicious insects or inhospitable soil, sizzling heat or other hindrances, man not only survived in Africa—in many ways and in many places he flourished. It is these men, these African Negroes and their achievements that we will observe briefly in the next chapters. But first, we should examine one important point—race.

THE MEN OF AFRICA

What is (or was) an African Negro? The twentieth century people of Negro ancestry in Africa range from the shortest to the tallest men in the world. These are, respectively, the Negrillos or pygmies and the towering, aristocratic Nilotes. Many types of Negro stock are well known, such as the West Africans and Bantu-speaking groups of East and South Africa, but many types have yet to be studied. In general, authorities describe Negroid characteristics as: dark skin, wiry hair, broad nose, thick lips, rounded forehead, protruding upper jaw, less prominent chin, narrow skull and pelvis.

The second major group of men in Africa was and is the so-called Hamites. The name comes from the Bible—these are the supposed sons of Ham, Noah's second son, who was (according to Genesis 10) the ancestor of the nations of Kush (Ethiopia), Mizraim (Egypt), Punt and Canaan. In other words, the peoples of Palestine and the lands to the south were supposedly descendants of Ham.

As a racial description, "Hamites" is about as exact as "a country mile." Today the term is used to refer primarily to peoples who speak a "Hamitic language." In the past, it meant a branch of a "Mediterranean race" which included the Nubians, Bejas, Abyssinians, Gallas, Somalis, Masais and others, as distinct from a northern branch that included the Fulani and Berbers. Some scholars include the Hottentots, mainly on the grounds that their language qualifies them.

Among the physical characteristics of the Hamites these have been listed: brown people with frizzy hair; lean and sinewy; slender and muscular; thin, straight, even aquiline nose with delicate nostrils; thin lips and without prognathism (protruding upper jaw). Other authorities call them tall, dark or even black-skinned, with wavy hair and oval faces; dolichocephalic with long face and narrow nose (one authority cites this as a typically Negroid feature also), though some have a short face and still others have even shorter faces and more prominent noses.

There are opposing theories about the origins of the Hamites. One school says they came from North Africa and moved into the Middle East; the other view is that they came to Africa from Arabia across the Red Sea. In any case, the Hamitic languages are spoken now by one out of five Africans, and the label "Hamites" is pinned on the Berbers and Tuaregs of North Africa and the Egyptians, Gallas of Ethiopia and the Somalis of the Horn.

The mixing of these two stocks has gone on for thousands of years with no discernible negative results. As British anthropologist Sonia Cole puts it, "the Nilo-Hamites [of eastern Uganda, Kenya and Tanzania] are the result of crosses between Nilotic Negroes and Hamites. Their fine features and graceful build, their pride and independence, [have] won the admiration of many a pioneer traveler and devoted administrator." Such crossings, she says, have happened very frequently "with the result that every grade of skin color from light brown to black is found among them, as well as every kind of hair from slightly wavy to frizzy."

Who or what, indeed, is a Negro? The term itself endures. "Negro" comes from the Latin *niger* and is Spanish and Portuguese for the color black. It is a descriptive term. And it is so inexact as to be terribly confusing, if not useless. Evidence of this is abundant, whether we hark back to the "Moors" who were considered black (or Negro) by the Spaniards but were in fact mostly Berbers from North Africa and were brown. But in comparison to a Songhay warrior, a Spanish Berber Moor seems white—particularly to another Songhay.

Webster's Collegiate Dictionary (Fifth Edition) says "Negro" means:

1. A person of the typical African branch of the black race . . . inhabiting the Sudan, or loosely, of any of the black races of Africa, including, besides the Negroes proper, Bantus, Pygmies, Hottentots and Bushmen.   2. A black man; esp., a person having more or less Negro blood.

Encyclopaedia Brittannica (1956 Edition) adds to the confusion:

Negro, the designation of the distinctly dark-skinned, as opposed to the fair, yellow and brown races of mankind (from Lat. *niger,* black). In this sense it embraces the dark races of the intertropical and subtropical regions of the eastern hemisphere, from Senegambia, West Africa, to the Fijian Islands in the Pacific. . . .

And the *Random House Dictionary of the English Language* (1966) tells us that "Negro" means:

1. A member of the Negro race, esp. of Africa. 2. a person having some Negro ancestry, esp. one having dark skin pigmentation.

"The anthropological adjective," adds *Random House,* means,

3. of, pertaining to, or characteristic of the black race of mankind, esp. the indigenous peoples of Africa, generally characterized by brown to black pigmentation, broad flat nose, prognathism, everted [turned outwards] lips, and wooly or crisp hair.

In short, skin color is the single common factor cited in all definitions and it is the criterion most used by most people when they conclude that a man is a Negro or "black." We shall accept this criterion. Keep in mind, therefore, that the men of Africa described in this book were "black" men (unless otherwise stated), whether they were Egyptian, Bantu, Malian, Nubian, or Ethiopian. On the basis of their skin color alone, none of them would be allowed to marry a white woman in most segregationist holdout areas today. The laws and local customs would prevent it, strictly on the basis of race.

Let us see, then, what wonders black men achieved in ancient Africa.

Generations pass away and others stand in their place
  since the time of them that were of old....
Rejoice, and let thy heart forget that day when they shall
  lay thee to rest.
Cast all sorrow behind thee, and bethink thee of joy
  until there comes that day of reaching port in the
  land that loveth silence.... Lo, none
may take his goods with him, and none that hath
gone may come again.

SONG OF THE HARPER
(c. 1850 B.C.)[1]

◁▷ ◁▷ ◁▷ ◁▷ ◁▷ ◁▷ ◁▷ ◁▷ ◁▷ ◁▷ ◁▷ ◁▷

BLACK EGYPT

◁▷ ◁▷ ◁▷ ◁▷ ◁▷ ◁▷ ◁▷ ◁▷ ◁▷ ◁▷ ◁▷ ◁▷

II

Throughout the centuries no educated Western man has questioned the fact that Egypt was the homeland of a civilization that scaled almost incredible heights. We all know that Egyptians had a calendar of 365 days five thousand years ago, that they invented paper, had a written language and excelled in the arts—sculpture, architecture, painting and literature—more than four thousand years ago. We know something of their powerful kings from reports in the Bible, and we have seen proof of their achievements in museums, photographs and books.

Yet Egyptian civilization has been considered a thing apart from the continent which gave rise to it and which provided its greatest achievements. Located on the African continent, peopled by human beings with dark skin, ancient Egypt and its culture have never been thought of as the products of African genius.

But the facts, the records, the archeological evidence, Egyptian art and legends give us ample proof that they were. To begin at the beginning: Who were the people of ancient Egypt?

From the cemeteries dating back before 3200 B.C., anthropologists have identified remains they label "Europoid" (including those of Cro-Magnon types), "Negroid" and some Asian types, with the "Europoids" predominating in the north and the "Negroids" predominating in the south. As one expert puts it, "the races were fused on the banks of the Nile well before pharaonic civilization came into being."[2] These people were black by the operating definition of skin color as well as by the general physical characteristics they had then.

The Greeks were surprised twenty-five hundred years ago to discover that the Egyptians were the darkest skinned peoples of the so-called Near East. Typically, they were—and are today—not homogeneous. Their skin color ranges from red-black to yellow. Their hair is black and wavy, curly or woolly; their eyes are bright and black; their bodies are lean and muscular, generally tending to tallness. Egyptian noses usually are large and straight, but frequently aquiline; their jaws generally tend to thrust forward with fleshy lips, often curled back. We can say without the slightest hesitation that the ancient Egyptians would have been considered Negroes by American standards, and until the passage of the Civil Rights Act of 1964 not one of the Egyptian Pharaohs could have bought a cup of coffee in a white drug store in the Southern states of the U.S.A.

Africans and Egyptians

What African elements can be discovered in the extremely sophisticated civilization of Egypt? Among others, the complicated religious beliefs wherein tribalism, animism and taboos had extraordinary force—with special rites for the major activities such as planting, harvesting, fishing, hunting and war, in addition to the *rites du passage*—birth, marriage, death.

We think of African witch doctors with fantastic, colorful costumes. Look again at a formal portrait of a Pharaoh. Note that he wears an enormous headdress. From this "double crown" sprout the head of a vulture and the "fire-spitting" flared head of a female hooded cobra, supposedly capable of consuming rebels in flames. The Pharaoh was the son of the falcon-god, and was considered a falcon himself, endowed with magical powers and an all-seeing eye. From his waist hangs an animal tail; on his shaven chin he wears a false beard which is, itself, considered a god. In his hand he carries a scepter with the head of the god Seth atop it—recognizable in the curious curved snout, long, straight ears and almond-shaped eyes. In processions, banners are carried before the king. These banners bear the symbols of the many powerful brother gods who have blessed him and whose aid is his to command.

The Egyptians believed that their king was superhuman. As a god, he was irresistible on the battlefield and could slay

hundreds of enemies at a stroke all by himself. "His eyes scruti-
nize the depths of every being." Nothing is impossible for him:
"Everything which he ordains comes about." Because the whole
world depends on him, his health is all-important. At the end of
a period of his reign a jubilee festival is celebrated. At one stage
in Egyptian history this took place in the thirtieth year and was
repeated every few years. Some anthropologists see in this a dim
holdover of the tribal ritual in which an aged and enfeebled
chief is disposed of. In the Egyptian refinement, the king ritually
renews his vital force and succeeds himself, appropriately surrounded by representations of his fellow gods in statue form.

The god-king required complete and abject self-
humiliation of his subjects. A person approaching him threw
himself on the floor, "smelling the earth, crawling on the ground
. . . [and] invoking this Perfect God and exalting his beauty."
The king was empowered to give or take life: "He gives breath to
whomsoever he pleases." And, of course, he was responsible for
the annual Nile flood as well as all other weather phenomena. He
had many powers and much responsibility, but, as one Pharaoh,
Achthoes II, summed up to his son, "royalty is a good profession."

At harvest time the king had the duty of performing the
magic ceremony of protecting from serpents the cattle used in
threshing. And the butchering of the cattle was symbolic of the
destruction of the enemies of the god, to whom portions of the
beast were offered on the altar. The cow was worshipped in
Egypt, and not only as a source of food, but as the sky, the
celestial mother and wife of the sun. The cow-god Hathor,
"which is the sky," watched over the underworld of the dead and
nourished the Pharaoh with milk.

In the tombs, from the time of the New Kingdom, about
1580 B.C., when the Egyptian civilization had reached new

heights of power and sophistication, the "book of the dead" was an indispensable aid to the wealthy and royal deceased. Placed in the coffin or mummy wrappings, it was full of magic incantations and formulas with drawings to make them even more powerful, and to insure a happy afterlife. The texts helped the dead one kill serpents, crocodiles and human enemies. With them he could escape the net and triumph over obstacles. He might, if he followed the diagrams and incantations, turn himself into a god by means of a spell "transforming himself into whatever he likes." And he could slip by the guardians of the gates of the Underworld if he but remembered to call them by name in the prescribed manner. Other spells activated the many protective amulets and little "slave" figurines intended to serve the dead person in after-life. Some kept him from walking upside down (in which case his soul would have escaped him!); still others gave him various powers such as the ability to drive away locusts; another made it possible for him to return to view his earthly house; still a third was intended to prevent a second death.

To the present day, Africans in other parts of the conti-nent have traditions and beliefs similar and in some cases aston-ishingly close to those of the Egyptians. For example, the Egyptian concept of *ka*, often translated as a "double," or "vital energy," was comparable to the "vital force" which the Bantu, Ule and other African peoples even today find so impor-tant. The Egyptian believed the body was animated by a vital energy, a force which came into the world when he was born, accompanied him throughout his earthly life and, at death, went with him into the Underworld. In the tombs and chapels, the *ka* is an exact double of the living person, sometimes painted, sometimes sculpted. Variations of this general belief still exist among a number of African peoples, though they usually represent the "vital force" by a stylized, doll-sized sculpture or relic of the dead person placed in a shrine hut or tree. In addition to the *ka*, Egyptians believed in a soul, which they conceived as something in their vicinity, perhaps an animal, flower or bird. If this sounds confusing it is because it confused the Egyptians also. They could no more explain the exact differences between the *ka*, the soul, their shadow and their physical being than most Christians can delineate the fine shades of difference between the soul, the spirit, the Holy Ghost, God, Christ and physical man.

How could a civilization two thousand years old continue to have faith in such naive beliefs? The answer, though not a satisfactory one, perhaps, is that these beliefs seemed to serve the Egyptians as well in their day as our beliefs serve us today.

BACK TO THE STARTING POINT

As Egypt slowly emerged, the thing that made it different from Babylonia and the Indus River Valley of the same time was an African organizational idea. This concept was that of divine king-ship—an idea so familiar to us from Western history that we scarcely think of it as first emerging in Africa, but such was the case. While the city-states of Babylonia and Mohenjo-Daro were rich, well-fed, keeping written records and able to communicate among themselves, there was a major difference between them and their counterparts in Egypt. The Egyptian towns and cities were unified under one ruler, a god-king, and because of this unity their civilization was leaping forward while the Babylonians and Indians were squabbling among themselves, jockeying for power. Throughout African history in various parts of the conti-

nent this belief in a god who becomes man and king of the
nation occurs repeatedly. It exists among African peoples to this
day. And its effect on the history of the West is incalculable.

The antecedents of the Pharaoh idea are clear enough in
the tribal chieftain's role. His duties included using his magic,
or god-powers, to control weather and nature, to protect and
increase his people and their cattle and crops. Over the centuries
these functions were refined to the point that the Pharaoh was,
as a god, the source of justice, understanding and creativity in
the land.

Traditionally, the semi-historical founder of the Egyptian
I Dynasty, Menes or Narmer, is given credit for the first dam-
ming of the Nile to control the annual flood waters. What this
says, essentially, is that the Egyptians did not or could not
cooperate to effect this fundamental water control until political
organization and centralized government under one ruler made
it possible. The rapid advances in living standards and technology that resulted from this unification of the country and this
new-found communality may very well have seemed so spectacular as to appear miraculous and, therefore, evidence of the
supreme magic of the divine ruler Menes, the Pharaoh.

Another basic element in kingship, the regeneration that
occurs when one reign ends and another begins, is symbolically
treated in the Osiris myth. This myth is one that has overtones
reaching into the here and now of Christianity and back into
the unfathomable eternity of African tribal folklore. According
to the Egyptians, Osiris was god of the world of the dead.
He had in ancient times been a king who was killed and ritually
cut into pieces, but who arose from this to rule the Underworld.
It was Osiris' son Horus who, in the form of the Pharaoh, ruled
on earth. As each Pharaoh died, he "became" part of Osiris,

joining his ancestors in the Underworld. At the same moment, his son became the new Pharaoh-Horus and there was a "rebirth" in the land (as there is with any new administration, whether in Egypt or the U.S.A.). In the Osiris-Horus myth we should not overlook the parallel with the God-Christ relationship—each god giving his own son to rule over earthly beings and then returning to his father upon "death."

A prehistoric element in the Osiris myth, developed as noted above, is the African tribal practice of placing overwhelming responsibility on the shoulders of the divine chieftain. It is the chief's magic that qualifies him for his position. Thus, it is he who must produce game, domestic animals, fish and above all crops and the rain that brings the crops. If he fails, if his magic wanes, his fate, in some societies, was ceremonial death and ritual dismemberment, with possibly token tasting of his flesh or blood to infuse his people with his magic. Thus, though his people do not go to the Underworld and "become" him, by ritual partaking of his flesh or blood he does become part of them all and they "share" him and thus are part of a brotherhood unit. Parallels may be found in the practices of certain religions even today.

We have glanced briefly at some of the spiritual and supernatural aspects that are fundamental to both Egyptian and African cultures beyond Egypt's borders and have done so initially because such links are often ignored. The greatness of Egypt lies, we generally believe, in the astonishing quality and quantity of its history and artistic and cultural achievements, so let us turn to these. Because of the length and prodigious output of Egypt's ancient dynasties ours can be, at best, only a highly selective, hasty sampling.

Out of the Mists

Like some irregular furrow in the endless crust of Africa, Egypt was a country some six hundred miles long and about seven miles wide. Only in the delta area, the hundred miles nearest the sea, was it broader. Enclosed by the limestone cliffs and deserts on either side, the first cataract of the Nile on the south and the Mediterranean Sea on its north, this verdant land of some ten thousand square miles—about the size of Maryland— was in prehistory really two kingdoms. One was Lower Egypt, the Delta area, whose king wore a Red Crown. The second was Upper Egypt, whose king wore a White Crown. It was Menes (or Narmer), king of southern Egypt, who conquered the Delta and unified the country, thus founding the first dynasty about 3200 B.C.

Menes was a skillful politician as well, for instead of ruling harshly as a conqueror, he established his capital city, Memphis, at a convenient site on the border between Upper and Lower Egypt, combined the symbols of the Red and White lands: the cobra and papyrus of the north, the vulture and lotus of the south. Menes wore the "double crown" representing rule over both Upper and Lower Egypt. He adopted and promoted the customs and gods of the north while retaining those of the south; took over the harem, maintained two palaces, two granaries, tombs and other symbols of the independence of both regions. This duplication was continued for thirty centuries and until the very end the kings of Egypt called themselves the Lords of the Two Lands.

The next historical breakthrough came about 2700 B.C. with an advance so staggering that, to put it in modern terms, it was as incredible to the people of that time as sending a

*Here is King Narmer, supposedly the first
Pharaoh. He wears the crown of Lower Egypt,
carries a flail and an animal tail tied to his waist,
His attendants carry falcons and lotus. This is
from a stone carving dating back to about
3100* B.C.   COURTESY BELLEROPHON BOOKS.

mission to the moon and back is in our time. The achievements were those of a black king, Zoser, and his black grand vizier, Imhotep. Imhotep (meaning "he who comes in peace") was a man about whom many legends and myths, cults and rituals developed. He was the forerunner of what was later called the Renaissance Man, the man of accomplishment in many fields. Imhotep was, as vizier, the most powerful man in the land, second only to the god-king, the Pharaoh himself. But in addition to executing his official duties, he achieved fame as wise man, scribe, architect and physician. He became so famous and honored that soon he became a demigod of medicine and eventually was made a god (one of the handful of non-royal humans so honored) and to him were built shrines and temples in many parts of Egypt and Nubia. Even the Greeks worshipped him, calling him Imouthes, and identifying him with Aesklepios, their god of medicine.

This extraordinary being was born to human parents near Memphis. However, when he was made a god, his father was relegated to a position much like that of Joseph in the story of the birth of Jesus. Imhotep officially became the son of a mortal mother by the Egyptian god Ptah, the creator of the world and of men. The cult temples of Imhotep were popular places to which the afflicted of all ages flocked, just as in Greek times they went to the shrines of Aesklepios and in Christian times to miraculous shrines such as Lourdes. The great tradition of miraculous cures was earliest associated with Imhotep's temples, and innumerable messages testifying to his healing powers have been found. Also plentiful are small statuettes of the man in his role as god of medicine. Not only did his shrines attract the afflicted; by 500 B.C. they were medical "colleges," where students gathered to learn medical techniques and professors taught basic and sophisticated medical practices.

Imhotep is credited with originating proverbs by the bushel—many of them popular centuries later. He became the patron saint of Egypt's scribes, and it was customary to pour out a tiny bit of water from the writing kit (consisting of water jar, pen and papyrus scroll) as a way of invoking Imhotep's spirit before the scribe began writing. Perhaps no serious collection of Egyptian art in the world today lacks at least one statue dedicated to Imhotep, so plentiful were they in ancient times. He is seen seated, reading a scroll stretched across his knees.

With King Zoser and Imhotep, civilization took an enormous step forward. Imhotep cast aside the prevailing use of sun-dried brick for royal tombs and went all-out to construct the "house of eternity" for his king, Zoser, out of stone, a logical choice for a structure intended to last forever. (The Egyptians never did build structures for the living entirely out of stone—this material was reserved for temples and the abodes of the dead. This explains why stone palaces do not exist as relics of ancient dynasties.)

The Step Pyramid

The original design made for Zoser's tomb was a *mastaba*, a flat-topped rectangular stone mound thirty-eight feet high and measuring 227 feet by a length we are not sure of. Now the *mastaba* was a familiar form and previous kings had been put to eternal rest in such tombs made of brick. In fact, Zoser's father had a *mastaba* tomb. It was built of the traditional dried brick, but had one innovation, considered a huge advance at the time. In the tomb was one room built of stone, which measured ten by seventeen feet.

Somewhere in the process of building Zoser's tomb, Imhotep and his royal master changed their original plan. The *mastaba* concept was expanded, and the size of the base was enlarged to 352 by 296 feet. In the base and below it were constructed galleries, hallways, rooms, chapels and chambers for the king, his necessary furniture and the symbolic and ritual objects he would need in the afterlife. Then upon this base was built another smaller *mastaba* and upon it yet another, and on this one still another, and another until six of these solid stone plateaus had been placed one atop the other, reaching some 210 feet into the sky at Sakkara, outside Memphis.

Consider the leap here: from a chamber ten by seventeen feet to a mass of masonry 210 feet tall! Because each of the succeeding *mastabas* is smaller than the one on which it rests and is set back, the pyramid is called, aptly, the Step Pyramid. In addition *Figure 7* to this, Zoser and Imhotep constructed a wall surrounding a vast rectangular compound in the center of which was the pyramid itself. The wall was massive—thirty-eight feet high and more than a mile in perimeter. There were buildings and courts copied from the chambers of Zoser's palaces. There were chapels surrounding a Jubilee Court in which statues of the king looked out blindly on a marshalling of architectural and artisan intelligence and skill such as the world had never before seen.

The outside of the surrounding wall featured bastion after bastion, passing in silent rows for thousands of feet. Set into these vertical revetments were fourteen doorways in the same style— but only one of them opened, the rest were dummies. In the Jubilee Court, the various buildings were each duplicated (one set for Upper, the second for Lower Egypt) and represented the lightly constructed pavilions used for celebrations and for coronation ceremonies. Inside the pyramid in the myriad rooms were statues large and small of Zoser, panels showing him conducting ceremonies (including the traditional sprint on his Jubilee day), rooms full of literally thousands of vases, bottles and jars of the most precious stones, of exquisite workmanship, walls of glorious faïence tiles, some of them simulating the colored reed curtains of the king's palace. What the tomb might have contained of valuable metal work—gold, silver, bronze—we will never know, for tomb robbers took all such items.

Here then, thrusting out of the sand and dominating the landscape for miles around, just as it affected architecture and the crafts for centuries, was a masterpiece that galvanized the resources of a nation. The planning, organization, execution of this innovation made possible the architectural and artistic triumphs that followed—and rightfully earned Imhotep the awe in which he was held.

So indelible was Imhotep's impact on history that nearly three thousand years later, when the priests were about to rebuild a certain temple at Edfu they used his name to insure that the king would approve the plan. The building was a faithful reproduction, they told the Pharaoh, of the plan which "descended to Imhotep from heaven to the north of Memphis" in Zoser's time. Not surprisingly, Imhotep's words were also venerated. Considered sage, philosopher, aphorist, his words were heard in the songs of Egypt for millennia. It was fitting that a temple was built in his honor not far from Zoser's pyramid at Sakkara.

The Great Pyramid Builder

Next we come to one of the most well-known of all the Pharaohs, the king who achieved immortality by building the most immense monument of antiquity. He was Khufu, or Cheops, as Herodotus

wrote him down, the builder of the Great Pyramid at Giza. He *Figure 6*
was the second king of the IV Dynasty—ascending the throne
about 2650 B.C.

Herodotus, the Greek historian, visited Egypt some two
thousand years after Khufu's death and reported the legends
that existed about him. According to these reports, Khufu was
supposed to have shut down the temples and rounded up his
subjects, impressed them into forced labor gangs to work on his
huge tomb and even forced his daughter into prostitution to
help pay for the mammoth work. It was said that a hundred
thousand Egyptians slaved ten years to build the massive
structure.

Actually, little is known about Khufu and other kings of
this dynasty, and there is no proof for Herodotus' reports. On one
point there is rebuttal: No king could have enslaved so many of
Egypt's subjects at that stage in her development and put them to
work exclusively on a non-productive project such as building the
pyramid. No doubt tens of thousands of workers did labor on the
building for many years, but all the evidence indicates that they
worked on it when the crops had been harvested and they were
not needed for other agricultural or essential seasonal activities.
Far from acting like scourged slaves, the work gangs proudly
signed the huge stones they sweated over.

We have no portrait of Khufu, but from his tomb there are
portrait heads of members of his family. One of these, of a
princess, is serene, beautiful and has definitely Negroid facial
characteristics, leading to conjecture that Khufu also may have
had a similar appearance.

Statues of Khafre, Khufu's son or brother who succeeded
him as king, do exist. They show Khafre as a powerful, intense
and remote man with wide cheekbones, fore-thrust mouth and

jaw and long, broad nose. He built Giza's second pyramid and his sculptors built the Sphinx.

TRANSITION

Menkaure, the son of either King Khufu or Khafre, was one of the last of the IV Dynasty kings. His is the third pyramid at Giza. There are several statues of him in existence and he is shown as a powerfully-built, determined man with a wide, oval face, heavy-lidded, rounded eyes and large mouth.

By 2280 B.C., the Old Kingdom had come to an end and Egypt was racked with revolution, led by contending princes. One observer wailed:

... The King has been carried off by beggars. Behold, men without faith or law have come to despoil the land of its royalty ... the Palace has been devastated in the space of an hour ... the man who could not even afford a coffin now has a tomb ... the man who could not build himself a hovel is now the owner of a house. ... Behold the judges of the land have been driven across the country. Behold, the owners of wardrobes are now in rags. The man who never wove anything for himself now has fine linen. Behold the man who could not build a skiff for himself now owns several boats, while their former owner looks on; they no longer belong to him. Behold the man who could not even play the zither now possesses a harp ... the country turns like the potter's wheel. ... [4]

It took more than two hundred years for someone to emerge with sufficient strength to subdue the dissidents and reunite the country. This was King Mentuhotep I, founder of the XI

Dynasty, a member of the Antef family who lived far up the Nile, close to Nubia in Upper Egypt. With this black king began the Middle Kingdom, sometimes called the First Theban Empire, for he established the capital in that city. Apparently he ruled for some fifty years and was deified and worshipped in Thebes for a thousand years after. He was succeeded by two other Mentuhoteps who let the political situation deteriorate to the point that the grand vizier was finally forced to take over the government.

This usurper was Amenemhet I, founder of the XII Dynasty. It was written that he was:

. . . a commoner who had become governor of the South, [he] seized the throne for himself and founded the XII Dynasty. He was one of Egypt's ablest and most energetic rulers. Amenemhet's reign was supposed to have been prophesied many years before, according to a papyrus which states:

"A king shall come forth from the south called Amuny [a familiar form of the name Amenemhet] the son of a woman of *Figure 8* Nubia and born in Upper Egypt . . . He shall receive the White Crown and wear the Red Crown. . . . Be glad, ye people of his time! The son of a high-born man will make his name for all eternity. . . . There shall be built the 'Walls of the Prince' and the Asiatics shall not again be suffered to go down to Egypt. They shall beg again for water for their cattle after their custom. . . . And Righteousness shall come into its own again and Evil shall be cast out."
The broad face, high cheekbones and widely-spaced eyes . . . suggest his parentage and were inherited by the other kings of this dynasty, as was his brooding, introspective expression.[5]

Amenemhet brought order to a period of chaos and restored unified administration to the country, sending it off on a renewed period of achievement and regenerating its creative impulses. This was the beginning of the Middle Kingdom, about 2000 B.C. in which a flowering of art took place, great irrigation works were accomplished and military and trade expeditions went into Kush and probed the borders of the Middle East.

Amenemhet was assassinated in a palace plot and was succeeded by his son Sesostris I whose quick action foiled the plot and apparently quenched an incipient civil war. There were two other kings with this name during the XII Dynasty but the third king was the greatest. He stripped the provincial nobles of their power, conquered and annexed lower Nubia to the Second Cataract (the Nile has five cataracts between the Mediterranean and the junction of the White and Blue Niles at Khartoum, some two thousand miles upstream; these cataracts have served as natural dividing points and places to locate forts for some six thousand years), and consolidated Egypt's hold on Palestine and Syria. He, plus the other two Sesostris kings, became one in the memories of Egyptians, and were merged as the subject of sagas and hero-legends in which the Pharaoh was the most magnificent king Egypt ever had and the world had ever seen, one who conquered all the peoples of that time. No wonder he was deified and worshipped in Nubia. †

Through the years the land of the blacks—Nubia—became increasingly important to the kings of Egypt. First of all, it supplied goods that were in constant demand in the Nile

†Nubia was later called Kush. It was the region south of the Nile's First Cataract and sometimes known as Wawat, a land rich in gold.

To the east of Kush, extending along the Red Sea in what today is the coast of Sudan, Ethiopia and Somalia, was the land known to the ancients as Punt.

kingdom: ebony, ivory, skins and pelts of animals, ostrich plumes, gold and silver, gems and metals, the precious scents of myrrh, aromatic trees, fragrant resins and wood, all so scarce in Egypt. Second, Nubia was a prime source of manpower. The "people imports" were workers, slaves, soldiers, and even "dwarfs" (probably pygmies) who were highly prized for entertaining the nobles with dances and comical antics.

The expeditions by the Egyptians went further and more frequently into these once remote areas. Garrisons were established, then trading posts and towns; viceroys were installed, temples were built and Nubia, Kush and Punt became integrally important to the Egyptian empire.

After the XII Dynasty, Egypt again lapsed into confusion, contention and internal strife. This time is known as the Second Intermediate Period. One of those who seized power and ruled in the south was black. He tells us so himself in his cartouche, or signature, which bears the word *Nehesi* or Nubian. But besides this we know nothing more about him.

It was during this time that foreign invaders swept into Egypt, taking over the Nile kingdom. These Asiatic conquerors were called Hyksos by the Egyptians, and they held a major portion of the country for nearly two hundred years. Meanwhile, the royal family and many noble families had fled before the invaders, settling in the south. First one prince then another contended for power and soon any man strong enough to rally support made an attempt to seize control. The city of Thebes, five hundred miles south of the Mediterranean, rose to eminence as the home of the most powerful of these southern princes while the Hyksos remained in the north.

The Egyptians made every effort to build up their power, cementing bonds with nearby princes and potentates in the traditional way, by dynastic marriages between princely families. There is evidence of much intermarriage with Nubians in the next dynasty. Meanwhile, one family established its dominance over the Egyptians in exile and became overlords of the Egyptian princes, the vassal kings of the land beyond Hyksos dominion.

The Hyksos, or Asiatics, as the Egyptians also called them, were not blind to the growing strength of the Theban dynasty. At length the Hyksos ruler deliberately provoked a fight with the Theban king, Seqenenra, in an eccentric way. He sent an official delegation to Seqenenra with this extraordinary message:

> King Apepa sends to thee to say: Give orders that the hippopotamus-pool which is in the flowing spring of the city be abandoned; for they [the voices of the hippos] do not allow sleep to come to me either by day or by night; but their noise is in mine ear.[6]

Now it was apparent to the "Prince of the Southern City," as Seqenenra was called, that either King Apepa was blessed with superhuman hearing to be disturbed by hippos three hundred miles away, or that he was attempting to make a fool of Seqenenra, or to goad him to battle, for which the Egyptian was not yet ready. Though we cannot be certain of the first possibility, the latter two are indisputable, for we know that the battle began and that Seqenenra, along with unknown numbers of other Egyptians and Asiatics, was killed in the fighting.

The mummy of Seqenenra was discovered in 1881 and, when unwrapped, confirmed this. Sir Gaston Maspero, the great director-general of Egypt's Antiquities in the nineteenth century, in a typical bit of archeological detective work, deduced this from the mummy:

> Two or three men, whether assassins or soldiers, must have surrounded
> and despatched him before help was available. A blow from
> an axe must have severed part of his left cheek, exposed the
> teeth, fractured the jaw and sent him senseless to the ground;
> another blow must have seriously injured the skull, and a
> dagger or javelin has cut open the forehead on the right side,
> a little above the eye. His body must have remained lying
> where it fell for some time. When found, decomposition had
> set in, and the embalming had to be hastily performed as best
> it might.[7]

Seqenenra's successor was King Kames who continued the fight
against the Asiatics. We know this from a fragment of a school-
boy's writing tablet found in a rubbish heap near a plundered
tomb. The youngster had copied a victory monument set up by
Kames to commemorate his campaigns. In it the king speaks to
a council he has called and bemoans his situation. "What use is
my power to me when there is one prince sitting in Avaris [in
the Nile Delta] and another in Kush; while I sit cheek by jowl
with an Asiatic and a Negro! Each has his slice of Egypt and
divides the land with me . . . ."

Kames tells his counselors that he wants action against
the Hyksos: "I will grapple with him and rip open his belly; for
my desire is to deliver Egypt and to smite the Asiatics." But his
counselors caution patience: "Behold, even if it is true that the
Asiatics have advanced as far as Cusae and have put out their
tongues all together at us, yet we are in quietness, holding our
own part of Egypt." In other words, things are not so bad. But
the counselors do promise to fight "if any man cometh up-river
and attack us, him we will oppose."

The king rejects these faint-hearted replies angrily and swears to fight "with these Asiatics, for the whole land weepeth—men shall hail me as the mighty ruler in Thebes, Kames, the Protector of Egypt." Then he sets out to make the prediction come true:

> Then sailed I downstream as a champion to overthrow the Asiatics by command of Amen, wise of counsel. My brave army marched before me like a blast of fire; troops of Mazoi were our vanguard in order to spy out the Beduin [Hyksos] and destroy their lairs. East and West brought fat and wine and the host abounded in victuals everywhere. I sent on a strong troop of Mazoi in advance, and I abode on guard in order to coop up Teta, the son of Pepy [Apepa] within Nefrusi [near Hermopolis]. I was not going to allow him to escape, and I held off the Asiatics. . . .[8]

Kames sent his troops against the city of Nefrusi at "the time of perfuming the mouth"—breakfast—and swept over the defenders. The fragment ends on this note of triumph. We do not know how far Kames carried his campaign, but his successor, Ahmose I, succeeded in driving the Hyksos out of Egypt at long last (they had been in control for about 220 years). Through a series of victorious battles, Ahmose I pushed the invaders back into Palestine where he finally defeated them. All in all, the reconquest took perhaps fifty years. Then he turned his sights south and sent his armies against the pretender to the throne in Nubia. Again he waged a successful campaign, crushing this opponent in what one of his generals called a "great slaughter."

THE NEW KINGDOM

With Ahmose I, about 1580 B.C., there began a new era in Egypt's history called the "New Kingdom." Ahmose was the first king in the famous XVIII Dynasty. He ruled from Thebes for at least twenty-two years. Besides dealing with usurpers, invaders and pretenders, he focused Egypt's energies on building and repairing the ravages of two centuries of foreign occupation.

At this point the position of women as royal consorts reached a new stage. For the first time the Great Wife is mentioned prominently in the official announcements and records of the Pharaoh. And this practice continues with more or less emphasis during the reigns of the XVIII Dynasty kings. It is a departure in Egyptian history and one that may well stem from the association of the Egyptian royalty with the Kushites. For in Kush then, as in later times, the queen was considerably more important than in Egypt.

Whereas Egypt had a tradition of male rulers and only male rulers (broken spectacularly in this XVIII Dynasty), Kush was frequently ruled over by women throughout its history. It is likely that the association of the exiled Egyptian royal families and the kings and queens of Kush and the dynastic marriages that linked the two regions ever more closely produced a new attitude toward the importance of the Great Wife, an attitude that may have caused the Egyptian kings to elevate the role of the queens in the eyes of their subjects.

In the court of Ahmose I there were three living queens. Two of these were dowagers—his grandmother Tetashera, his mother Ahotep, and his sister-wife, the Great Wife Nefertari. Protocol at the royal receptions, state occasions and banquets must have been a headache for the grand chamberlain, whose responsibility it was to determine who should precede whom. But of these three women it was Nefertari who became widely venerated as the founding mother of the XVIII Dynasty. She is often shown in pictures of the court with a dark, almost black skin. This is highly unusual, for Egyptian tradition always assigned a fair skin to females, whatever their actual skin color, and a red-brown skin to males. One explanation for the unusual treatment of Nefertari by artists is, of course, that because she was so highly regarded they painted her in her "true colors," faithful to her real skin tone. Another theory is that as she became more and more venerated she was assigned divine status and was shown as one of the gods of the Underworld, represented

Figure 13   in blue-black colors. Perhaps her husband, to settle questions of who outranked whom among his womenfolk, ordered this particular god-treatment to give Nefertari undisputed primacy.

After Ahmose I, Egypt's borders were expanded "from the Horns of the Earth to the Marshes of Asia" by Thutmose I. By this poetic phrase the king meant that he had conquered from the swamps of the Euphrates to the "Horns of the Earth." (A geographical reference that has puzzled scholars through the centuries, although most believe this refers to some place[s] in Kush.) Thutmose did send expeditions deep into the south, and in fact, one of his inscriptions was turned up near the Nile's Fifth Cataract, one thousand miles from the Delta as the bird flies. Some scholars believe that Thutmose's expeditions reached Meroe, the capital of Kush, beyond the point where the Atbara flows into the Nile.

Whatever the specific details of this other extreme of Thutmose's conquests, it is a fact that under this Pharaoh, Nubia was elevated to a new, unprecedented level of importance in the

Egyptian scheme of things. The king established a new office of great importance, and an administrative bureaucracy to tend it. This office was equal in its significance to that of the king's vizier, or prime minister, we are told. And furthermore, Thutmose recognized the value of the south by decreeing that the prince of Kush was, from that time on, the Right Hand of the Pharaoh in the entire lands south of Elephantine (modern-day Aswan), located at the First Cataract.

The Queen-King

The next ruler of great importance was quite extraordinary: first, because of great ability; and second, because she was a woman. She was Queen Hatshepsut, the Great Royal Wife of Pharaoh Thutmose II, Ahmose's grandson. Unquestionably the most famous historical woman of antiquity, Hatshepsut ruled Egypt as the wife of her short-lived half-brother for fourteen years. Then she ruled as regent with her stepson Thutmose III for an additional twenty-one years. As the chief architect of the realm, one of her key counselors, Ineni, put it:

> Having ascended into heaven, he [Thutmose II] became united with the gods, and his son, being arisen in his place as king of the Two Lands, ruled upon the throne of his begetter, while his sister, the god's wife Hatshepsut governed the land and the Two Lands were under her control; people worked for her, and Egypt bowed the head.[9]

This period of the Thutmose Pharaohs threw the official record-keepers and historians into a tailspin. It was a time of great expansion, great wealth and of monumental building projects that made Egypt an imperial power, Thebes and many temple

The celebrated expedition to Punt during the reign of Hatshepsut is described in words and pictures in her tomb at Deir al-Bahri. This is one of the Egyptian ships she sent to bring back the legendary riches of Punt about 1500 B.C.
COURTESY BELLEROPHON BOOKS.

areas magnificent showplaces, and that saw the transformation of a cliff-lined, barren gulch into the Valley of the Kings—a staggering collection of tombs and temples. Hatshepsut played a central part in these activities. But Egyptians had a deeply ingrained prejudice against being ruled by a woman. Only twice before in their history had Egyptians been ruled by women. All the customs and rituals were geared to rule by kings. Therefore they (and Hatshepsut) went to extraordinary lengths (resulting in considerable confusion) to disguise the fact that she was female. In the annals and on the monuments she was referred to as "king"; she was shown in sculpture wearing the short kilt, pectoral and double crown of a king, with a man's body and the ceremonial beard; the official lists of Egypt's rulers are unbroken from Ahmose I to his son Amenhotep I, to his son Thutmose I and from him to Thutmose II and his son Thutmose III. No-

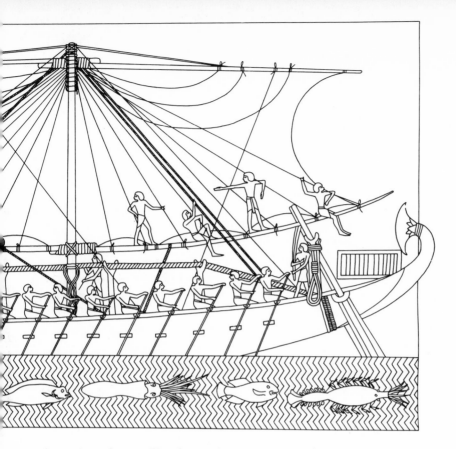

where does Queen Hatshepsut's name appear!

Across the Nile from Thebes beyond the cultivated land, beyond the strip of desert west of the ribbon of green, rise the silent, yellow cliffs. And in the base of this deeply-fissured stone backdrop is a masterpiece of architecture. It is the temple, now three thousand years old, that Hatshepsut built for her monument. In it she records her version of her life—in fact, she goes even further back. To confound her critics and give herself clear title to the throne, she has placed on the walls a series of scenes and inscriptions showing how she was conceived by the great god Amen. Another god, Khuum, the creator of men, is then shown fashioning the baby and its *ka* out of clay—but both tiny figures are obviously boys! Panel after panel portrays the high points of Hatshepsut's life. One of these series shows in remarkable, delightful detail an expedition sent to the land of Punt.

Figure 9

The scenes tell the story from the moment of casting off of the lines to the triumphant return. We see the voyage, arrival at Punt, the meeting with the king of the Puntites over a pile of trade goods. The queen of Punt, incidentally, is shown as an *Figure 12* obviously overweight (by our standards) little woman. The artist who did this scene drolly shows nearby a poor, spindly-legged, emaciated beast that would totter under the weight of an empty saddlebag. This the artist has labeled, with tongue in cheek, "the queen's donkey."

The king of Punt greets Hatshepsut's expedition much as the Aztecs greeted Cortez and his men:

Why have ye come hither unto this land, which the people know not? Did ye come down upon the ways of heaven, or did ye sail upon the waters, upon the sea of God's Land [Punt]? Have ye trodden the ways of [the god] Re? Lo, as for the King of Egypt, is there no way to his Majesty, that we may live by the breath which he gives?[10]

The Egyptians were taken for demigods, or representatives of the distant king-queen who must be a god. Similar responses by Africans were reported as recently as the last century when British expeditions told native chiefs about the Great White Queen Victoria.

At any rate, the Puntites showered the riches of their realm on the Egyptians:

The loading of the ships very heavily with marvels of the country of Punt; all goodly fragrant woods of God's Land, heaps of myrrh-resin, with fresh myrrh-trees, with ebony and pure ivory, with green gold of Emu, with cinnamon wood . . . eye cosmetic, with apes, monkeys, dogs and with skins of the

southern panther. . . . Never was brought the like for any
king who has been since the beginning. . . .[11]

The expedition returned to Thebes and was received triumphantly by the king-queen to whom the chiefs of Punt brought
tribute and gave obeisance. This splendid achievement, this
exciting and hugely successful expedition, of which the queen
was so obviously proud, was organized and led by one of her
most trusted lieutenants, identified in the scenes and the records
as Chancellor Nehesy or Nehesi (Nubian or black).

Thutmose III

Nehesy became one of the handful of Hatshepsut's key counselors and administrators. So long as she lived, they were the most
powerful men in the realm. When she died, after ruling for
thirty-five years, her young nephew/husband/stepson Thutmose III, having endured twenty-one years of her regency,
lashed out with hatred so stunning and thorough that its scope
staggers the imagination. Some authorities conjecture that the
queen's demise may have been arranged for her. There is no
direct evidence of this, but there *was* the thundering hatred of
her stepson. He had had enough of her in life and wanted to
insure that he would be free of her in death or in the afterlife of
the Underworld.

The immediate victims of his fury were the officials of
Hatshepsut's reign who had kept him away from power. Nehesy
and that select handful of the queen's trusted lieutenants were
stripped of rank. Thutmose then proceeded to obliterate Hatshepsut's features and her name wherever they were to be found
in the kingdom. In this way he destroyed her *ka* and all the
necessities for her afterlife. The statues of Hatshepsut in museums

today have been reassembled from the smithereens in which they were left by Thutmose's royal wrecking crews.

Though this vindictive beginning for his reign might have been taken as an indication of his character, it would have been misleading. Thutmose III turned out, in the thirty-two years of his actual rule, to be the greatest warrior-king ever to direct the destinies of Egypt. Far from being petty and vindictive, he displayed magnanimity and compassion—for his time—to foe and vanquished, and piety of a high degree, judging from the extensive temples he built and his support of the priesthood.

Chubby, short (five-feet-five-inches tall), powerfully built, with a nose like a battleship rudder, Thutmose III launched seventeen military campaigns during his rule. He conquered the Libyans of the western desert, the Nubians of the south, the Syrians of the north, the Mitanni and other Asiatics in the east. Plunder and tribute poured into Egypt and the monuments multiplied and rose stone on stone, or were carved in the immortal rock. Under the king the army had become a professional service and the elite units in it were the fierce Mazoi, the black warriors. They had the honor and responsibility of guarding the king himself, as his personal bodyguards. They also served as the police force for the royal capital.

Books could be written about Thutmose III and his achievements, but the significant points for our purposes are his extraordinary achievements as warrior, administrator and leader. It is also interesting that he was not of pure "solar blood." Far from it. His father was undoubtedly Thutmose II—the family profile with that unmistakable nose proves that. But his mother was an obscure secondary wife or concubine of humble parentage. Her name was Aset and it appears that through her Thutmose III received a further inheritance of Negro blood.

From the standpoint of power politics his claim to the throne was weakened by his having been the offspring of a girl who was not a royal princess. Thus it was necessary to assure his claim. This was done by marrying him to one of Hatshepsut's daughters and by a trick engineered by the priests of Amen, when the young man was serving as a chief priest of Amen's main temple. As the figure of Amen was carried around the temple in the annual ceremony by the priests, it suddenly stopped in front of young Thutmose III and bowed to him—a sign from the great god that this was to be the true ruler of Egypt, recognized by the god himself! This dramatic scene is recorded for all time in stone in one of the king's temples.

The empire established by Thutmose brought an influx not only of booty and wealth, but beauty and manpower. From the corners of this huge empire flowed the works of art and artisans, the craftsmen and skilled workers and the slaves—women and children, particularly. The royal harem expanded and so did those of the court nobles and chief functionaries. The result, of course, was that Egypt, from top to bottom, experienced the leavening effect of an infusion of ideas, arts and people from distant lands.

We can see something of this impact in the almost sensational arrival on the scene of the queen of Thutmose III's great grandson, Amenhotep III.

The Great Royal Wife

Seemingly out of nowhere and into prominence always given only the Great Royal Wife came Amenhotep III's chief consort, Queen Tiy. It was almost scandalous that she was a commoner—the king knew it, the court nobles and high persons of the land knew it, and the king made certain that all his subjects knew it by flaunting the fact. He issued a series of commemorative announcements, engraved in the traditional way on small blue scarabs and distributed by the thousands, saying:

> May he live, Amenhotep III, given life, and the King's Great Wife Tiy, who lives. The name of her father is Yuya, the name of her mother is Tuya; she is the wife of a mighty king whose southern boundary is as far as Karoy (the region around Napata in Kush) and northern as far as Naharin![12]

The thrust of this wording is to warn all persons that though this woman may be of insignificant background, she now carries all the strength and prestige of her mighty husband, the king.

Tiy was, to say the least, a woman of unusual power and influence. She was also beautiful, with a personality that reaches out across the centuries. And she was black. There are two excellent portrait heads of her, one as a young girl, wearing a flat-topped, shoulder-length headdress. In this there is a slightly petulant look, a cast of arrested expectancy, as though she is drumming her fingertips on the chair arm as the sculptor goes about his time-consuming business.

Figure 14 Tiy's is a strong face, with determination written on it, though its pouting, sensual lips and matter-of-fact eyes are absolutely feminine. The later portrait shows a woman whose symmetrical lips and almond-shaped eyes are her most compelling features. We see that impatience still sits on her brow, though experience has made her more knowledgeable. Tiy wears a hair arrangement in this portrait that we would today call an "Afro." Any Sunday morning you may see her modern counterpart proudly entering America's Negro churches across the land.

Queen Tiy's prominence was a breakthrough. She was

the first commoner in Egyptian history to be announced and accepted as the Great Wife. Many kings had followed a fancy for an attractive peasant girl or untitled commoner by adding her to their harem, and so might have Amenhotep III. The difference was that the two were married when in their childhood or early teens at the latest. Thus this was a state wedding, arranged with the attention to the political and dynastic implications by the officials of the court.

Why these counselors selected Tiy, the daughter of a comparatively obscure "prophet and overseer" of the temple of a distinctly minor god, Min, is a puzzle. The family lived in a town in Upper Egypt called Ipu (modern Akhmim), and one Egyptologist has found evidence that three generations of Egypt's kings took wives from this town and this same family.

Whatever the reasons for the choice of Tiy as a wife for Amenhotep III, her elevation to Chief Wife had been done with the advice and planning of the boy-king's mature counselors, as well as his own (apparently enthusiastic) acquiescence. Furthermore, from this point on Amenhotep placed Tiy's name alongside his at the head of official announcements and royal documents—an unheard-of thing. And from this point on her influence continued throughout his reign and into that of her son. It was an unparalleled period in which, in official acts, public occasions and at affairs of state, Tiy and the queens who were her immediate successors were prominent as were no other Egyptian queens before or after.

Tiy and Amenhotep III reigned over a world of unrivaled wealth, luxury and splendor for thirty-seven years. It was a magnificence built upon the conquests and continuing tribute from the Near East, Libya, Punt and Kush. Only once during this period did the king put on his armor and that was for a brief expedition to Nubia to quell an outbreak of unrest. He maintained garrisons, of course, in the occupied areas—Syria, Lebanon, Israel, Nubia. But such was the power of the Lord of the Two Lands that kings of other powerful empires wrote to him begging letters. The King of Babylon, for instance, wrote "send me a great deal of gold . . . If, during this harvest, you send the gold concerning which I wrote to you, then I will give you my daughter."[13] Evidently, sufficient gold was sent to Tushratta, the king of Mitanni, for he gladly sent his daughter with a host of 317 handmaidens for marriage to Amenhotep. The king married the girl and added the Mitannian maidens to his harem, which was extensive. As is so often the case with inveterate collectors, Amenhotep's zeal to add to his harem seemed to know no bounds. He wrote, for instance, to Milkiu, prince of Gezer, sending trade goods, silver and gold, ordering forty concubines at forty silver shekels apiece, saying "so send very fine concubines in whom there is no blemish. . . ." Later, he even wrote to Tushratta again for another princess, niece of the last one the Mitannian sent, and Tushratta speedily complied— including with this prize a strong suggestion that more gold would be welcome.

Figure 10

Though his harem consisted of hundreds of concubines, and his secondary wives were numerous, Amenhotep seems to have been devoted to Tiy, who shared his enthusiasms and his honors and, significantly, his responsibilities. This, to bear part of the duties of the king, was truly revolutionary for a queen then and in most of recorded history. However, a letter from Tushratta of Mitanni upon the death of Amenhotep III clearly shows the important role Tiy played in foreign affairs: "Whatever were all the words of your father [Amenhotep III] which he wrote to me, Tiy, the Great Wife of [the king], the beloved, your mother, she knows all about them. Enquire of Tiy, your mother, with regard to all these things."[14] Letters from the kings of Babylon and Hatti are similar in their references to Tiy, and some are addressed to her alone.

Few kings in history have been as powerful and rich as Amenhotep III, and few so keenly devoted to their wives that they would virtually move heaven and earth for her. These things the king did for Tiy. In the spiritual sphere, she was made goddess of a temple at Sedeinga in Nubia, and worshipped as a deity. As for earth, "His Majesty commanded that there should be made a lake for the Great Royal Wife Tiy, living in her city of Zarukha . . . His Majesty made the festival of the opening of the lake in the third month of the harvest season, on the sixteenth day, when [he] sailed in the royal [yacht] *Tehen-Aten* [Aten Gleams], in its cabin."[15]

The commemorative inscription from which this is quoted gives the size of the lake as more than a mile in length by over a thousand feet in width. It also tells us that the elapsed time between ordering the building of the lake and the gala ceremonies celebrating this twelfth year of his rule was exactly fifteen days. The more one ponders those facts the more impressive Amenhotep's devotion to his queen becomes and the more impressive the administrative genius and technical skill that enabled him to turn a romantic whim into reality in just two weeks.

But this lake was simply a small, private construction to go along with the new palace built on the west side of the Nile for his queen. In addition, Amenhotep assigned his chief of public works and architects so many monuments and temples that they earned for him the title Amenhotep the Magnificent. In the brilliance of the court life he led he was the true spiritual predecessor of Louis XIV of France, *Le Roi Soleil*. Here is a catalog of some of the masterpieces of architecture the king built at Thebes alone: a monumental sanctuary for which his architects invented the basic elements of cathedral architecture, including nave, side aisles and clerestory; a —

massive pylon before the temple of Karnak . . . from the river an avenue . . . between two tall obelisks, and before it . . . his portrait colossus . . . hewn from a single block of tough gritstone sixty-seven feet long . . . a temple to Mut, the goddess of Thebes . . . and excavated a lake beside it . . . laid out a beautiful garden in the interval of over a mile and a half [between] . . . Karnak . . . [and] Luxor temple and connected the great temples by avenues of rams carved in stone, each bearing a statue of the Pharoah between the forepaws. . . . the brilliant hues of the polychrome architecture, with columns and gates overwrought in gold and floors overlaid with silver, the whole dominated by towering obelisks clothed in glittering metal. . . .[16]

On the other side of the river near the base of the cliffs the king built for himself the biggest temple of his reign. It was to stand through eternity and outside its entrance were placed two gigantic seated statues of the king, each about seventy feet tall, each carved from one solid piece of rock. These stand beside obelisks before the pylon entrance to which one climbs from the river via an avenue marked by parallel rows of stone jackals. About the court of the temple were other statues of the king; a thirty-foot sandstone tablet inlaid with jewels and gold was placed to show where the king stood during his ritual duties.

The temple had walls and floors:

> ... overlaid with gold and silver, displayed the most prodigal magnifi-
> cence ... the bronze hinges and other mountings of the vast
> cedar pylon-doors weighed together some tons, and required
> castings of unprecedented size; while the overlaying of such
> doors with sheets of bronze exquisitely [ornamented] in pre-
> cious metal with the figure of the god demanded a combination
> of esthetic capacity with mastery of ponderous mechanics,
> which is not too common even at the present day.[17]

Thus did Amenhotep III embellish the land. But such are the
ways of men that before two centuries passed, his own descendants pilfered his great temple (which has been called the greatest
work of art ever wrought in Egypt) like scavengers, in order to
build temples of their own. They did, however, leave his two
colossal statues (known as the "singing Colossi of Memnon" to
the Greeks and Romans) facing across the plain. They are now
largely shapeless and sand-bitten, and covered with graffiti and   *Figure 11*
tourists' names. The Emperor Hadrian is reported to have
camped beside them to hear them "vocalize." (The sounds were
caused by the heat of the sun at dawn striking the cold stone,
causing it to expand and "sing.") This was hardly what Amenhotep III had in mind when he carved on his once gold and be-
jewelled stele which lies shattered in the sand nearby: "My
majesty has done these things [to last] millions of years, and I
know that they will abide in the earth." †

One more highly significant feat of building must be
mentioned here. It is the immense temple Amenhotep built in
Nubia at Soleb, a major town in Kush, about as far south of

†Though this is reminiscent of Shelley's "Ozymandias," that poem refers to
another superegotist, Ramses II, and the Ramesseum at Thebes.

Abu Simbel as it is northwest of Napata. More than three hundred feet long, the temple has two halls and two massive pylons. The King of the Two Lands himself came to dedicate this building, so important did he consider it and Kush. Here the king was worshipped as a god. And, as we noted earlier, it was at Sedeinga, also in Kush, that Amenhotep built the temple for Queen Tiy, for her cult-worship.

The primary responsibility of a queen, of course, is to produce an heir to the throne—a male heir. In the first twenty-five years of their married life Queen Tiy bore the king four daughters. It was not until the twenty-sixth year that a boy-child was born to the queen. The royal couple and the government leaders sighed with relief and there was rejoicing throughout the land. There was one more baby, a girl, born still later. This last child was given the name Baktaten—an unusual name for a royal daughter because it included the term "Aten" (Creator of Mortals and Maker of their Life) and not "Amen."

THE HERETIC KING

Amen was the "resident" god of Thebes who superseded all others with the Thutmosid kings and vice versa. It was when Amen nodded to Thutmose III that his claim to the throne was strengthened immeasurably. So widespread had become the cult of Amen that he was first of the two thousand gods worshipped in Egypt, not to mention those imported from abroad with the conquests by the kings from Kames on. The cult of Amen was, in fact, the state religion. Even the royal family showed their allegiance to Amen by including his name in their children's names and in the official name of the King of the Two Lands himself: Amenhotep which means "Amen is satisfied." Furthermore, the Amenites—both priesthood and followers—had become powerful. The priests were wealthy, thanks to the floods of tribute lavished upon the cult in the religious observances and the triumphs of empire, i.e., booty from foreign wars. The scores of temples erected by the great builder-kings of the XVIII Dynasty were primarily for Amen, and so large did such construction loom in Egypt's economy that the major portion of her "Gross National Product" was intimately bound up with, if not actually dependent on, the worship of Amen.

So it must have been something of a shock to the Amen priesthood to find Amenhotep naming his youngest after this "upstart" god, Aten. However, he had named the Crown Prince Amenhotep IV, and since the male heir and not the fifth princess would rule Egypt, the priests probably tolerated this as a whim of the king—or perhaps his queen. Those who now look at the few straws in the wind which have been uncovered point out that even back in Amenhotep's twelfth year as ruler the name of Aten came in for royal mention on the festival boat launched on Queen Tiy's artificial lake: *Tehen-Aten.*

There are other inscriptions to Aten, inscriptions that were made before the end of Amenhotep's reign, at Soleb in Nubia and even in Thebes itself. In fact, one inscription tells us that Amenhotep III was responsible for the building or enlargement of a temple in Thebes dedicated to Aten. And one company of his personal bodyguards carried the name Aten also. This is significant because the matter of one god among two thousand became the all-consuming central issue of the next decades in Egypt. It was the center of the whirlwind caused by the coming to power of the Golden Pharaoh's son, as we shall see.

Amenhotep III had prided himself on his athletic prowess and skill as a hunter during the early years of his reign. One of his typically modest commemorative scarabs says:

Live the Horus [the god-king], the strong bull, arising in Truth, Lord of the Double Crown, establishing laws, making ready both plains. Horus on Nubti, great and mighty, smiting the Setiu, King of Upper and Lower Egypt. Nebmaatra, Son of Ra, Amenhotep Heq Uast, granted life, and the Royal Wife Tiy, who liveth. Reckoning of lions brought by His Majesty in his shooting by himself, beginning in the first year up to the tenth year, lions, terrible: 102.[18]

But by the thirtieth year of his rule Amenhotep's lion-hunting days were long past. Fat and flabby, suffering from abscessed teeth and, no doubt, the effects of overindulgence in the pleasures of the vine and the couch, the king brought his young son in to "rule" with him. His old correspondent, brother-in-law/father-in-law, Tushratta, having sent two wives, now sent still a third female, the sacred statue of the goddess Ishtar to heal the aging king. She was no more successful than Amenhotep's small army of secondary wives and concubines or his legions of priests. About the time the crown prince reached his teens the Golden Pharaoh, then approximately fifty, joined his ancestors. And so began the most incredible reign in Egyptian history—that of Amenhotep IV, who before long cast aside this illustrious name and adopted another: Akhnaten, meaning "Spirit of Aten."

Akhnaten was a heretic. About him and his queen rages one of the most heated controversies of Egyptian history. Almost every conceivable view of the man has been expressed by Egyptologists, whether amateur or professional. Some believe Akh-

naten all but destroyea Egypt; to others he was the greatest
innovator and philosopher in the history of the Two Lands. *Figures 15 -16*
One expert calls him a "young dreamer . . . the most remarkable
of all the Pharaohs, and the first *individual* in human history."[19]
Another brands him a fanatic who destroyed his country. Yet
another lauds him as a purely spiritual leader while still a
fourth concludes that he was a sexual degenerate. For every one
who calls him great there is another who denounces him as
hopelessly impractical or incompetent. The man inspired—and
continues to inspire—serious works of philosophy, religion, history, poetry, drama, fiction and fantasy.

Nefertiti

Perhaps second only to the interest in King Akhnaten is the
conjecture about his chief wife, Nefertiti, whose beauty is world
famous. The lovely portrait heads of her, discovered by a German
archeological team excavating a sculptor's studio in Akhnaten's
capital city just before World War I, are known in every civilized
land today. The portraits were also the center of a heated
international quarrel, because the Germans took them out of
Egypt illegally and did not officially acknowledge their existence
until 1924. Not surprisingly, this upset the Egyptians. They
demanded return of the queen's portrait heads, but the Germans
refused. During World War II there was real danger that the
priceless portraits would be destroyed with other objects in the
Berlin Museum or that they would be taken as loot by a conqueror. Fortunately for the world, Nefertiti's portraits survived
and today are among the chief treasures of the Berlin Museum,
to the continuing disgruntlement of Egypt.

Nefertiti, whose name means "The Beautiful Lady Has
Come," is one of the most sublime beauties in the history of this

planet. There is a quality beyond the merely mortal in the symmetry of her wide-set eyes and broad cheekbones, the curve *Figure 17* of the jawline, the ample lips, just one degree short of sensual, ending in Mona Lisa dimples. The quality of immediacy, of living, breathing humanity exists in the sculpture, and yet, she has an air of expectancy as well as patient resignation, of endurance and stoical acceptance which makes her at once compassionate, all-knowing, and somehow unreachable. If Akhnaten is the first "individual" in Egyptian history, surely she is the first woman to come to life in its art.

Who was she? Here again we step into the quicksand of conjecture and conflicting theories. We know for certain that she was Akhnaten's Great Royal Wife, that she bore six princesses, that she was shown in the official sculptures and pictures and cited in the official documents of her husband in a way and to a degree unlike any of her predecessors, even Queen Tiy. We know that in the last years of Akhnaten's rule she was in eclipse and she passed from the scene without a murmur or a trace when his rule ended.

As for the theories: (1) She was Tiy's daughter and Akhnaten's full sister (for proof, goes this theory, simply place the portraits of Nefertiti and Akhnaten side by side and their striking resemblance makes further discussion unnecessary); (2) Her real name was Tadukhipa and she was one of King Tushratta's Mitannian bride-shipments to Amenhotep III and a harem legacy to his son; (3) She was the daughter of Queen Tiy's brother, the cavalry commander Ay who took over the throne after Tutankhamen, and was thus a first cousin of Akhnaten. (This theory has a number of distinguished adherents.)

The King of the Two Lands apparently loved Nefertiti with a passion announced freely and publicly in a fashion seldom

*Figure 1. These rock paintings of
running men are from South Africa.
Similar prehistoric paintings in caves
and on rock are to be found in several parts
of Africa, including recently-discovered
examples in the Sahara.*
THE AMERICAN MUSEUM OF NATURAL HISTORY.

Figure 2. Here is a reconstruction of the "old man of Olduvai Gorge," in Kenya. He is Zinjanthropus, *the granddaddy of us all. Discovered by Dr. L.S.B. Leakey, this "man of Zanj" lived hundreds of thousands of years ago. Because of his enormous teeth he has been nicknamed "nutcracker man."*

RESTORED BY DR. HARRY SHAPIRO,
AMERICAN MUSEUM OF NATURAL HISTORY.

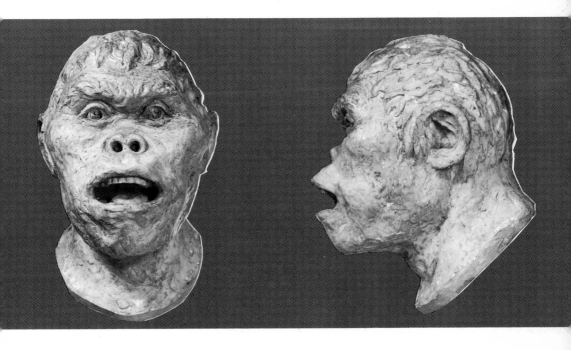

Figure 3. This is a reconstruction of Australopithecus, *a descendant of* Zinjanthropus, *found in a limestone cave in South Africa. Though his name means "African southern ape," he is truly a man: weight, seventy pounds; height, about four feet; brain, slightly larger than his Olduvai predecessor; arms shorter than an ape's; flat feet and no tail. More than six hundred have been found so far.*

RESTORED BY DR. HARRY SHAPIRO,
AMERICAN MUSEUM OF NATURAL HISTORY.

Figure 4. These are "manillas," curved bars of metal that were used as money in West Africa. Made of brass, copper or iron, they were exchanged for goods. The largest of these three, called a "king" manilla, was supposedly bartered for up to a hundred slaves. There were smaller versions of these that were shaped like bracelets and were much more common.
CHASE MANHATTAN BANK MONEY MUSEUM.

Figure 5. The cowrie shell, shown here, varies in size from about half an inch to several inches in diameter. Cowrie shells of the smaller sort served as money in Africa for centuries. Their value varied with their availability. Thus, their purchasing power was low near the sea but increased with the distance from the ocean. To make exchange easier, the cowries were generally strung together, with five strings of forty each, or two hundred, the normal unit in some areas. As recently as 1945, two hundred cowries were the equivalent of three British pence in Nigeria.
CHASE MANHATTAN BANK MONEY MUSEUM.

Figure 6. The Great Pyramid at Giza, built by Khufu (or Cheops), was completed less than a century after the construction of Zoser's tomb—the first "step" pyramid. The other two major pyramids were built by his successors, Khafre and Menkaure. Far from being the products of scourged and tortured slaves, these pyramids, it seems, were the ancient equivalent of the United States' effort today to send men to the moon.

EGYPTIAN STATE TOURIST ADMINISTRATION

Figure 7. The "first wonder of the world" might be the title for this forty-seven-hundred-year-old pyramid. Built by the Egyptian Pharaoh Zoser, it rises two hundred ten feet above the sands at Sakkara. Zoser's tomb originally was to have been only the lower section of the pyramid, but his architect, Imhotep, changed the design and this gigantic hill of stone, the first "step" pyramid, was the result. It required an organization of manpower and construction such as the world had never seen before.

EGYPTIAN STATE TOURIST ADMINISTRATION.

Figure 8. Amenemhet I, founder of the XII dynasty in Egypt. He was the son of a Nubian woman and seized the throne during a period of upheaval. He proved to be an excellent Pharaoh and his reign sent Egypt into another period of expansion and high achievement, known as the Middle Kingdom.

THE METROPOLITAN MUSEUM OF ART. GIFT OF J. PIERPONT MORGAN, 1912.

Figure 9. At Deir El-Bahri near Thebes is this temple of one of the most remarkable women the world has ever known, the queen-king Hatshepsut. On the walls of the structure, which was cut into the rock and extended hundreds of feet into the cliff, are murals telling the story of her conception, birth, life, and achievements as she wanted them told. Hers was a peaceful reign, and one of its high points was an expedition to Punt, reported on the walls of her magnificent tomb.

UNITED PRESS INTERNATIONAL PHOTO.

Figure 10. Amenhotep III, one of the richest and most powerful rulers in history. During his time, Egypt's borders included Kush, Libya, Punt and the Near East; riches flowed into his coffers, and art and architecture flourished. He was called Amenhotep the Magnificent.
THE METROPOLITAN MUSEUM OF ART. ROGERS FUND, 1956.

Figure 11. These two colossal sculptures are seated statues of the Golden Pharaoh, Amenhotep III. They are at Luxor, facing the plain and are called, erroneously, the "singing Colossi of Memnon," because of the sounds coming from them when the heat of the morning sun causes them to expand. Nearby in the sand is Amenhotep's stele which reads, "My majesty has done these things [to last] millions of years, and I know that they will abide in the earth."
EGYPTIAN STATE TOURIST ADMINISTRATION.

Figure 12. Here is the Queen of Punt, as seen by the Egyptian artist. She is decidedly fat, but it is quite probable that plumpness was a mark of beauty as well as wealth in her country, as it is today in many lands.
COURTESY OF THE AMERICAN MUSEUM OF NATURAL HISTORY.

Figure 13. Murals from the tomb of Queen Nefertari, wife of Ahmose I, the founder of the XVIII dynasty (about 1570 B.C.). Nefertari was venerated as the founding mother of this dynasty and her tomb is at Luxor.

EGYPTIAN STATE TOURIST ADMINISTRATION.

Figure 14. Queen Tiy, Great Royal Wife of Amenhotep III, played a prominent role in the reign of her husband and her son, Akhnaten.

EGYPTIAN MUSEUM, BERLIN.

Figure 15. Akhnaten, the heretic who succeeded Amenhotep III. It was this Pharaoh who overturned the religious system of Egypt and instituted the worship of one god. A new humanism entered Egyptian life and can be seen in the painting and sculpture of this time, which is called the Amarna Period, after the location of Akhnaten's palace and capital. This is a portrait of the king in the traditional style. Contrast it with (Figure 16), a naturalistic portrait done in the Amarna style.

THE METROPOLITAN MUSEUM OF ART.

ROGERS FUND, 1911.

Figure 16. This stucco portrait of Akhnaten was done sometime after 1375 B.C., and was used as a model for official portraits of the king. He has been called by some Egyptologists the first individual in human history.

EGYPTIAN MUSEUM, BERLIN.

*Figure 17. This is Nefertiti—
"great in favor, lady of grace,
sweet of love, ... beloved of the
living Aten [the king] ...," as
described by Akhnaten. This
portrait head in limestone was
found in a sculptor's studio in
Amarna. Compare it with the
portrait of Akhnaten from the
same period.*
EGYPTIAN MUSEUM, BERLIN.

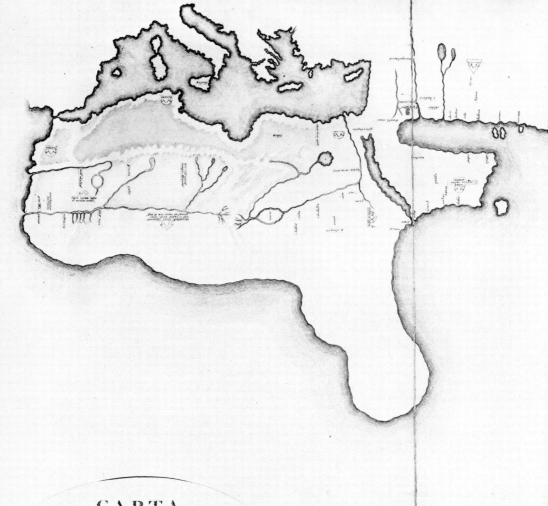

CARTA
DELL' AFFRICA
tratta fedelmente dall' Originale
del
Portulano Mediceo Laurenziano

Segnato di N.° 9 Gadd.° Rel.
e Baudin Catal.° Biblioth. Leopold. Laurent. T. II. Pag. 11.

Saggio del Carattere del Codice.

Vebi gracia p͞ma luna de m̄ c̄c̄li͂ secu͂ hue huit noua.
ad dies .b. vu mens ianuary. ad ⚹ ⚹ 2 vorra decce ut in isto
canleosio patet. 2 ꝛo diely ꝛ february. luna huit dies xv uede in tabula ista
in numero xv sub mens ianuary iuensis. cancer u͂ in cȃne eic luna zi gradily xv.

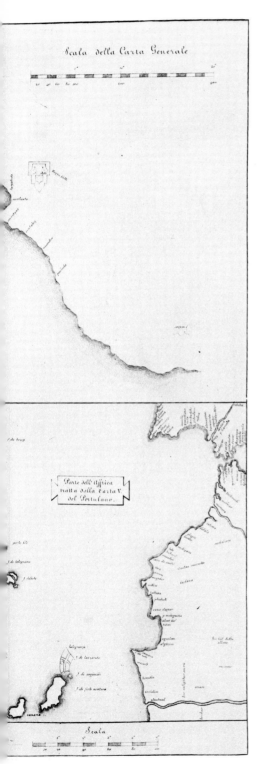

Fig. 18. This early map of "Affrica" printed in Italy is more accurate in its treatment of the Mediterranean coastline than in its depiction of the rest of Africa and Arabia. Among the few features shown with some degree of accuracy on the African continent are Tunisia, Morocco, the Nile and "nubia saracenos." Note the "island" of Meroe indicated in mid-continent. The inset map shows details of the Straits of Gibraltar and the coast southward, including the Canary Islands.
NEW YORK PUBLIC LIBRARY.

Figure 19. This Dutch map of 1573 shows the kingdom of Prester John, "emperor of Abyssinia." The plaque at the upper left is a listing of the titles of the mythical monarch, whose palace is not specifically located on this map. Among the curiosities shown on the chart are the Niger River, which was believed to flow underground for miles and then re-emerge. The "mountains of the moon" are shown at the bottom of the map, beyond which lies "unknown territory." Nubia is shown not only as a region but as a city on the Nile south of Assuan (Aswan). Bornu is shown as a region and city near Lake Chad (labelled Lake Borno on the map), and Benin, on the west coast, and Mozambique, Malinde and Mombasa on the east coast, are among the cities identified. The mapmaker warns that there are both sirens and tritons in the large lake labelled Lake Zaire (bottom, center).

Figure 20. This seventeenth century map carries far more detail about the African coast, evidence of the rapid collection of information from the expeditions then visiting the continent. The interior, however, continued to puzzle the mapmakers. Note on this map an island at Syene on the Nile and another at Meroe. Azania is placed inland from Melinde and Monomotapa is shown upstream on the Cuama (Zambesi) River. Both Ethiopia and Nubia are shown as important kingdoms west of the Nile beside the "Caramontes" along the Niger River. By this time Prester John's domain is not specified on the map, though the mythical ruler rates an explanatory footnote in the lower right corner.

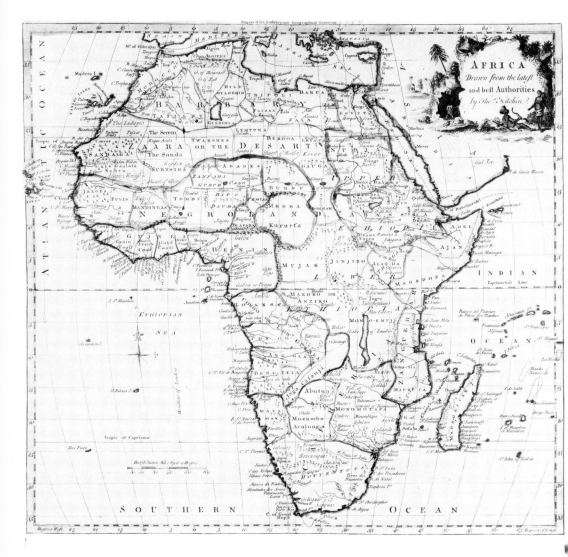

Figure 21. By the time of the American revolution the mapmakers had a pretty thorough knowledge of Africa's shape and coastal features. This map of that era shows Benin, Melli (Mali), Tombut (Timbuktu), Burnu (Bornu), and the region of the Mandingas in a wide belt labeled "Negroland." On the eastern portion upper and lower Ethiopia are shown, with "Antropophages or Men Eaters" located inland from Melinda (Malindi) and north of "Ft. of the Zimbas"—no doubt a reference to Zimbabwe—up the Cuamba (Zambesi) River, in the kingdom of Monomotapa.

NEW YORK PUBLIC LIBRARY.

equaled by rulers in all of history. To him she was:

> The heiress, great in favor, lady of grace, sweet of love, Mistress of the South and North, fair of face, gay with the two plumes, beloved of the living Aten [the king], the Chief Wife of the King whom he loves, Lady of the Two Lands, great of love, Nefertiti, living for ever and ever.[20]

Few women in public or private have received tribute so adoring as this stone love-letter from a king. And in the bas reliefs of royal family life Nefertiti kisses the king and clings to him as he drives a chariot. We see them in other pictures in tender domestic scenes of relaxed family dining, with the king and queen enjoying roast meat while their daughters play about them and sneak sweets from the table. The devotion and naturalness reach across the centuries and tell us that here, at this remote place thirty-two hundred years ago, lived men and women with the drives, passions and pleasures that we can all recognize.

This, the portrayal of domestic scenes, of human frailties as well as the superhuman qualities of the god-kings of Egypt, was a breakthrough in art. Before Akhnaten, the kings and their consorts and children march forth as to battle, in formal, stylized, lockstep. Rarely does a personality shine through the conventional figure portraits; rarely are the Pharaohs shown as anything but rigid, starched marionettes in scenes of formal triumph or religious observance. Akhnaten not only allowed the artists, but commanded them, to show his foibles and frailties. Previous kings are invariably broad-shouldered, slim-hipped Olympic stars, judging by their portraits. Here for the first time we see a king who actually eats foods that mortals eat; here is a king whose pot belly is conclusive evidence that he is no warrior or athlete.

But this was not the greatest of the revolutions Akhnaten caused. His most astonishing act was to overthrow the existing god worship in Egypt and elevate the minor worship of Aten to the status of state religion. Furthermore, the religion was one centered on a supreme god, Aten, whose High Priest was the Pharaoh himself. It was an all-embracing god, a god of all peoples, places and nations, not the parochial type of god which had grown in such profusion in towns and provinces of Egypt. Aten's symbol was the sun, and like the sun, Aten was universal, easily understood, and within the experience of all men.

To Egyptians this was a simple transformation and extension of Ra, the sun-god that had been with them from before time began. But in one major respect Aten differed completely from all previous gods: Aten demanded that the old gods be cast aside. Unlike all the hundreds of gods in Egypt's past who had lived complacently side by side with one another, Aten was a "jealous god" who tolerated no others. He was the one and only. And it was this intolerance, this insistence on exclusive obedience that caused the furious uproar that engulfed Aten, Atenism, its high priest, the King Akhnaten, and his family.

We have little space to cover this intricate subject and must confine ourselves to the outlines of the accomplishments of the heretic king. Over a period of years and in the face of what must have been tremendous opposition by the priests of the many religions, large and small—but particularly the entrenched, vastly wealthy cults such as Amen and Ra— Akhnaten established the new religion throughout the land. Temples were built to the worship of Aten—new, innovative structures, with the roofs open to the sun instead of closed and gloomy as in other places of god-worship. The arts flourished. We have already noted the contrast between the new naturalism, the flowing, stylized line in the painting and sculpture at this time, and the rigidly stylized art of all the centuries which preceded it.

Literature also took a giant step in the direction of humanism. We have several moving examples, one of the most famous being the so-called "Hymn to the Sun" in which Akhnaten, its author, shows us that his conception of the Aten god was of a "benificent father of all men"[21] rather than the national god who was a triumphant conqueror, crushing all peoples and driving them, laden with tribute, before Pharaoh's chariot. Here are samples from this revolutionary poem of religious philosophy which has proven so persistent an influence for three millennia. The hymn, found carved in the tomb chapels of the nobles, has many parts dealing with night, day, man's creation, *the* Creation, seasons, beauty and the knowledge of god. One passage reaches out to the peoples of other lands:

> *All distant lands, thou hast made their life*
>   *Thou has set a Nile-flood in the sky [rain]*
> *And it descendeth for them and makes waves upon the mountains*
>   *Like the Great-Green [sea] to drench their fields in their*
>   *villages.*
> *A Nile-flood in heaven, it is thy gift to the foreign countries. . . .*
>   *But the Nile-flood comes forth from the netherworld [earth]*
>   *for*
> *The land of Egypt.*

And here, universality and love are given as binding forces among men:

> *Thy dawning is beautiful in the horizon of heaven,*
>   *O Living Aten, Beginning of life!*
> *When thou risest in the eastern horizon of heaven,*
>   *Thou fillest every land with thy beauty;*

For thou art beautiful, great, glittering, high over the earth;
    Thy rays, they encompass the lands, even all thou hast made.
Thou art Ra [king of the gods], and thou hast carried them all
    away captive;
    Thou bindest them by thy love.
Though thou art afar, thy rays are on earth;
    Though thou art on high, thy footprints are the day.

Here is one part of Akhnaten's Aten hymn that should sound familiar:

When thou settest in the western horizon of heaven
The world is in darkness like the dead. . . .
Every lion cometh forth from his den,
The serpents they sting. Darkness reigns. . . .

Bright is the earth when thou risest in the horizon. . . .
The Two Lands are in daily festival,
Awake and standing upon their feet . . .
Then in all the world they do their work.

How manifold are all thy works!
They are hidden from before us.
O thou sole god, whose powers no other possesses.
Thou didst create the earth according to thy desire, being alone:
Man, all cattle, large and small;
All that are upon the earth.

Compare this with Psalm 104:

Thou makest darkness and it is night,
Wherein all the beasts of the forest do creep forth;
The young lions roar after their prey; they seek their meat
    from God. . . .

The sun ariseth, they get them away
And lay them down in their dens.
Man goeth forth unto his work
And to his labor until the evening. . . .

O Lord, how manifold are thy works!
In wisdom hast thou made them all;
The earth is full of thy creatures.

(This remarkable similarity is one of many that occur between
Bible verses and ancient Egyptian texts. Another of considerable
interest is the resemblance of the "Teaching of Amenophis" to
the Proverbs. As to the actual influence of the Egyptian writings
on the books of the Bible, there is heated controversy. Some
scholars contend that the Egyptian ancestry of the Bible verses
is absolutely clear; other authorities, equally well-qualified, vehe-
mently deny this and point to sources and citations that tend to
strengthen their argument.)

Understandably, a god as sensitive as Aten to the living
things that were his children rejected the prevailing sacrifices of
birds and beasts and preferred flowers and fruit—joyousness
rather than mystery and superstition.

In the sixth year of his reign, Akhnaten moved his court
across the river to a new capital city at a site now called
Amarna. Built from the ground up along the west bank of the
Nile, the city was called "Akhetaten" by the king. The title
meant "Horizon of the Aten." He set four boundary posts at
the corners of the city, inscribed with his oath never to go
beyond the borders of the new capital nor to allow any one to
induce him to do so. It was at this time that he formally
changed his name from Amenhotep IV to Akhnaten. Furthermore, he issued proclamations forbidding worship of Egypt's old

gods and launched a ferocious attack on the strongest cults of all, especially that of Amen. All over Egypt his men went, chisels in hand, to strike from tombs and monuments the now-banned name and those of other gods wherever they found them. The king even went so far as to remove the word Amen from the name of his father!

Clearly, without fanatical determination to pursue his goal of religious revolution, and without the indisputable power of the Pharaoh, Akhnaten would have been unable to make any dent whatsoever in the enormously rich and entrenched positions of the older religions. That he managed to accomplish so much in so brief a time is an undeniable testimony to his energy, dedication and ability. However, it is interesting that he was unable to read the depth of the reaction and resistance against the new religion.

The records tell us that in the twelfth year of Akhnaten's rule, the Queen Mother, Tiy, made a state visit from her palace. Some of the experts believe that this formal expedition to her son's palace was made expressly to counsel him to modify his stand, to slow the pace of his religious revolution. Perhaps. Other experts believe that Tiy was the master architect of the swing to Atenism; still others credit Nefertiti with this. It is more likely that all three had an interest, each to his own degree, in promoting Atenism. (Whatever Tiy's mission, we have a brilliant picture of a state banquet in which she and her youngest daughter are included in the family group with the king and queen and four of their princesses.) There is little evidence that Akhnaten heeded immediately any "go slow" counsel from his mother or anyone else.

The end of this remarkable period came some five years later. How and exactly why is a mystery. But conjecture based on a recent analysis of the evidence develops this hypothesis:

Akhnaten realized that he needed to arrange for a successor. He had fathered six princesses and no sons by his chief wife. A state marriage was arranged, between his eldest princess, Meritaten, and a boy named Smenkhkare, whose parentage is not explicitly known. However, the portraits of the youth show him with the unmistakable Akhnaten nose, chin and profile, and it is believed that he was the king's son by a secondary wife.

The king now arranged for a co-regency, in which Smenkhkare would share the throne with him. After the coronation, the prince and princess moved to Thebes, the former capital and the center and stronghold of the Amen cult. There Smenkhkare, as co-regent, held court. Thus Akhnaten, who was pledged never to leave his capital city, was able to do the next best thing: He sent his son to the very heart-root of opposition to Atenism as an indication that a reconciliation was desired.

Now, coincident with this, Nefertiti dropped from her conspicuous position of former years. She left the palace, taking her second daughter and son-in-law Tutankhaten (popularly known as King Tut, today) with her. In place of Nefertiti's names in the official pronouncements we now find Meritaten and Smenkhkare mentioned with unstinting praise and affection from Akhnaten.

The effort for reconciliation with the old order failed. Smenkhkare and his queen never returned to Akhetaten. Akhnaten shifted his attention to another successor—Tutankhaten. The boy, however, was only about nine years old and his wife but two years older. And who was Tutankhaten? The records do not state, but the portraits do. The Akhnaten profile is unmistakable—he appears to be a full brother of Smenkhkare—another son of the king.

Tutankhaten

The elevation of young Tutankhaten to co-regent must have come after Smenkhkare was dead and gone, aged about twenty-seven. It occurred in the last days of Akhnaten's troubled reign. Shortly afterward the heretic king died (a natural death?). He disappeared, unmarked by any known record of either burial or death. We do know that Tutankhaten continued to hold court at Akhetaten for three years, then, perhaps after a fight with, or the death of, Nefertiti, he moved his court back to the old capital city, Thebes, simultaneously severed Aten from his name and that of his queen and restored Amen not only there but on tombs and monuments and temples. He reconciled himself with the powerful priesthood of Amen by the simplest, most direct method possible—buying his way back:

> The temples of the gods and goddesses had gone to pieces [Tutankh-amen says, in an inscription]. The land was upside down, and the gods turned their backs upon this land. Their hearts were hurt, so that they destroyed what had been made. But I deliberated plans with my heart, seeking out acts of services to my father Amen. All the property of the temples has been doubled—tripled—quadrupled; their work is charged against the palace, and against the estate of the Lord of the Two Lands.[23]

But even though the boy-king made his peace with the gods, he was not allowed much time. Before his nineteenth birthday Tutankhamen was dead and the struggle to seize power, a struggle close to the surface from the time Akhnaten spurned Amen-Ra, now broke out.

In a desperate, stealthy attempt to hold on to the throne, Tutankhamen's widow sent this message to the king of the Hittites, eight hundred miles north of Egypt in central Anatolia: "My husband is dead and I have no son. People say that you have many sons. If you were to send me one of your sons he might become my husband. I am loath to take a servant of mine and make him my husband."[24]

Only absolute desperation would drive a queen to approach so naively the prime rival of her nation in this way. And only extreme distaste would cause her to mention the likely fate she abhorred even more—marriage to "a servant of mine."

But the wily Hittite ruler, incredulous at an offer that was beyond his wildest dreams, was suspicious. It was as though the bank robber, laboriously drilling his way into the bank vault, had been suddenly offered the combination by the president of the bank. Though the Hittite king had plenty of sons to spare, he sent a counselor to investigate, then replied cautiously to the widow. She wrote again, this pathetic message:

Why do you say "They may try to deceive me?" If I had a son, would
I write to a foreign country in a manner which is humiliating
to me and to my country? He who was my husband died, and
I have no sons. Shall I perhaps take a servant of mine and
make him my husband? I have not written to any other
country, I have written only to you. People say that you have
many sons. Give me one of your sons and he shall be my
husband and king in the land of Egypt.[25]

Finally satisfied that the offer was genuine, the Hittite king immediately shipped off one prince, complete with entourage. We can practically see the Hittite ruler clucking with glee and rubbing his hands as he calculated how soon he could incorporate

Egypt into his empire. But his temporizing had consumed too much precious time. The vultures who were seeking power learned of the queen's reckless gamble and, as the Hittite records (from which the queen's letters are quoted) report, the would-be bridegroom and his party were waylaid on their long journey and murdered "by the men and horses of Egypt."[26]

And what of the queen? The last daughter of Akhnaten of whom we know anything joined her other sisters, her mother Nefertiti and her grandmother Tiy in slipping from historical view. The one-time vizier and "fan bearer on the right of the king, master of all the horses," her uncle Ay, maneuvered his way to power and the magnificent XVIII Dynasty was no more.

Perhaps it was marriage to Ay or Ay's successor, the general Horemheb, that fueled the queen's desperation. Ay had served her father as a devotee of Aten; he had switched without a qualm to Amen again under Tutankhamen and was a good forty years older than the queen. A gold ring has been found on which Ay's name and the queen's are linked as they are for royal consorts. Perhaps it was Ay's hope that he could marry the girl to legitimize his ascent to the throne. Apparently he did not succeed in wedding her—his Great Royal Wife was the same Thuya, nursemaid to Akhnaten, who had been his spouse a generation or more before. Some experts believe the widow served as co-regent with Ay. Ay's reign was brief. He managed to complete a regal burial for Tutankhamen, as we know from the dramatic discovery of that famous tomb in 1922. But Ay soon was overtaken by death or General Horemheb, or both, and we do not have any solid information what happened to the widows of Amenhotep III, Akhnaten, Smenkhkare, Tutankhamen or Ay.

In 1907 a tomb was discovered in the Valley of the Kings and announced with great fanfare to be that of Queen Tiy. That was the legend on the gilded shrine in the rock chamber, so naturally the gold-encased mummy coffin with its precious royal mummy was thought to be that of the great queen. Instead, the bones turned out to be those of a young man! And the four canopic jars (in which the dead person's vital organs were placed) with their sensitively carved alabaster heads were confidently labeled youthful portraits of Tiy. Research rejected this theory and they are now known to be portrait heads of Princess Meritaten, daughter of Akhnaten and Nefertiti. The markings in the tomb are confusing, bearing the names of Tiy, her husband (obliterated and/or altered), their son Akhnaten (obliterated), and a reference interpreted as Smenkhkare. Conjecture about the mummy case is that it was made for Tiy, Nefertiti or Meritaten and revamped for Akhnaten or Smenkhkare. The experts believe the body in the mummy case is that of Smenkhkare. Thus our knowledge of the great and fascinating XVIII Dynasty ends in a welter of confusion and mystery in a jumbled rock tomb in the Valley of the Kings.

THE RISE OF THE SOUTH

As we have seen, the south was of the greatest importance to Egypt. It was the source of its fiercest and most dependable troops, and it was the essential source of wealth—gold and other strategic materials. Its key position is evident from the establishment of the viceroyalty of Kush in the XVIII Dynasty. The viceroy was called "The King's Son of Kush" and was considered second only to the Pharaoh in the hierarchy. His other titles included "Prince of Kush, First Royal Herald, Steward of the Peasantry, Overseer of the Treasury and Overseer of the Gold Lands of the Lord of the Two Lands."

With access to and control over great wealth and manpower, the viceroy was in a position of strategic importance. He could be, and he was, a "king-maker," often using his power to work with or against the priesthood in backing a candidate for king, or in influencing the policies of the king. He had to be a shrewd, outstanding administrator and political strategist; he was supposed to be of untarnished reputation and loyalty to his king.

An indication of the power of the viceroy and the Nubians is found in the XX Dynasty, when a civil war broke out. The viceroy, Pa-Nehesi, collected his troops, rushed north and put down the revolution. After victory, Pa-Nehesi led his armies back to Kush.

Over the generations the responsibility for the defense of the empire fell increasingly on Nubian troops. By the time of Rameses II, the Great, who ruled until 1225 B.C., the backbone of the Egyptian army was its Nubian soldiers. By the time of Rameses XI, one soldier who rose to become viceroy of Nubia was Herihor. With the power of Nubia, he pressured the priesthood into naming him High Priest. This, plus his military and civil rank, made him second only to the Pharaoh in the country, and, in truth, the power behind the throne. When the king died it was easy for Herihor to take over, which he did, thus starting a new dynasty, the XXI, about 1090 B.C.

It is of considerable significance that the days of Nubia's violent rejection of Egypt were, in general, previous to the XVII Dynasty. It was then, when the Hyksos were thrown out of the Two Lands, that the capital permanently shifted to Thebes, far to the south of the Delta. Also, the Nubian troops carried the spears and swords that drove the interlopers back into the Middle East. It is fair to estimate that many Nubians were in positions of importance from this time onward. During the XVIII Dynasty, in addition to the forts built in Nubia, temples and towns were built by Egyptian kings and administrators. Trade increased and reached a new peak. The boundary was set far south, at the Nile's Fourth Cataract. The princes of Nubian families were brought to the Egyptian court and trained and educated as royalty. Elaborate buildings and temples were sponsored by the Pharaoh, and his son in Kush was truly a powerful man.

The trade, construction, expeditions, training and education of the royal heirs, and the acculturation of Nubians in the Egyptian army and police forces had profound effects on Kush. It became an Egyptian province, with Egyptian gods, arts, administration and influence imposed, seeping in, sifting down and infiltrating extensively. In fact, it was here, as Egypt weakened and declined after 1000 B.C., that the empire of Kush rose to world importance. From their capital at Napata near the Fourth Cataract, came the Nubian carriers of Egyptian tradition who attempted to restore Egypt's greatness.

NOTES

1. *Song of the Harper*, trans. by T. Eric Peet in *A Little Treasury of World Poetry*, H. Creekmore (ed.), (New York: Scribner's Sons, 1952), p. 7.
2. Georges Posener, *Dictionary of Egyptian Civilization*, (New York: Tudor Publishing Co., 1959), p. 237.
3. *Ibid.*
4. *Lament of Ipuwer*, c. 2200 B.C.
5. Egyptian Collection, 1969. New York: Metropolitan Museum of Art.

6. *Papyrus Sallier*, i. 1–3, British Museum; quoted by Jas. Baikie, *A History of Egypt*, (London: A & C. Black, 1929), 1: 415.
7. *Ibid.*, p. 417.
8. J. H. Breasted, *Ancient Records of Egypt*, (Chicago: University of Chicago Press, 1906–1907), Vol. 2.
9. Leonard Cottrell, *Lady of the Two Lands*, (New York: Bobbs-Merrill, 1967), p. 40.
10. *Ibid.*, p. 41
11. Breasted, *Op. cit.*, 11:862; text from royal scarabs issued in Amenhotep III's reign.
12. Baikie, *Op. cit.*, 11:207.
13. *Ibid.*, p. 179.
14. *Ibid.*, p. 191.
15. J.H. Breasted, *A History of Egypt*, (New York: Scribner's, 1937), pp. 343-349.
16. *Ibid.*
17. Baikie, *Op. cit.*, p. 184.
18. Breasted, *Op. cit.*, p. 356.
19. Cottrell, *Op. cit.*, p. 102.
20. Breasted, *Op. cit.*, p. 377.
21. *Ibid.*, pp. 371.-376.
22. C. Desroches-Noblecourt, *Tutankhamen*, (Greenwich, Conn: New York Graphic Society, 1963).
23. Cottrell, *Op. cit.*, p. 196.
24. *Ibid.*, 197.
25. *Ibid.*
26. *Ibid.*

Look, all the birds of Punt
are descending on Egypt,
scented with myrrh.
The first bird that lands
fooled by my bait
is fragrant with the perfume of Punt
his claws steeped in balm.

THE BIRD CATCHER[1]

Egyptian

◁▷ ◁▷ ◁▷ ◁▷ ◁▷ ◁▷ ◁▷ ◁▷ ◁▷ ◁▷ ◁▷ ◁▷

THE KUSH
MILLENNIUM

◁▷ ◁▷ ◁▷ ◁▷ ◁▷ ◁▷ ◁▷ ◁▷ ◁▷ ◁▷ ◁▷ ◁▷

III

KUSH IS ONE OF THE TANTALIZING MYSTERIES
of antiquity. That it was a rich, powerful land of black people,
that it existed for at least a thousand years before its decline
and disappearance, we can be sure. But we know only bits and
pieces of its history, only fragments of information about its
periods of greatness, its mighty kings and their achievements.
Although they left behind them impressive evidence of their
highly developed religion, wealth, skill and written language

before fading into the unknown, we do not know what became of its royalty, leaders, artists, architects, artisans and scribes.

As one expert puts it, "[Kush] was an African civilization, firmly based on African soil, and developed by an African population. That an urban, civilized, and literate state existed deep in the African continent and lasted nearly a thousand years in itself constitutes an achievement of outstanding importance."[2]

Kush's history is inextricably interwoven with Egypt's. In fact, "Kush" is the name Egyptians gave the land far to the south of their country. Five hundred miles below Alexandria, near the First Cataract of the Nile is the city of Aswan, known in antiquity as Syene and Elephantine (though it has been tens of centuries since elephants were last found in the area) and famous today as the site of Abu Simbel and the great High Dam. From Aswan south through the trackless sands and the green trail of the Nile's waters for more than seven hundred miles extends what the ancients called the lands of Nubia and Kush. Most of this area is now the Republic of the Sudan.

The borders of Kush were the Libyan desert to the west and the Ethiopian highlands on the east, Maharraqa and Dakka in the north and Senna in the south. It was then, as now, mostly sandy desert and parched hills, plateaus and forbidding rock formations. But more than two thousand years ago whole sections in the south, particularly around the rivers Nile, Atbara, White and Blue Nile, were green with meadows and forests. The official records at Senna near the Second Cataract show that the annual Nile floods were some twenty-six feet higher than they are today, so there must have been more rainfall upstream in those days.

Though we know from archeological finds that there

were Stone Age men living in Kush, the first written record is
an Egyptian report carved in rock near the Second Cataract. It
tells of King Zer's conquest of lower Nubia about 3000 B.C.
Another record tells of a raid in 2750 B.C. by Pharaoh Senefru
who constructed a fleet and "hacked up" the homeland of the
Nehesi (Nubians). Senefru boasted of the loot he brought from
Kush, especially the prisoners and cattle. Some scholars believe
that such raids devastated an existing civilization that had blossomed in the late Stone Age and the period just before Egypt
was united under one strong king—about 3200 B.C.

During the next eight hundred years Kush became increasingly important to Egypt. The Pharaohs sent military expeditions, then trading missions, and later established forts and
trading posts. Finally, about 1570 B.C., Ahmose I and his
successor Thutmose I occupied important sections of Kush and
made it part of Egypt. From then on, Egyptianization of Kush
proceeded at a rapid rate. The Pharaohs built temples and
towns in Kush down to Kurgus, nearly 350 miles south of Aswan.
Famed Abu Simbel, the site of the two immense temples built
by Rameses II, is one such town, located in the northernmost
part of Kush.

Meanwhile, an area on the Nile called Napata, about
350 miles south of Aswan but nearly two hundred miles west of
Kurgus, developed as the capital of Kush. Scores of Pharaohs
built temples and monuments in the Napata area and a place
called Jebel Barkal, a butte that rises three hundred feet above
the surrounding countryside, became a holy burial ground. As
the decades ticked away the black people of Kush prospered,
developed leaders and a royal family. The Pharaohs ruled Kush
through their viceroys and the children of the Nubian chiefs
were taken to the Egyptian court not merely as hostages but

with due honor, and they were given high rank and were educated as royalty.

A Prosperous and Powerful Land

Kush was an important source of gold, raw and finished goods, slaves and soldiers for Egypt. The records of the time tell of the annual tribute from Kush. These payments included quantities of wood, ebony, gum, ivory, ostrich feathers and ostrich eggs (the shells were used for necklaces and jewelry), carnelian, red ochre, amazon stone, perfumes and oils, grain, cattle, leopards (and leopard skins), giraffes (and giraffe-tail fly whisks), dogs and baboons. A temple decree at Nuri, near Jebel Barkal and Napata, dated about 1320 B.C., describes local occupations. Most of the people in the area were farmers or fishermen; some kept bees, others built boats and were sailors or oarsmen in the Nile traffic. Traders were listed also, and many worked at washing for gold.

As we noted in reviewing Egypt's history, Kush became increasingly strong, rich, and independent until by the end of the XXII Dynasty (950 B.C.), as the strength of the Pharaohs diminished, Kush broke away from Egypt. It was a time of great upheaval in the kingdom on the Nile. There was great pressure from outside the country. Pirates raided Egypt's Mediterranean coast and Assyrians forced back Egypt's Middle Eastern frontiers. Egypt lost its empire to invaders from Europe and the East. Law and order broke down in the Two Lands. Thousands starved because of drought and crop failure; roaming bands of soldiers terrorized the people; the grasping priests, exorbitant taxes and corrupt officials squeezed farmers and merchants unmercifully. Even the tombs of the Pharaohs were not safe from ransacking. Libyan invaders seized the throne of Egypt and droves of Egypt's priests, leaders and artisans fled to Kush.

In the midst of these circumstances a black leader named Kashta came to power as king of Kush, and in 751 B.C. conquered Upper Egypt. Not much is known about Kashta. He took the title of king but not Pharaoh. As part of his price for peace, Osorkon III, the Libyan ruler of Lower Egypt, was "persuaded" by Kashta to make his daughter high priestess of Amen-Ra, the state religion. This formally established Kashta's right to the throne.

Incidentally, at the very time Kashta was campaigning successfully in Upper Egypt, Rome was founded at a bucolic river crossing on the Italian peninsula. While Kashta, using some of the most advanced organizational and military techniques of his day, was conquering one of the world's greatest civilizations, the Romans, consisting of several tribes of farmers and shepherds, were living in straw huts on the hills overlooking the swamp that one day would become the Forum.

By this time Kush had been under increasingly strong Egyptian influence and domination for more than a thousand years. Especially during the New Kingdom, Kush, as an integral part of Egypt, had been thoroughly Egyptianized in religion, art, literature, administration and organization. Thus, when the Two Lands tottered under the onslaught of pressures from outside and inside the country, Kush became a haven and refuge in which the basic elements of Egyptian civilization were cherished and continued. When Piankhi, who was Kashta's son, became king, he therefore viewed the reunification of Egypt and the ousting of her enemies as his principal challenge. With puritanical zeal, carrying the "true" Egyptian values back to the motherland, Piankhi led his legions into Egypt in an attempt to liberate the country from the foreign yoke imposed by the Libyan kings and to restore the greatness of the Two Lands.

Opposition to the Libyan usurpers had built up in the north of Egypt also, and in the Delta, the region between what is now Cairo and Alexandria, a prince named Tefnakht arose and rallied a rebellion. He marched out of the Delta and subdued large areas of Lower Egypt, moved on into Upper Egypt and captured Hermopolis, three hundred miles south of the Mediterranean, and meanwhile placed the strategic city of Herakleopolis, 180 miles from the sea, under siege.

Piankhi, in his capital at Napata, eight hundred miles south of Herakleopolis, realized that this was a challenge too strong and an opportunity too important to miss. He ordered his armies north. One army was to stop the southward advance by land of Tefnakht's troops and recapture the key city of Hermopolis. The second army was sent down the Nile to prevent Tefnakht's assault on Thebes, the capital of Upper Egypt.

Piankhi's forces intercepted Tefnakht's fleet north of Thebes, defeated it soundly and then raced to Herakleopolis to reach it before the city surrendered to Tefnakht's siege. Here again Piankhi's troops were successful and drove Tefnakht's army back into the Delta. However, the fact that Tefnakht and his army managed to escape and retreat to safety enraged Piankhi. He left for Egypt immediately, devoutly celebrated a feast day at Thebes, and hurried on to take command of his troops in their siege of Hermopolis. His armies soon overpowered the weakened defenders and Hermopolis surrendered. The queen of Nemarath [Nimrod], the prince of Hermopolis, then pleaded with one of Piankhi's six wives that the life of the defeated prince be spared, and it was done.

Engraved in a stone pillar is Piankhi's official description of the events of his reign. We glimpse the man's character from his report of this moment of triumph. During his tour of the captured palace Piankhi inspected the stables. The report tells us he was furious to find that Nimrod's horses had not been properly fed and cared for while the city was under siege. (No doubt the horses had been slighted in the pressure to keep citizens alive.) Anyway, Piankhi was incensed: "I swear as Ra loves me . . . it is more grievous in my heart that these horses have suffered hunger than any evil deed that you have done in the pursuit of your ambitions."

A horse is engraved on Piankhi's stele—very unusual in Egyptian or Kushite art. But Piankhi was unusually fond of horses and he insisted that they be included in the pictures on the wall of the huge temple of Amen at Jebel Barkal, the great religious center of Kush. It was this temple that Piankhi rebuilt to celebrate the conquest of Egypt. Furthermore, in the royal graveyard at Kurru the remains of twenty-four horses have been found. They were buried in rows, side by side, standing and facing south. Wearing silver headbands, plume carriers and rich trappings, these horses were the teams for the royal chariots of Piankhi and his three successors.

After Hermopolis surrendered, Piankhi hurled his troops and fleet against Memphis, the ancient capital of Egypt. Determined to crush all resistance, Piankhi overwhelmed the city in an all-out assault. When it fell, many princes of the Delta surrendered and Piankhi moved on to Heliopolis. There his armies captured the city, and Osorkon IV, last of the Libyan kings of Egypt, capitulated. Prince Tefnakht, meanwhile, scurried to safety on a remote island at the mouth of the Nile. From this refuge he sent a surrender message to Piankhi, who was satisfied in the fullness of his triumph to leave Tefnakht alone.

Piankhi's victory was immense by any standard. He had conquered all of Egypt and was now, as king of Upper and Lower Egypt and Kush, lord and master of a land that stretched from the Sahara to the borders of Ethiopia and from the shores of the Mediterranean fourteen hundred miles to the middle reaches of the White and Blue Niles, beyond modern Khartoum.

Flush with victory and laden with riches, Piankhi withdrew to his capital at Napata. It was then that he erected that stone pillar recording his conquest. Piankhi was now Pharaoh and wore the double crown, symbolic of his rule over both Upper and Lower Egypt. The full panoply and pomp of Egyptian tradition were restored and his name, as founder of the XXV Dynasty, took its place alongside the greats of Egypt's illustrious history.

When Piankhi returned to the capital of Kush he had been satisfied to leave the princes of the Delta alone, only requiring, of course, that they pay annual tribute to him. As he might have foreseen, this allowed them altogether too much leeway. With Piankhi a thousand miles away, Prince Tefnakht once again rebelled and declared himself king of Lower Egypt. He did not live to make good that claim, but about 720 B.C. his son Bekenrenef claimed these royal titles and continued the insurrection.

Though Pharaoh Piankhi struck back, he died before the rebellion could be crushed. His brother Shabako then came to the throne. Shabako ruthlessly smashed Bekenrenef's revolt and, as an object lesson to dissidents, burned the rebel leader alive. But more important, he moved his capital from Napata five hundred miles north to Thebes from which he could govern more effectively and keep a wary eye on the Delta princes and others who might be contemplating revolt.

Pharaoh Shabako was not satisfied to let the Delta princes hold power, as Piankhi had allowed. He installed a Kushite administration over the entire country to tighten control and prevent another uprising. Futhermore, to secure his claim to the throne of Egypt, he saw to it that his daughter was adopted as high priestess of Amen-Ra. Shabako could truly call himself king of Kush and Egypt and thus was he known throughout the ancient world.

This was a time—about 700 B.C.—of great trouble not only in Egypt but all through the Middle East. It is the period we read of in the Old Testament of the Bible, particularly in II Kings and Isaiah. The Hittites in Asia Minor had given way to the Sumerians and Phrygians and they in turn were under attack from the Assyrians, Cimmerians, Medes and Scyths. Wars were practically continuous, with battles raging in Iraq, Iran, in the Caucasus and throughout the eastern end of the Mediterranean. Among the small nations caught between the superpowers of the time many were familiar from Biblical history: Israel, Judah, Damascus, Sidon and Tyre.

The major expansionist power of this period was the Assyrian empire. During the years we have just glimpsed, Assyria overwhelmed Babylon and, at the opposite end of its frontiers, conquered Damascus, sacked Samaria and deported the ten tribes of Israel to Iraq. This left the tiny kingdom of Judah between Assyria and Egypt. The Book of Kings tells of Hezekiah's fateful decision to cooperate with the Egypt of the Kushite Pharaohs against the Assyrians.

Sennacherib, King of Assyria, invaded Judah, extorted a payment of silver and gold and went on to besiege Jerusalem. Pharaoh Shabako dispatched an army to break the siege and repel the Assyrians. Taunting his enemies, Sennacherib said to

Judah, "Now behold thou trustest on the staff of this bruised reed, even upon Egypt, on which if a man lean, it will go into his hand and pierce it; so it is Pharaoh king of Egypt unto all that trust on him."[3]

As the king of the Assyrians gathered his troops and prepared to attack Judah and Egypt, a miracle occurred, the Bible tells us. The Angel of the Lord struck Sennacherib's armies, killing fifteen thousand men overnight. Apparently the "miracle" was a plague that devastated the troops and in 701 B.C. the Assyrians hastily fled from Palestine.

When Shabako died five years later, the threat of war with Assyria still haunted Egypt. Piankhi's son Shebitku became Pharaoh after his uncle Shabako's death. His younger brother Taharqa joined him on the throne at Thebes. Taharqa was only twenty at this time, but by his twenty-fifth year Shebitku was dead and the young man was sole ruler of Kush and Egypt.

Taharqa

No new sovereign could have had more encouraging omens for the beginning of his reign. Famine, drought and pestilence had plagued Egypt for scores of years. But as Taharqa came to the throne in 690 B.C. there occurred an unprecedented flooding of the Nile. Pharaoh Taharqa described this historic event:

It [the flood] penetrated the hills of Upper Egypt, it overtopped the
mounds of Lower Egypt, and the land became a primordial
ocean . . . moreover the sky rained in Nubia, it made all the
hills glisten. Every man had abundance of everything, Egypt
was in happy festival. . . . For the inundation came as a cattle
thief, it inundated the entire land, the like of it was not found

in writing in the time of the ancestors and none said "I have
heard from my father [of such a flood]."[4]

Taharqa did not exaggerate. The heavy rains in Kush brought
the water level of the Nile at Karnak, near Thebes, to an
astonishing three hundred feet. This high water mark is still
visible. Not only did this massive bath irrigate vast areas of
land, it drowned rats and other vermin. The result was a record
harvest, a surge of popular support for the new ruler, and
widespread belief that the new reign was blessed by the gods.

Because of the Assyrian threat, Taharqa moved his court
to the Delta where he could keep an eye on events in Asia
Minor. He schemed with other rulers against the Assyrians and
encouraged Assyria's vassal states, especially Tyre and Sidon, to
rise up against their oppressor. Sidon rebelled in 677 B.C. and
Tyre the next year. There is no record that Taharqa helped
either country. The Assyrians crushed both revolts and executed
the king of Sidon. Five years later the Assyrians, under King *Figure 22*
Esarhaddon, finally launched their attack on Egypt. Using camel
trains, Esarhaddon's armies crossed the Sinai desert, struck the
massed Egyptian armies at the frontier and defeated them
soundly. Pursuing their advantage, the invaders pushed on and
in a mere two weeks reached Memphis, surrounded it and laid
siege to the city. It fell to a powerful Assyrian attack and
although Taharqa fought his way out, his children and harem
were taken by the invaders.

The princes of the Delta then vowed loyalty to Esarhaddon, who proclaimed himself king of Upper and Lower Egypt.
He erected a victory pillar on which he showed the princes of
Egypt paying tribute to him and Taharqa as a captive being
led by a ring through his lips. However, Esarhaddon then made

the same mistake Piankhi had committed eighty years before: He left Egypt.

Taharqa hurled fresh armies against the Assyrians and not only retook Memphis but swept through the entire Delta area. Hearing this, Esarhaddon returned to subdue Egypt. However, he died en route and his son Ashurbanipal continued the expedition. This time the Assyrians were more thorough and ruthless. They smashed Taharqa's army in the Delta and took Memphis. Taharqa fled to Thebes and Ashurbanipal descended on that city in forty days, driving Taharqa from it in 666 B.C.

In 664 B.C. Pharaoh Taharqa died in his forty-sixth year, ending the reign that had begun with such promising omens. In his quarter century of rule Taharqa had been a great builder in Egypt, but even more so in Kush. He restored temples, built new ones, added colonnades to others, constructed the largest pyramid of his dynasty and a mammoth temple hewn out of the rock at Jebel Barkal, an expanded copy of the famous temple of Rameses II at Abu Simbel.

The vast temple at Kawa, about 120 miles north of Napata, is an example of Taharqa's interests as well as his building activities. An inscription tells how Taharqa noticed the sorry state of the Kawa temple on his way to Egypt at the beginning of his reign. At that time the modest mud brick structure was deteriorating from the rain and was half covered by sand. After his coronation at Memphis the next year, Taharqa sent a small army of experts and craftsmen to build a huge temple on the site. It was constructed of sandstone, some of it overlaid with gold leaf. The landscaping included a lake, which had to be dug, plantings of trees and vines, and gardens and vineyards—gardeners were brought from Lower Egypt. Taharqa dispatched experts in telling time by star-transits (astrologers) and in addition to the priests and attendants normally attached to a temple of this importance, he sent the captured wives of Delta princes who had resisted him, assigning them to serve the gods, while serving as hostages.

Tanwetamani

Taharqa's nephew Tanwetamani succeeded him. Even before the Pharaoh's death Tanwetamani had dreamt that he saw two snakes rise, one on either side of him. Officially, this dream was interpreted to mean that Tanwetamani would have an illustrious reign and would unite all of Egypt, wresting it from the Assyrians.

Therefore, when he became king, Tanwetamani was crowned at Napata and went down the Nile to Elephantine where he was received tumultuously. His welcome at Thebes was triumphant. At Memphis he met in battle the ever-rebellious princes of the Delta. His armies chased them back into their fortified towns. Returning to Memphis, he received tribute from the princes he had defeated.

Then disaster struck. The Assyrian armies arrived and Tanwetamani ran before them. For awhile he stayed at Thebes. When the Assyrians neared, he hurried to Napata. The invaders determined to make an example of Thebes and they pillaged and sacked it. We read of their action in the words of the Biblical prophet Nahum who warned Nineveh later:

Art thou better than populous [Thebes] that was situate among the
  canals and that had the Nile round about it for a rampart
  and a wall? Kush and Egypt were her strength, and it was
  infinite. . . . Yet was she carried away, she went into captivity:

> Her young children also were dashed in pieces at the top of all
> the streets; And they cast lots for her honorable men, and all
> her great men were bound in chains.[5]

The Assyrians put one of the Delta princes on the throne of
Egypt and from 654 B.C. he ruled the Two Lands, thus ending
the Nubian XXV Dynasty, so far as control of Egypt was
concerned. This dynasty continued to rule over Kush for a
thousand years more, however. Though Tanwetamani was not
captured by the Assyrians, there is no information about what
happened to him. His pyramid is not in Taharqa's cemetery,
but with his ancestors at Kurru.

How were the Assyrians able to conquer Egypt with
such speed? They had developed iron weapons and scale armor
which were far superior to the bronze swords, spears and arrows
of their enemies. Furthermore, the Assyrians had refined military
organization to the point that they used special units for special
tasks—engineer units for siege, ordnance units for outfitting and
supplying troops, transport units for managing travel. They had
divisions made up of light and heavy bow, spear, cavalry and
infantrymen and their heavy chariots were the ancient equivalent
of our modern tank and armored units. In addition, the Assyrian
soldiers were tough, wiry peasants who had been fighting in the
constant Assyrian campaigns of conquest for years. Well-trained,
well-disciplined, experienced and equipped with the latest in
weapons and military techniques, they were truly formidable.

Taharqa's armies, with their bronze and brass weapons,
were at a distinct disadvantage in pitched battle against the
Assyrians. It was after this time that iron objects were made in
considerable quantities in Kush. Egypt had little iron ore and

practically no wood for fuel. In contrast, the area around Meroe, the great city of Kush, more than three hundred miles upstream from Napata and eleven hundred miles south of the Mediterranean, had timber and rich iron ore deposits. Meroe is on the east bank of the Nile, between the Fifth and Sixth Cataracts, about 120 miles from present-day Khartoum. After 600 B.C. Meroe became a large ironworking center. Even today the hills of slag produced by the ancient iron production are so impressive and unique that Meroe is often called the Pittsburgh of ancient Africa.

For a millennium after the Assyrian conquest, the sixty-six descendants of Tanwetamani who ruled over Kush continued to style themselves "King of Upper and Lower Egypt" as well, though they no longer had such power. They continued the forms of Egyptian civilization—the religions and court ceremonies, writing, art, architecture—but with strong African elements unique to Kush. Kush was a rich land and these kings were powerful even though they no longer had the resources of Egypt. They still aspired to reconquer Egypt for some years and when Pharaoh Necho II was defeated by the Babylonian king Nebuchadnezzar in 605 B.C. the king of Kush decided to try again. The Kushites drove as far as Abu Simbel, only 250 miles from Thebes. Now Egypt was simultaneously threatened from south and north, and the Pharaoh decided to send his Greek and Carian mercenaries against Kush. In the fierce, desperate fighting that followed, the Kushites were driven back deep into their country while the Egyptian expedition sacked Napata, the capital. Damage to the statues of the kings at Jebel Barkal and Napata dates from this event, as far as we can tell. The capital of Kush was transferred at this time to Meroe.

MEROE

Today, the ruins of Meroe may be observed from the railroad that runs north from Khartoum. In view are two or three small temples and beyond them is the extraordinary stone platform thought to be the Temple of the Sun described about 430 B.C. by Herodotus. Still farther on are the ruins of the pyramids of the Western Cemetery where the leading citizens of Meroe were buried. And about a mile beyond this point is a long hill with *Figures 23–24* the royal pyramids built on it. Here are the kings and queens who ruled from 300 B.C. onward. On the far side of the ridge is a valley and across it are still more pyramids. These structures are the grave sites of numerous relatives of the XXV Dynasty rulers.

Meroe benefits from the floods of two rivers, the Nile and the Atbara, and also is at the northern limit of the rainfall belt. Because of these conditions it is a fertile area and in ancient times this accounted for its wealth. Here cattle, sheep, and goats could be raised and crops grown. In addition, caravan routes crossed the river near Meroe going west; others, many others, went east to the Red Sea ports. These factors, plus the ironworking industry, made the city one of the most important in Africa for many centuries. It has been partially excavated, and the cemeteries have revealed scores of kings, queens and princes and their way of life.

Inscriptions on pillars erected by these black kings tell us of attacks by rebels and raiding tribes in what must have been a no-man's land between Kush and Egypt for centuries. They tell also of temples built and festivals inaugurated, of increasing insecurity in the land. By 330 B.C. looters were able to take gold objects from the temples in the cities of Kawa and Tare, precious items that had been in the shrines for 250 years. So depleted were the king's powers that he was unable to capture the raiders and had to content himself with replacing the stolen objects with goods from his own treasury.

And yet there was a resurgence of wealth and power about 250 B.C. King Ergamenes and the five black rulers who succeeded him flourished in a period when friendly relations with Egypt were at an all-time high. A Greek dynasty, the Ptolemies, was on the throne of Egypt and temple inscriptions in Nubia prove that Ergamenes and Ptolemy IV were unusually friendly. In fact, at the town of Philae near the First Cataract, Ptolemy built the inner hall of a temple and Ergamenes the entrance hall; at Dakka, a few miles south, the situation was reversed. Ergamenes built the inner hall of a temple and Ptolemy constructed the entrance.

Figure 29

There was a revival of Egyptian culture in Kush at this time and the chapel of Ergamenes' pyramid was decorated by artists and scribes who must have been Egyptian. We know this because the Meroitic writing was distinctly different from the Egyptian by this time. (Both Meroitic hieroglyphs and so-called cursive writing can be read, incidentally; they were deciphered in 1909 by Griffith, who was able to determine the phonetic value of the script. However, though the written language can be read phonetically—like Etruscan—the meaning of the words is not known.) But over the next five reigns there was a general prosperity which deteriorated drastically during the rule of King Tanyidamani, from 120 to 100 B.C. One archeologist has theorized that there was a split in the kingdom at this time over who had the right to the throne. But whatever the cause, from this point on a sudden impoverishment is noticeable in the tombs, their furnishings and decoration.

In 30 B.C. Rome conquered Egypt and governed the

Kush border from Syene. About 24 B.C. the Roman governor, Gaius Petronius, took a military force to Arabia, leaving this frontier lightly defended. Seizing the opportunity, the Kushites attacked Philae and Syene, sacked them and carried away the bronze statues of the Emperor Augustus which the Romans had placed in the market squares.

When Petronius returned, he launched an expedition to punish Kush. The Greek historian-geographer Strabo described this reprisal mission and said the poorly-armed Kushites could not withstand the Roman might and were driven before Petronius' advance. The Romans captured the towns of Premnis and Pselchis and the queen of Kush (called "candace" in Meroitic) offered to return the statues. Petronius ordered his troops on, however, and they looted not only Premnis and Pselchis, but Napata, which they utterly destroyed. The candace sent her general to surrender and the Romans moved back to a fortified garrison at Premnis.

Figure 32

Just nineteen hundred years later Strabo's report was verified when archeologists excavating a small temple in a palace complex in Meroe discovered a fine bronze head of Augustus. It was definitely Roman work and was hidden in a pocket of clean sand under the threshold of the building. Today it is in the British Museum, and a cast of it is in the Khartoum Museum.

The Roman attack was not a death blow to Kush. In fact, under King Netakamani (2 B.C. to 23 A.D.) there was a resurgence of prosperity that enabled him to build temples, shrines and chapels, and to reconstruct the temples at Napata destroyed by Petronius. Netakamani brought in Egyptian craftsmen for much of this work and it was the final revival of the Egyptian tradition in Kush. This was a last flush of prosperity, though twenty-two more rulers followed Netakamani before the dynasty sputtered out in poverty and oblivion three centuries later.

Kush's Art

For centuries the ancient world knew Kush for her art as well as her raw materials. Her craftsmen were skilled in working precious metals and her gold, bronze and silver jewelry, implements and utensils have strong, beautiful designs. Her potters *Figure 31* were masters of their craft. The finest pieces were relatively small and delicate, turned on wheels, with compelling scenes or designs in earth colors. Often Kushite pots carry sketches of hunters, animals, plants, flowers and intricate patterns. Many have decorations stamped into them and some have designs incised into their surfaces and filled with white or red pigment.

Today the pottery of Kush is her best-known product. One authority states it "ranks with the finest products of ceramic art of the ancient world both in the quality of its fabric [manufacture] and the style of its decoration, and, together with the later and related pottery of Christian Nubia, forms the main contribution of the ancient Sudan to the artistic heritage of the Nile Valley."[6]

Though there have been no definitive studies of Kush's art, we are able to deduce that there was a strong local tradition of vigorous expression in stone and paint and architecture. In these media the influence of Egypt was greatest and we see this in the tomb pyramids, the forms of the temples and the trapezoidal pylons, the familiar stylization of the figures marching in profile. Yet, within these conventions there are elements that are unmistakably Kushite. Both men and women, for instance, are stocky and heavy-limbed, with prominent rear-ends and folds of fat at their necks. The regalia of the kings and queens is decidedly different from the Egyptian, though many of the same gods attend them.

We see in the Lion Temple reliefs at Naqa the royal couple wearing close-fitting, helmet-like hats, held by a narrow

Figure 26 band about the brow, with ribbons flying behind. On their upper arms they have bracelets and at the wrist and forearm they wear elaborate cuffs or bracelets. About their necks are waist-long strings of large, ball-shaped beads. A bird-wing pattern is used on the kilt of the king and skirt of the queen. The king wears a thumb ring (and these are frequently found in the graves), carries a sword and decorative mace; the queen carries a sword in each hand! (Egypt's queens never carry such weapons.) And King Sherkarer in one relief smites his enemies, wins the flower of victory from the sun-god and wears curious lion-head kneecaps in his hour of triumph.

Perhaps the most distinctive features of Kush's art are the representations of the lion and elephant. The kings are always seated on lion thrones and in temple reliefs the enemies of the king are pictured as subdued by and in some cases devoured by lions. There is also evidence that in the lion temple at Musawwarat es-Sofra, tame lions were kept as living symbols of the lion-god Apedemek, who is shown on the walls as larger than humans, receiving tribute from the king and leading the other gods. He carries a bow and quiver in one scene, a staff in another and wears the familiar three-part crown and a plain gown from breast to knee.

On the pylons of the great Lion Temple at Naqa (other lion temples are found at Musawwarat and Meroe) there is a

Figure 25 huge, unique bas-relief of Apedemek—wearing his three-part crown — with the body of a cobra emerging from a lotus. This use of the snake and lotus and other representations of Apedemek with three heads and multiple arms suggests influences from India where the triple-lion image has been venerated for millennia and is found to this day. It has been speculated that Indian goods must have come to Kush via the caravan route from the Red Sea ports.

Another element suggestive of Indian influence is the use of the elephant in sculpture and building arrangement at Musawwarat es-Sofra. There, large enclosures with ramps, walls terminating in elephant figures and reliefs show elephants in many ceremonial activities, including the carrying of a king. It is thought that this particular site may have been a place for training elephants for military use. Kushites were the trainers for the elephants used by the Romans in warfare.

Figure 30

Kush's architecture is extensive in its variety and quantity. The usual building materials are brick and stone and the buildings are similar in design to the Egyptian temples, pylons, courtyards, shrines and pillars. Throughout Kush at the important towns and cities are all of these constructions, plus palaces, baths, tombs, forts, houses and cemeteries. The most outstanding sites are at Nuri, Jebel Barkal and Kurru where the gaunt ruins of pyramids remind us of Kush's past glories. Napata, Meroe, Karima, Faras, Amara East and Kawa are rich in buildings and unexcavated ruins. All of these give evidence of wealth, power and prestige. Yet, there were times of real poverty. Both Pliny and Seneca tell of one or two reconnaisance missions from Rome into Kush sent by Nero about 61 A.D. to evaluate whether to conquer the region and add it to the Roman Empire. The representatives from Rome traveled around the country, visiting the cities of Kush, talking to the people. They returned to Rome and reported that Kush would not be worth the effort.

Figure 27

THE FALL OF KUSH

What caused the downfall of Kush? Although there is no definitive record on this, there were several major factors that must have combined to bring about its end. One was the ruin of the land. Lengthy and extensive grazing of cattle and goats on the countryside had this effect. The cattle overgrazed the grassland. The goats ate the tiny shoots of trees, thus preventing the replacement of mature trees which aged and died or were cut for timber or fuel. Without trees, the root systems to anchor the soil are lacking and grazing crops are more susceptible to the elements. Erosion increases and the soil quickly washes away. Another probable factor in the decline of agriculture was the dwindling rainfall and the effect of the ensuing drought on the growth of crops.

Still another factor was the impoverishment of Egypt under Roman rule and the impact this had on trade between Kush and its northern neighbor. Egypt prospered during the first century of Roman control but the taxes became increasingly harsh, until Egyptians actually fled the farms and villages and penniless peasants took up banditry. Poverty was general throughout Egypt and there were riots in the major cities.

The pressure from other tribes and nations was a major factor in Kush's demise. In fact, in 296 A.D. Rome's Emperor Diocletian called in a tribe called the Nobatae or Noba and encouraged them to "protect" Egypt's southern frontier. This was an open invitation to launch raids and prey upon Kush, with Upper Egypt as a sanctuary. This action indicates that the Romans had decided Kush was so insignificant, unpromising or troublesome as to warrant no further interest. Cutting Kush off from Egypt could only weaken the black land and hasten its ultimate downfall.

There were other peoples who harrassed, invaded and probably captured portions of Kush. One of these tribes was the Blemmyes on Kush's eastern border, who apparently became strong enough, along with the Nobatae, to seize control of one of the large northern Kush provinces. More important than any of these, ancient pre-Ethiopia, called Axum at this time, had gained power and, in the opinion of some experts, actually took over effective rule in Kush.

Trade with India, the Middle East and the Roman world in the goods of Africa made Axum wealthy as Kush declined. That decline is dramatically illustrated by the differences in the pyramids of the last rulers of Kush. From tall and stately stone *Figure 28* monuments with elaborate painted and carved decoration in their tomb chambers, the pyramids became shorter, smaller, less decorated (with poorer craftsmanship) until the final ones are little more than small mounds of plastered red brick.

Whether Kush was nibbled away by these various forces or fell in one cataclysmic collapse is uncertain. We do know that Ezana, the king of Axum, claimed to be king of Kush and sent an expedition to punish and subdue the Noba who were in the area and had revolted. Here is a part of Ezana's inscription describing the expedition of 350 A.D., shortly after Constantine had moved the Roman capital to Byzantium:

. . . I, Ezana, . . . king of kings . . . made war upon Noba for the peoples
  had rebelled and had boasted of it. . . "They [the Axumites]
  will not cross the River [Atbara]" said the peoples of Noba. . .
  And as I had warned them and they would not listen but
  refused to cease from their evil deeds and betook themselves
  to flight, I made war on them . . . and fought with them on
  the [Atbara] at the ford of Kemalke. They fled without

> making a stand and I pursued them for twenty-three days,
> killing some and capturing others. . . I burned their towns,
> both those built of bricks and those built of reeds, and my
> army carried off their food and copper and iron . . . and
> destroyed the statues in their temples, their granaries and
> cotton trees and cast them into the river [Nile]. And I came
> to [Kush] and fought a battle and captured prisoners at the
> junction of the rivers [Nile] and [Atbara]. And the next day I
> despatched [five armies] up the [Nile] to raid the country and
> the cities built of bricks and of reeds . . . and after that I sent
> [two armies] down the Nile against the four towns of the
> Noba which are made of reeds. . . And my peoples reached
> the frontier of the Red Noba and they returned in safety,
> having defeated the Noba and spoiled them by the might of
> the Lord of Heaven. And I planted a throne in that country
> at the place where the [Nile] and [Atbara] join. . . .[7]

At this point silence descends on ancient Kush and it disappears
from sight. One of the tantalizing mysteries of history is the
question of its fate. What happened to its priests, its royalty, its
skilled craftsmen? Did they become wanderers in strange lands?
Did they migrate westward and manage to put down roots?
These and other tempting questions may be answered when the
scholars have excavated the key places and solved the riddle of
Meroitic language. Meanwhile, there are some intriguing clues.

For instance, the name "Kush" went out of use after the
fall of Meroe. Yet there are Negro peoples west of the Nile
today whose names have "Kush" as part of their own. The
Kagiddi, the Kaja and the Kajjar all included the phrase "Kash"
or "Kaj" which means "people of Kush."

The Kagiddi have a legend that they came from somewhere in the east and were led westward by a queen. The queen, according to their belief, is buried in a grave mound and the location of this grave is well known. Perhaps excavation of this site will uncover evidence about the Kagiddi's connection — if any—with the fall of Meroe.

The institutions of the Darfur, a black people centered about six hundred miles west of Meroe, have many direct parallels with those of Kush. The royal palace at Uri, for instance, has stone work like that in the royal palace at Meroe. Several of the Darfur tribes use cattle brands approximate to the royal property marks used at Meroe. Some of the names used by Darfur royalty seem to stem from Meroe also.

These are but a few of the curious facts that point to revelations yet to come about the end of Kush. Certainly a people who maintained a high level of civilization for a thousand years must have left some traces that will tell us their fate. But for now the final chapter of the story of Kush's greatness and disappearance remains unwritten.

NOTES

1. *The Bird Catcher*, B. Aaftjes, *Der Blinde Hafner;* in U. Beier, *African Poetry*, (Cambridge: Cambridge University Press, 1966), p. 49.
2. P. L. Shinnie, *Meroe*, (New York: F. A. Praeger, Inc., 1967), p. 169. Shinnie used the date c. 431 B.C. for the start of this period which extended to about 340 A.D. because this was the time during which the city of Meroe was Kush's capital. Kush was far older, however, and the Kushite kings conquered Egypt from their capital at Napata in 751 B.C.
3. *II Kings*, xviii, 21.
4. A. J. Arkell, *A History of the Sudan*, (London: Athlone Press, 1961), pp. 121–141.
5. *Old Testament;* Nahum III, 8, 9, 10.
6. Shinnie, *op. cit.*
7. *Ibid.*

We lived in freedom
Before man appeared:
Our world was undisturbed,
One day followed the other joyfully,
Dissent was never heard.
   Then man broke into our forest
   With cunning and belligerence,
   He pursued us
   With greed and envy:
Our freedom vanished.

SONG OF THE TURTLE
Traditional Ghanian poem

◁▷ ◁▷ ◁▷ ◁▷ ◁▷ ◁▷ ◁▷ ◁▷ ◁▷ ◁▷ ◁▷ ◁▷

GHANA:
LAND OF GOLD

◁▷ ◁▷ ◁▷ ◁▷ ◁▷ ◁▷ ◁▷ ◁▷ ◁▷ ◁▷ ◁▷ ◁▷

IV

AOUKAR, WAGADU, SONINKE, *KAYA MAGHAN*—
if these words sound strange, perhaps it is the fault of our
historians and educators. Aoukar or Wagadu were terms for the
ancient empire founded by the black Soninke people of West
Africa. Their leader was called *kaya maghan*—king of the gold;
or *ghana*—war chief.

Over the centuries, as the wealth of Aoukar became
famous, the term for its powerful king—*ghana*—became synony-

mous with the country itself. Even today the word lives on in the name of the Republic of Ghana on the Gulf of Guinea. This young nation purposely chose to associate itself with the glory of a past empire that was rich and powerful, even though in reality modern Ghana has no historical links with ancient Ghana. It is far southeast of the nation that developed from about 200 A.D. and flourished until smashed by an invasion in 1075.

The original Ghana was in the western part of the *Bilad es Sudan*—Land of the Blacks, as the Arabs called the belt that spans Africa from the Atlantic to the Red Sea, bordered on the north by the Sahara and on the south by the tropical rain forest. This first empire of the Western Sudan nestled in the wide "U" made by the mighty Senegal River on the west and the headwaters of the Niger on the east.

What was great about Ghana? It was a land of ambitious and able black people who governed a large territory of interior, grassland Africa with a well-developed system of administration and taxation. It was a prosperous land with far-reaching trade relations in all directions. Ghana's rulers had organized extraordinary numbers of warriors. Equipped with iron-pointed weapons, these soldiers had expanded the empire's boundaries and maintained a degree of peace in the country that was marveled at by friends and foes alike.

Because written records are lacking for the early centuries, we have to rely on archeology, reports of observers and oral history (the chronicle passed on from generation to generation by the professional "storytellers" or historians). The reports are often fabulous and frustrating because they raise so many additional questions. Often archeological findings verify portions of the reports. And in future years, as more and more scientists dig in the ruins of ancient Ghana and more written reports (now in libraries and private collections) are translated, we will have increasingly accurate information about the wonders of Ghana.

That it was a Land of Gold cannot be denied. The yellow metal was plentiful in Ghana and especially in the areas to the south of it. Because of the king's control of the precious metal, Ghana was rich. The trade in gold to the north and salt to the south made the empire a vast trading center and a crossroads for caravans.

Reporting about 1520 A.D., a Moslem Soninke named Al Kati told in his famous history *Tarikh al-Fettash* about one king, Kanissa'ai, who ruled Ghana in its days of glory.

The King

Al Kati wrote that Kanissa'ai was "one of the lords of the gold." It was his custom to come out of his palace every evening to hear his subjects and talk with them. This he did, however, only after the necessary preparations had been completed. "A thousand faggots were gathered for a fire, so that all might be lit and warmed." So spectacular was the fire that its flames lighted "the space between heaven and earth." After this, Kanissa'ai would appear in his ceremonial dress and take his place upon "a balcony of red-gleaming gold." Then he would give orders "to bring forth food sufficient for ten thousand people."[1]

According to Al Kati, King Kanissa'ai could well afford such prodigal generosity. Even the king's horses lived royally. Kanissa'ai owned one thousand horses, Al Kati reports, and each one slept on a mattress of its own "with a silken rope for a halter" in a stable that was as spotless as the king's palace. Each steed had its own copper urinal and three body-servants to tend to its needs around the clock!

What about such a report? How accurate can this possibly be? Allowing for exaggeration and mis-translation of quantities, there is still no reason to doubt the general outlines of Al Kati's information. As to the extraordinary care of the king's horses, we can believe it up to a point. In the days of Kanissa'ai, horses represented wealth in every part of the world. Thus it would have been prudent for a king to amass as large a number as possible, (1) as evidence of his wealth and superiority; (2) to control his people and protect his power. In his wide-flung state, the king needed horse patrols to keep order and check on the caravans. Then, as was true until the time of the gasoline engine, he who had the most cavalry was generally the most powerful. (3) Since his horses were so valuable, they deserved, and got, extraordinary care. (4) Care of the horses provided work for many hands, creating a nucleus of loyal retainers.

What about Kanissa'ai's audiences? Audiences with his people were part of a king's duty to his subjects in many areas of Africa, though every night of the year would have been an unusually demanding schedule. In fact, the description of Kanissa'ai's audiences tallies with that of another historian whose book, published in Cordoba in 1067, described the Ghana of that time:

The king who governs [Aoukar, or Ghana] at present . . . is called Tenkaminen; Tenkaminen is the master of a large empire and a formidable power. . . The king of Ghana can put two hundred thousand warriors in the field, more than forty thousand being armed with bow and arrow. . . . [Note that this was just a year after a certain Norman duke named William fielded between ten thousand and fifteen thousand warriors in a battle at Hastings and conquered the tiny island of England.]

When he gives audience to his people to listen to their

complaints and set them to rights, he sits in a pavilion around which stand ten horses with gold-embroidered trappings. Behind the king stand ten pages holding shields and gold-mounted swords; on his right are the sons of princes of his empire, splendidly clad and with gold plaited in their hair. The governor of the city is seated on the ground in front of the king, and all around him are seated his viziers. The door of the pavilion is guarded by dogs of an excellent breed who almost never leave the king's presence and who wear collars of gold and silver, ornamented with the same metals. The beginning of a royal audience is announced by the beating of a kind of drum which they call *deba*, made of a long piece of hollowed wood. The people gather when they hear this sound. . . .[2]

This report was written by the illustrious Moorish geographer Al Bekri, in the monumental *Book of Roads and Kingdoms*. This was a compilation of the most up-to-date and authoritative information on Africa at that time. Al Bekri had never set foot in Ghana himself. His information came from the caravan leaders, Moslem merchants and travelers who had made the journey, and he set down their descriptions with scrupulous attention to detail. We can trust his reports because archeologists have verified many of his statements. Furthermore, the statistics in his book have been checked and have been found remarkably accurate.

The Kingdom

The geographer described the capital of Ghana, for instance, as made up of two towns situated on a plain. In one lived the king and his court, and in another, about six miles distant, the Moslem traders and merchants lived. The Moslem town, according to Al Bekri, had twelve mosques with paid staffs of Koranic readers and learned men. Surrounding the town were "wells of sweet water from which they drink and near which they grow vegetables." The king's town, he continues, included "a palace and a number of dome-shaped dwellings, the whole surrounded by an enclosure like the defensive wall of a city."

In 1914, at a place known today as Kumbi Saleh, about two hundred miles north of the capital of the Republic of Mali in present-day Mauritania, the ruins of a town were unearthed. French archeologists excavated them in the 1950's and found numerous fine stone buildings, many of them two stories high. The scientists are convinced that this is the town of the Moslem traders and the search is on for the twin town of Ghana's kings. This will be more difficult to find, for the Ghanians used baked clay and wooden beams for construction—materials far more susceptible to deterioration than the masonry used by the Moslems.

Why this separation of towns? The kings of Ghana were not Moslems, though they enjoyed friendly relations with the Moslem traders and there was mutual respect between Ghanians and Moslems. Apparently the kings of Ghana welcomed the merchants and traders so long as they paid their taxes and observed the laws, but they did not want foreign influences in the capital. It was, after all, a fortress with a rich treasury and they wanted no aliens within the walls perhaps plotting to overthrow the monarch and raid the vault. It was safer, therefore, to keep them at a distance where they could be watched.

One of the major achievements of the Ghanians was their organization of the empire. From Al Bekri and other sources it is evident that by the mid-eleventh century the king of Ghana ruled through a functional hierarchy. He had a group of executive officers, his viziers; he had a governor to manage his

capital city; and he had as part of his court the sons and heirs-
apparent of the kings and princes who were loyal to him. No
doubt these princes were present not only to enjoy the court life
but also as hostages to insure that their fathers remained loyal
to the "king of kings."

So the small but energetic tribes that began with the
advantage of ironworking and iron-tipped weapons about 200
A.D. developed a proverbially prosperous, extensive empire over
the next millennium. Their strategic location gave them control
of the north-south trade. From the south came ivory and slaves,
as well as gold for the Western world. The traders and merchants
exchanged these for the products of North Africa: salt (that
essential commodity unavailable to inland peoples), copper,
dried fruit and cowrie shells (used as money or a medium of
exchange).

This trade enriched not only the merchants but the king
and his government. Al Bekri explains:

The king extracts [a tax] of one *dinar* of gold on each donkey-load of
salt that enters his country and two *dinars* of gold on each load
of salt that goes out. A load of copper carries a duty of five
mitqals and a load of merchandise, ten *mitqals*.[3]

In addition to this export-import tax revenue, the king also had
another sizable source of income. Al Bekri continues:

The best gold in the country comes from Ghiaru, a town situated eighteen days' journey from the capital in a country that is densely
populated by Negroes and covered with villages. All pieces of
native gold found in the mines of the empire belong to the
sovereign, although he lets the public have the gold dust that
everybody knows about. Without this precaution, gold would
become so abundant as practically to lose its value. . . .[4]

In other words, the Ghanians understood the effectiveness of a monopoly for maintaining the price of a commodity—in this case, gold. They controlled the bulk of the gold and prevented it from becoming so plentiful as to drive the price down. Modern-day monopolists do the same, whether the commodity is diamonds (controlled by a small group of companies and released to the market in a small trickle to keep prices up) or oil (where, as an instance, a Texas regulatory commission decrees that oil may be extracted only three days a week and cuts this limited production schedule even more when the supply threatens to drive prices down).

Not all of Ghana's gold came from its own mines. From Wangara, a district just south of Ghana, Mandingo natives exchanged the yellow metal for salt and other necessities. This was done by the "silent trade" or "dumb barter" system. The Ghana merchants would come to a specified place on the bank of a particular river, put down their wares and leave, moving completely out of sight. The gold miners would then warily come and examine the goods. Beside the items they desired, the Wangarans would place an amount of gold dust they considered fair. Then they would retire and the merchants would return. If satisfied with the amount of gold left by the miners, a merchant would pocket it and leave the object. However, if he considered it insufficient, he would again go out in hopes that the Wangarans would increase their payment.

Primitive as this system seems, it worked well for centuries. And it should be noted that this west African area was the primary wellspring of gold for the Western world until the conquistadors of Spain found new sources in the Americas. African miners in this same area today, using the same methods as their ancestors, have produced as much as 140,000 ounces of gold a year! The medieval gold coins of Italy, France or England probably began in ancient Ghana as barter in exchange for salt.

By the beginning of the eleventh century great changes were under way in western Africa. A flood of Arabs had rolled across North Africa destroying, looting, raiding and seizing property, sending the people of these areas fleeing before them. One group that they literally ran off their land was the Berbers. Meanwhile the friction between Berbers and Ghanians had increased along their borders. The Soninke town of Audaghost on the ever-shifting border between the two peoples had been taken over by one of the Berber tribes long before. The Berbers had built Audaghost into a trading center that rivaled Ghana's capital. When the Ghanians captured the city in 990 A.D., Berber tribes united to oppose the Soninke.

The leaders of the Berbers converted to Islam of an extremely puritanical sort. The Berber masses, however, rejected this rigid, narrow interpretation of the Moslem religion. Then arose a devout, fiercely severe leader named Abdullah ibn Yasin. According to tradition, Ibn Yasin withdrew from the world to a "hermitage" on an island in the River Senegal. Here he breathed the fire of holy war—*jihad*—into his loyal followers who were called "the people of the hermitage" (Almurabitun, in Arabic), later known as the Almoravids.

The Almoravids

These Moslem fanatics directed by Ibn Yasin slowly converted more and more of the Berber tribesmen at sword point until most of their villages and towns in the west were Almoravid strongholds.

The Almoravids had two goals. The first was to reform

and press on the Moslems of North Africa and Spain their new, "pure" Islam. Their second goal was to convert all unbelievers— and incidentally conquer in the process. Though the main thrust of the Almoravids was north, one wing under a leader called Abu Bakr aimed south and east. Abu Bakr captured the city of Audaghost in 1054 and after twenty-two years of bitter fighting his troops took the capital of Ghana. Though he laid claim to the entire empire, Abu Bakr found he could not even hold the portion he had taken. Revolt after revolt sprang up and the Almoravids were kept off balance rushing about to quell the "unruly" people of Ghana. Abu Bakr, in fact, was killed in 1087 as he attempted to put down one of the many revolts.

However, in the thirty-three years of battling the Almoravids, the strong central control of the king of Ghana over his empire had been shattered. All but two of the former provinces had asserted their independence and were by then separate kingdoms. One of these, Kaniaga, became prominent because of able leadership by members of the So clan of the Fulani people. Before the thirteenth century began, Kaniaga managed to annex another kingdom, Diara. Then, in 1203 A.D. their king, Sumanguru, led them in a successful drive to capture Ghana's capital, Kumbi Saleh. He claimed the lands and territories of the former empire and enslaved the Ghanians.

But Sumanguru was scarcely as successful as the Almoravids had been in putting the empire back together and controlling it. Immediately after his seizure of Kumbi Saleh, the Moslem traders packed up and left. They re-established their trading center at Walata, far to the north, beyond easy reach of Sumanguru's soldiers. The departure of the Moslem merchants and traders was a serious blow to the commerce of the old empire of Ghana. But Sumanguru's conquests prepared the way for emergence in the Western Sudan of a new empire, even greater than Ghana: the empire of Mali.

NOTES

1. Mahmoud Kàti, *Tarikh al-Fettash*, (trans. by Houdas and Delafosse) (Paris: E. Leroux, 1913).
2. Al Bekri, *Description de l'Afrique Septentrional*, (trans. by de Slone) (Paris: Impr. Imperiale, 1859).
3. *Ibid.*
4. *Ibid.*

Black Askia's fetish was his people's health:
The world his world, he gave the Bengal light
Of Books the Inn of Court in Songhay. Beba Mzigo!*
The law of empathy set the market price,
Scaled the word and deed: the gravel-blind saw
Deserts give up the ghost to green pastures!

Solomon in all his glory had no Oxford,
Alfred the Great no University of Sankore:
Footloose professors, chimney sweeps of the skull,
From Europe and Asia; youths, souls in one skin,
Under white scholars like El-Akit, under
Black humanists like Bagayogo. Karibu wee!†

The Good Gray Bard in Timbuktu chanted:
"Europe is an empty python in hiding grass!"

---

* "Lift the loads!"
† "Welcome!"

LIBRETTO FOR THE REPUBLIC OF LIBERIA
by Melvin B. Tolson[1]

◁▷ ◁▷ ◁▷ ◁▷ ◁▷ ◁▷ ◁▷ ◁▷ ◁▷ ◁▷ ◁▷ ◁▷

THE
MAGNIFICENCE
OF MALI

◁▷ ◁▷ ◁▷ ◁▷ ◁▷ ◁▷ ◁▷ ◁▷ ◁▷ ◁▷ ◁▷ ◁▷

V

IN THE MIDDLE OF THE ELEVENTH CENTURY
in Asia, the Mongol hordes were terrorizing vast stretches of
land. In the Middle East the Seljuk Turks were conquering
Baghdad and laying siege to Damascus. In Europe, Duke William was preparing to sail for England, and French troops were
battling the Moors in Spain.

In Africa the Almoravid hosts had swept north through
Morocco and Spain and south into the Sudan. Ghana was
mortally stricken and Sumanguru, king of Sossos, was imposing

his rule on the Ghanian domains. In so doing, Sumanguru put harsh levies on the conquered peoples. He set high taxes in gold and in foodstuffs, in slaves and in women—requiring the most beautiful girls and young women be turned over to him. Such actions won him few friends, of course. Among those who most resented Sumanguru's severity were the people of Mali, the land south of Kumbi Saleh on the Niger River.

The Mandinke who lived there were a tribal branch of the same family group that included the Sosso and the Soninkes and all three spoke the Mande language. The Mandinke were different from the other two, however, in that they had accepted Islam willingly and early in the Almoravid invasion. The Soninke had become Moslems only under threat of death and the Sossos had rejected Islam and retained their tribal religion. This point is important, for it tells much about the flexibility of the Mandinke and their willingness to embrace new ideas. It also points up a basic strength of the Mandinke as they proceeded to build a powerful state: their position in, and support by, the burgeoning Moslem world.

Now Sumanguru had a sizable portion of Mandinke territory under his rule and his harsh taxes and seizure of women made these people furious. Sumanguru had taken over Mali when its king, one of the Keita clan, had died. He quickly established a reputation for avarice, cruelty and ruthlessness. His potential rivals were summarily executed, and he was hated and feared because of his ability with witchcraft.

The Hungering Lion

When the victorious Sumanguru visited his newly-conquered domain he saw the son of the late king, a boy called Sundiata, meaning "Hungering Lion." Never was a child more misnamed: Sundiata was weak, and he suffered from a type of paralysis that made it impossible for him even to stand up. All the healers in the land had examined Sundiata and had pronounced him an incurable invalid. So when Sumanguru saw the boy he spared his life, certain that this cripple would never be a threat to him.

The legend of Sundiata tells how the young prince fought against his physical disability. Through sheer determination, after months of effort and untold suffering, he forced himself to stand with a cane. After that, he managed to walk. After still further agonized effort, he was able to abandon the cane. His strength grew with his age and he overcame his earlier lameness completely. In fact, he earned fame as a hunter and horseman, and for his courage and knowledge of military life.

All this time, Sumanguru's taxes, his requisitioning of Mandinke women and his harsh rule were biting ever more deeply into the minds of Malians. Sundiata was spending his time to good advantage, training troops, gaining the friendship and support of other tribes, preparing for the inevitable day when Sumanguru's reign would be challenged. In 1230 A.D. Sundiata was named king of Mali. With the aid of an army loaned by a neighboring king, Sundiata moved into Mali to claim his throne and began girding for the confrontation with Sumanguru. It was five years before the showdown came.

Sumanguru commanded a huge, well-equipped army and in addition he was supposedly impervious to weapons and therefore invincible in battle because of his magic powers. Sundiata led a coalition of forces determined to end Sumanguru's power over them. The legend of the climactic battle between these armies is told in an ancient, anonymous Arabic manuscript.

This is its story:

As Sundiata advanced with his army to meet Sumanguru, he learned
that Sumanguru was coming against him with an army prepared for battle. They met in a place called Kirina. When
Sundiata turned his eyes on the army of Sumanguru he
asked, "What is this cloud on the eastern side?" They told
him it was Sumanguru's army.

As for Sumanguru, when he looked in Sundiata's direction
he exclaimed, "What is that mountain of stone?" And they
told him "It is the army of Sundiata, which lies to the west of
us."

Then the two columns came together and fought a murderous battle. In the thick of the fight, Sundiata uttered a
great shout in the face of the warriors of Sumanguru. At once
these men ran to get behind Sumanguru. He, in return, uttered
a great shout in the face of Sundiata's warriors, all of whom
fled to get behind Sundiata. Usually when Sumanguru
shouted, eight heads would rise above his own.

When they had done this, Sundiata said to one of his
captains, "Have you forgotten the taboo?" [He was referring
to a prophecy that told of Sumanguru's end.] As soon as
Sangaran Danguinia [the captain] heard Sundiata's question
he came to the front of the army, halted, grasped the [spear]
armed with the spur of a white cock and threw it at Sumanguru. As soon as it had struck Sumanguru, Sangaran said,
"This is the arrow of him who knows the ancient secrets. . . ."
While he was saying this, Sumanguru vanished and was seen
no more. Now he had had a gold bracelet on his wrist and
this fell on that spot. A baobab tree grew out of it and carries
the mark to this day. . . . As for Sundiata, he defeated the

army of Sumanguru, ravaged the land of the Sosso and subjugated its people.[2]

The year of Sundiata's great victory was 1235, just twenty years after a group of unruly barons forced King John to sign the Magna Carta at Runnymede in faraway England. Sundiata led his armies throughout the lands formerly under Sumanguru's sway. Finally he assaulted the capital city of the Sosso, a place reputed to have 188 strong points and therefore to be absolutely beyond capture. Formidable it must have been, for the siege was a difficult one. Attack after attack failed over a period of many months of constant fighting. Finally, in a burst of determination, Sundiata's forces breached the walls and overcame the city. Then, retaliating for their years of exploitation under Sumanguru's cruel reign, the Malians took revenge by killing the people of the Sosso capital. No doubt this was excused as *jihad*, or holy war and thus forgivable, for the Sosso were infidels in the eyes of the Moslem Mandinkes. Not long after, in 1240, Sundiata's forces sacked the city of Kumbi Saleh. This ended the relatively short-lived Sosso Empire and left Mali in the prime position of power in the Western Sudan.

▷ *Where the King Lives* The Mandinke homeland, the small state of Kangaba, had as its capital a city named Jeriba. But this· was too remote from the center of the new empire so Sundiata moved the capital to a new city farther down the Niger. It was called Mali in the Mandinke tongue, meaning "where the king lives." This term superseded Kangaba as the name of the rising empire.

After 1240 Sundiata did not personally lead any campaigns. He did not have to, so powerful were his armies. But he kept his generals on the move to extend the borders of the realm. They succeeded handsomely and became the military governors of new provinces. Sundiata turned to the primary problems of his empire—establishing peace and the conditions for trade to flourish; and encouraging agriculture for a reliable food supply.

He was quickly successful. The caravans once again made their way to and through Mali in safety and with great profit. Cultivation of new lands and harvesting crops of peanuts, rice, sorghum, taro, yams, beans, onions, calabash and grains gave a substantial base to Mali's economy. These food crops plus staples such as cotton made the empire enviably rich by the time of Sundiata's death in 1255. "Hungering Lion" lives on to this day in the legends and folk tales and dances of West Africa, as well he should for his achievements. He set the course for Mali's greatness.

One of Sundiata's sons, Uli, succeeded him and ruled for fifteen years. They were years of steady expansion in which territory was added to the empire. By 1270, when Mansa Uli died ("Mansa" is a title meaning "emperor" or "sultan"), Mali's borders had been pushed outward to encompass the gold-rich Wangara and Bumbuk districts, most of Diara to the northwest and down the Niger to Lake Debo. Furthermore, Mansa Uli realized the importance of broader contacts in the Moslem world. He therefore made the holy pilgrimage, the *hajj*, to Mecca in Arabia. Thus began a tradition that most subsequent Malian emperors followed.

Mansa Uli's death brought another of Sundiata's sons to the throne. He was named Karifa and was quickly judged insane when his horrified subjects saw him shooting arrows at people in and out of court, simply for amusement. This began a period in which there was a fight for power among a number of contenders. All in all, there were seven emperors over the next forty years, six of them undistinguished, if not incompetent. Only one of them, Sakura, who ruled from 1285 to 1300, managed to add to the realm. But he had seized the throne and was, therefore, a usurper. The condition of the empire was desperate and its future looked bleak. But at this moment of crisis a remarkable man came to the throne. He was Mansa Kankan Musa I who came to power in 1312 (about twenty years after the first Crusade ended). "Musa" is Arabic for "Moses," and Mansa Musa proved to be just such an inspired leader to the peoples of Western Sudan.

BLACK MOSES

Mansa Musa built Mali into one of the greatest and most famous empires of the world of that time. In his reign of twenty-five years this extraordinary man stamped his personality indelibly on African history. He was, says an Egyptian contemporary, Al Omari, "the most important of the Moslem Negro kings; his land is the largest, his army the most numerous; he is the king who is the most powerful, the richest, the most fortunate, the most feared by his enemies and the most able to do good to those around him."

The greatest challenge he faced was to bring stability to the land. Peace and safety within Mali's borders were urgent needs, and Mansa Musa rapidly established law and order throughout his domain. He then sent his armies into the field to extend the empire. They carried the banners of Mali west into Tekrur, clear to the Atlantic coast; north to the Sahara, taking cities such as Walata; and even across the desert to the salt-mining outpost of Taghaza. They advanced eastward, beyond the cities of Timbuktu and Gao to the borders of Hausaland. To the south Mansa Musa's troops continued Mali's firm grip on the gold-producing regions. At the height of Mansa Musa's power, Mali was (according to Al Omari's report) "square in shape, being four months [of travel] in length and at least as much in breadth. . . ." It measured perhaps fifteen hundred miles by a thousand miles, roughly the size of all of Western Europe.

Governing this mammoth area was a gigantic task that took keen judgment, wisdom and administrative skill. Kankan Musa had all of these. His domains were as varied as their people. At the close of his reign, there were twenty-four semi-independent kingdoms within the empire of Mali. Most of these had tribal chiefs whom Musa had left in power so long as they demonstrated their loyalty to him; the others had governors whom the emperor had placed in power. Some of these governors were generals who had conquered the territories. Mansa Musa made other men governors in recognition of outstanding services to him and the empire.

In addition to these kingdoms, there were territories under the direct control of the Emperor. Within each of these there were further subdivisions into provinces placed under the administration of *ferbas* (governors). The major towns and cities were under *mochrifs* (mayors). *Ferbas* and *mochrifs* were appointed by the Mansa.

Mansa Musa was able to maintain peace throughout his lands—a major accomplishment. It took a huge army to do this. The upkeep on a vast standing army required a good deal of money, but the money was available, thanks to Mansa Musa's efficient tax system and the prosperity of the empire.

Now the caravans of Morocco, Egypt and North Africa came to Mali and the emperor sent his ambassadors and agents to reside in Fez, Morocco's capital, in Cairo, and other important centers. Mansa Musa's capital became a major crossroad of the Moslem world and daily the city was thronged with merchants, traders and scholars from North Africa and Egypt who had come on business or had settled there. As a devout Moslem, Mansa Musa welcomed the men of Islam from whatever quarter they came. It was a time of general expansion for the Moslem world, a time when it led the West in learning, arts and culture. Religion and trade also went together. Mansa Musa recognized these vital elements of Islam and encouraged them to the utmost.

The man proved himself a wise ruler. We have a word picture from Al Omari of the restraint exercised by Mansa Musa in governing his domains. It is a picture of practical statesmanship of the kind needed to rule thousands of diverse peoples scattered over the face of West Africa:

> The sultan of this country [Mali] has sway over the land of the "desert of native gold," whence they bring him gold every year. The inhabitants of that land are savage pagans whom the sultan would subject to him if he wished. But the sovereigns of this kingdom have learned by experience that whenever one of them has conquered one of these gold towns, established Islam there and sounded the call to prayer, the production of gold dwindles and falls to nothing; meanwhile it grows and expands in neighboring pagan countries. When experience had confirmed them in this observation, they left the gold country in the hands of its pagan inhabitants and contented themselves with assuring their obedience and paying tribute.[3]

Al Omari also tells us something about the great emperor and the customs of the court:

[Mansa Musa] is known to the people of Egypt as the king of Tekrur
but he himself becomes indignant when he is called thus,
since Tekrur is only one of the countries of his empire. The
title he prefers is that of lord of Mali, the largest of his states;
it is the name by which he is most known. . . .

The Sultan [Mansa Musa] holds court in his palace on a
great balcony called *bembe* where he has a great seat of ebony
that is like a throne fit for a large and tall person. On either
side it is flanked by elephant tusks turned towards each other.
His arms stand near him, being all of gold, saber, lance,
quiver, bow and arrows. He wears wide trousers made of
about twenty pieces [of material] of a kind which he alone
may wear. Behind him there stand about a score of Turkish
or other pages bought for him in Cairo. One of them, at his
left, holds a silk umbrella surmounted by a dome and a bird
of gold: the bird has the figure of a falcon. His officers are
seated in a circle about him, in two rows, one to the right and
one to the left; beyond them sit the chief commanders of his
cavalry. In front of him there is a person who never leaves
him, who is his official executioner; also another who serves
as intermediary [spokesman] between sovereign and subjects,
and who is named herald. In front of them again, there are
drummers. Others dance before their sovereign, who enjoys
this, and make him laugh. Two banners are spread behind
him. Before him they keep two saddled and bridled horses in
case he should wish to ride.

Arab horses are brought for sale to the kings of this country
who spend considerable sums in this way. Their army numbers one hundred thousand men of whom there are about ten

thousand horse-mounted cavalry; the others are infantry having neither horses nor any other mounts. They have camels in
this country but do not know the art of riding them with a
saddle. . . .

The officers of this king, his soldiers and his guard receive
gifts of land and presents. Some among the greatest of them
receive as much as 50,000 *mitqals* of gold a year [1 mitqal =
⅛ oz.], besides which the king provides them with horses and
clothing. He is much concerned with giving them fine garments and making his cities into capitals.

It is one of their customs that whenever someone charged
with a certain task or important affair reports to the king, the
latter questions him on everything that has happened from
the time of his departure to the time of his return and in
great detail. Legal cases and appeals also go up to the sovereign
who examines them himself. Generally he writes nothing but
gives his orders, most of the time, orally. He has *qadis*, secre-
taries, offices.[4]

From this we have a portrait of a man who has the qualities of
a great leader: attention to detail, concern for justice, liberal
rewards to his loyal servants, availability to his subjects; a person
aware of his responsibilities and of his empire and unwilling to
see them diminished or slighted by thoughtless word or deed.
▷ *The Fabulous Journey* We also see Mansa Musa as a devout, practicing Moslem. This is clear from his pilgrimage to
Mecca—a journey of some three thousand miles via Cairo over
some of the most infernal territory on the face of the globe. But,
as might be expected of so unusual a man, when Mansa Musa
made the pilgrimage it became an event of international importance, one of the most famous trips in history. It spread his

name far and wide and was a topic of conversation for a century.

Musa's *hajj* was the stuff of legend and fable from the outset. It was spectacular in size because the emperor brought along friends, family, doctors, savants, princes, tribal chiefs and governors of the empire. Some of the latter made the journey at Musa's insistence, in part as hostages to prevent attempts to take over the kingdom, in part to allow his son to rule without hindrance during his absence. There are varying reports on the number of people who went with Mansa Musa: One report put the figure at eight thousand; another estimated sixty thousand!

Outfitting thousands of people and animals for a journey of about nine thousand miles for upwards of a year was a monumental task. For months food and supplies were gathered from all over the empire. Gold dust from the royal treasury was divided into three hundred-pound loads—a typical camel burden—and there were one hundred of these! Musa had five hundred slaves with him and each of them carried a staff in which there was gold weighing five hundred *mitqals*. (The *mitqal*, *miskal* or *miscal* was a measure of gold and varied from about 59.7 grains in Tunis to 74 grains in Aleppo. About 4.81 grams seems to have been an accepted standard.)

The Emir, el Mehmendar, tells about Musa's visit to Cairo on the first leg of his pilgrimage in July, 1324:

When I went out to greet [Mansa Musa] in the name of the glorious Sultan el Malik en Nasir [of Cairo], he gave me the warmest of welcomes and treated me with the most careful politeness. But he would talk to me only through an interpreter [although he could speak perfect Arabic].

I suggested that he should go up to the palace and meet the Sultan. But he refused, saying, "I came for the pilgrimage

and for nothing else and I do not wish to mix up my pilgrimage with anything else." He argued about this. However I
well understood that the meeting was repugnant to him because he was loath to kiss the ground [before the Sultan] or to
kiss his hand. I went on insisting and he went on making
excuses. But imperial protocol obliged me to present him [at
the Egyptian court] and I did not leave him until he had
agreed.

When he came into the Sultan's presence we asked him to
kiss the ground. But he refused and continued to refuse,
saying, "However can this be?" Then a wise man of his suite
whispered several words to him that I could not understand.
"Very well," he thereupon declared. "I will prostrate myself
before Allah who created me and brought me into the world."
Having done so he moved towards the Sultan. The latter rose
for a moment to welcome him and asked him to sit beside
him. Then they had a long conversation.

Mansa Musa's reluctance to kowtow to a local sultan was understandable pride. In terms of gold and monetary wealth, Mali
was incomparably richer than Egypt. And so far as territory
was concerned, Musa's realm was many times larger. He was
truly the khan of Africa, ruling a vast empire second in the
world of that time only to that of Genghis Khan in Asia.

El Mehmendar's description of Mansa Musa's departure
from Cairo makes it clear that it was costly to have a rich and
powerful guest in those days. Consider the size of Musa's caravan
and the requirements of protocol for the host to such an emperor:

When the time of pilgrimage [departure] arrived, [The Sultan of
Egypt] sent [Mansa Musa] a large quantity of *drachmas* [silver
coins], baggage camels and choice riding camels with saddles

and harness. [The Egyptian Sultan] caused abundant quantities of foodstuffs to be bought for his suite and followers, established posting-stations for the feeding of the animals, and gave to the emirs of the pilgrimage a written order to look after and respect [the Emperor of Mali]. When the latter returned it was I [el Mehmendar] who went to greet him and settle him into his quarters.

This man spread upon Cairo the flood of his generosity: There was no person, officer of the [Cairo] court or holder of any office of the [Cairo] sultanate who did not receive a sum in gold from him. The people of Cairo earned incalculable sums from him, whether by buying and selling or by gifts. So much gold was current in Cairo that it ruined the value of money.

Does history record any other case of a royal host's hospitality being repaid so liberally by his imperial visitor's generosity that the economy of the host's country is ruined? Al Omari, writing in Cairo, provides a footnote to this shower of gold:

Gold in Egypt had enjoyed a high rate of exchange up to the moment of [Emperor Musa's] arrival. The gold *mitqal* that year had not fallen below twenty-five *drachmas*. But from that [arrival] day onward, its value dwindled; the exchange was ruined and even now it has not recovered. The *mitqal* scarcely touches twenty-two *drachmas*. That is how it has been for twelve years from that time, because of the great amounts of gold they [Mansa Musa's entourage] brought to Egypt and spent there.[5]

No doubt Mansa Musa gave substantial amounts of his gold as alms in Mecca, as the pilgrimage was the central purpose of his trip. Perhaps his generosity had similar impact there. An embarrassing moment occurred when the great emperor discovered (as who has not?) that he had spent all his money. Egyptian merchants were eager to loan him enough gold to complete his journey. No one had the slightest doubt about his ability to repay the loans.

Certainly the emperor's trip was the sensation of the Moslem world. It literally put Mali on the map. Maps of Africa after this time almost always show Mali and many have drawings of Mansa Musa. They usually show him as a black emperor with robe, crown, scepter and orb of gold. Mali became fixed in people's minds as the Eldorado—country with limitless gold, and as a result there was an even greater flow of traders, merchants, religious leaders and scholars to the empire.

On his return journey Mansa Musa brought a number of outstanding Moslem scholars to Mali. Among them was a famous poet and architect, Al Saheli of Cordoba, whom Musa engaged to build a palace and a great mosque at Timbuktu. As the huge caravan approached Mali on the return trip, messengers came with news that the major city of Gao, capital of the Songhay people, had been captured. It had been under siege by Musa's troops for many years. Delighted at this news, Mansa Musa made a special visit to the conquered city. He took back to his capital two Songhay princes as hostages to insure Gao's loyalty. But they also were honored as princes of Mali.

Mansa Musa had forged an unprecedented empire in Africa. One the most widely-traveled of the Moslem writers of the Middle Ages, a Berber named Ibn Battuta, wrote about his visit to Mali and his judgments are instructive.

Among the admirable qualities of the Malians, Ibn Battuta noted several: They abhorred injustice and the Sultan forgave no one who was guilty of it. Peace and order prevailed in the land and no one needed to fear "brigands, thieves or ravishers." If foreigners died in Mali, their possessions were placed with a trustworthy man until they could be claimed by a qualified person. The people of Mali were highly devout. They wore fine white garments on the holy day; they memorized the Koran. "One festival day," says Ibn Battuta, "I visited the *qadi* and saw children [chained] and asked him, 'will you not let them free?' He replied, 'only when they know their Koran by heart.' "

In short, Ibn Battuta found the people of Mali honest and just, living by laws, Allah-fearing, devout and determined to educate their children in their religion. Of course not all that Ibn Battuta saw pleased him. Several customs he found "deplorable" from his Berber perspective:

> Women go naked into the Sultan's presence without even a veil; his daughters also go about naked. On the twenty-seventh night of Ramadan I saw about a hundred women slaves coming out of the Sultan's palace with food and they were naked. Two daughters of the Sultan were with them and these had no veil either, although they had big breasts.
>
> The blacks throw dust and cinders on their heads as a sign of good manners and respect.
>
> They have buffoons who appear before the Sultan when the poets are reciting their praise-songs.
>
> And then a good number of Negroes eat the flesh of dogs and donkeys.[6]

Mansa Musa is known to have desired to settle in Arabia to meditate at Mecca after his pilgrimage. He expected to install his son formally as his successor and then return to the holy city. But the demands of his mammoth empire prevented this and he never left Mali again. In 1337, the year Edward III of England challenged the French King Philip VI in what became the start of the Hundred Years' War, Mansa Kankan Musa died. His twenty-five years of exceptional leadership had created a phenomenally great empire. Its leadership now went to his son, Maghan.

The Fall of Timbuktu

But hardly had Mansa Musa been buried when his empire began to go to pieces. Emperor Maghan lacked his father's extraordinary qualities. The first major evidence of this was when Mossi warriors from the Volta River area raided the fabled city of Timbuktu. They overwhelmed the Mandinke garrison defending the city and put the torch to Timbuktu. This was a signal disaster, because it was so prominent a place, so important a market and cultural center and because it was considered to be nearly impregnable. The fall of Timbuktu sent a tremor throughout the empire and gave fuel to the ambitions of other tribes and kingdoms who were thinking about independence.

Mansa Maghan's rule ended in just four years. His uncle, Mansa Sulayman, succeeded him when Maghan died, and brought strong leadership to the throne again. Sulayman made the *hajj* to Mecca in 1351—about the time the Black Death was scourging Europe. Both coming and going he re-established his control over the eastern regions of the empire. He was faced with a revolt by the city of Gao, however, which he was unable to recapture. And there the Songhay power began to grow.

By the time Sulayman died in 1359 he had done much to shore up the weaknesses in the empire. But the emperors who came after Sulayman had neither the vision nor the vigor to keep Mali together. The northern kingdoms soon felt the lash of the Tuaregs, the raiding Berber tribesmen of the desert. Walata, Arawan and Timbuktu fell to them. In the west, at Tekrur, the Tucolor and Woloff tribes threw off Mali's control. The Mossi from the south struck out in raids on garrisons and caravans. Meanwhile the Songhay continued to gather strength around their base at Gao.

This does not mean that Mali collapsed in a heap overnight. Its decline was slow and far from steady. By the time the Turks took Constantinople in 1453, Mali's power had been severely cut. Even so, the noted Leo Africanus described the capital of Mali in 1510 as a town of six thousand houses with several mosques and Koranic schools. The people of the town were merchants and artisans and Leo called them superior "to all other Negroes in wit, civility and industry."

The Songhay power was increasing rapidly, and the rulers of Mali, casting about in desperation for assistance, approached the Portuguese. Sailors from Portugal had landed on Mali's Atlantic coastline and the Malians proposed an alliance with the Europeans. The purpose was to thwart the Songhays. Nothing came of this effort, and though the Mali dynasty continued, by the time Cromwell and the Roundheads had seized England in 1645, Mali had shrunk to the size of its original territory, the small state of Kangaba.

NOTES

1. Melvin B. Tolson, *Libretto for the Republic of Liberia*, in *African Heritage* by Jacob Drachler; (New York: Collier Books, 1964) p. 182.
2. Anonymous, quoted in *A History of West Africa* by Basil Davidson; (Garden City, New Jersey: Anchor Books, Doubleday & Company, 1966).
3. Ibn Fadl Allah al-Omari, *Masalik al Absar fi Mamalik al Amsar*, Cairo, c. 1342; (Paris: Gaudefroy-Demombynes, 1927).
4. *Ibid.*
5. *Ibid.*
6. Ibn (Mohammed Ibn Abd Allah) Battuta, trans. by H.A.R. Gibb, *Travels in Asia and Africa, 1325–1354;* (New York: R.M. McBride and Comp., 1929).

The drunkenness of youth has passed like a fever,
   and yet I saw many things,
Seeing my glory in the days of my glory.
The feet of my war-horse
Drummed upon the cities of the world;
   I sacked great towns like a hot wind
And fell like thunder upon far lands.
The kings of the earth were dragged behind my chariot
   And the people of the earth behind my laws;
But now
The drunkenness of youth has passed like a fever,
   like foam upon sand.
Death took me in a net;
   My armies warred against him in vain,
My courtiers flattered him in vain.
   Listen, O wayfarer, to the words of my death,
For they were not the words of my life:
   Save up your soul
And taste the beautiful wine of peace,
   For tomorrow the earth shall answer:
He is with me,
   My jealous breast holds him for ever.

INSCRIPTION AT THE CITY OF BRASS[1]
Anonymous

◁▷ ◁▷ ◁▷ ◁▷ ◁▷ ◁▷ ◁▷ ◁▷ ◁▷ ◁▷ ◁▷ ◁▷

THE SONGHAY
ASCENDANCY

◁▷ ◁▷ ◁▷ ◁▷ ◁▷ ◁▷ ◁▷ ◁▷ ◁▷ ◁▷ ◁▷ ◁▷

VI

ALI KOLON AND SULAYMAN NAR. THOSE WERE
the names that made Mansa Maghan furious. They were the
names of two princes of the Dia line who had been brought as
hostages from Gao by the great Mansa Kankan Musa when he
returned from his *hajj* and stopped for a triumphal inspection of
the newly-conquered city in 1325.

Gao was a rich city, the Songhays were resourceful and
powerful people, and their Dia kings were able leaders. They

had to be, to keep Gao independent over the centuries, as they had managed to do so successfully until Mansa Musa's armies had finally overwhelmed the city. So the great emperor deliberately selected two of the sons of Songhay King Dia Assibai to take back to Mali's capital. Musa had been willing to leave Assibai as titular ruler of Gao so long as the taxes and tribute were paid on time and the king and his people remained loyal to Mali. But to insure that the king did not forget his obligations Musa kept the two princes, Ali Kolon and Sulayman Nar, at his court. Just in case.

This was not a captivity in which the princes were locked up and fed bread and water. On the contrary, these princes, along with those from other kingdoms of Mali's empire, were respected and important members of Musa's court. They were part of the imperial entourage and were trusted—in a limited way. In fact, they were given increasingly vital assignments as they demonstrated their loyalty and skill. Prince Ali Kolon, for instance, showed remarkable ability as a soldier and leader of men. Therefore the emperor sent him on military expeditions.

The legends state that on each new mission Ali Kolon purposely guided his expedition closer to his homeland, Gao. Apparently no one in Mansa Musa's court noticed this interesting pattern. And no one saw—or revealed—that the prince was carefully hiding weapons and other necessities along the route to the city of Gao.

It was after Mansa Musa's death that a period of confusion began, during which time Mansa Maghan tried to grasp the complex responsibilities of the empire. This was when Ali Kolon saw his chance. Secretly he plotted with his brother and a small group of trusted friends and, when Mansa Maghan and most of his armies were distracted with events elsewhere, Ali

Kolon and his band of followers raced for Gao, the Songhay homeland. Maghan, as soon as he heard of the escape, roared for his generals and hurled his cavalry after the princes. But Ali Kolon had planned thoroughly, and his planning paid off. The fugitives eluded Maghan's soldiers and slipped into Gao.

Here further complications faced them. The histories are not explicit about precisely what happened. But it is clear that the princes had arranged their return in advance with friends and relatives. They could not have been accepted in the city of Gao otherwise, for during the years they had been in genteel captivity at Musa's court, control of Gao had changed. Their father, Assibai, had died and four other kings of the Dia line had come to the throne after him. So when Ali and his brother arrived at the gates of the city there was a Dia king reigning. This king, of course, might have preferred to turn the two princes over to Mansa Maghan and thus eliminate a dangerous threat to his own power. Perhaps he tried to do so. All we know from the histories is that Ali claimed to be the rightful ruler, was elected chief and ousted the last of the Dia kings.

Ali then established a new dynasty, the Sunni ("restored") kings. Sunni Ali Kolon and his followers consolidated their hold on Gao and from that time on successfully repulsed the Malian attempts to retake the city. It was something of a stalemate, because though Mali was unable to capture Gao, the Songhay were not strong enough to break out of their city and the environs on the Niger River and enlarge their kingdom.

Songhay Stronghold

Today there is a section of the Niger River from Lake Debo to Busa that is one thousand miles long. This section is marked off naturally by rapids at both ends. Just as the Nile provided the necessities for people to live and develop in what otherwise would have been a desert, so the Niger provides for its area. It is a waterway that replenishes the land during flood season, waters the entire area all year, is full of fish and makes it possible to raise crops and feed animals. The Songhay traditionally have lived on the middle Niger and today there are about half a million of them still in that area.

The histories say that the Songhay first settled in large numbers in a place called Kukya, near the northwest border of modern Nigeria. This town grew, and during the seventh century drew settlers and traders from far and near. The Songhay people grew so strong that they attacked the Sorko people and captured Gao, their most important town. It was at this time that the Songhay established their ruling Dia dynasty.

Gao grew and prospered as the trading center for caravans from Tunis to Cyrenaica on the central Mediterranean coast, and from Egypt. Most of these traders, if not all, were Moslems, and over the decades and centuries more and more Moslems settled in Gao and Kukya. They became an increasingly important element in the culture and economy of the Songhay. In 1009 the king, Dia Kossoi, accepted Islam as his religion. Kossoi also decided to live part of the year in the thriving metropolis of Gao. This was an important move on his part: It brought royal protection to the city and thus reassured the Moslem traders that the irritating and often devastating raids by nomads would be reduced or prevented entirely. The king's residence in Gao gave the city new prestige, of course, and it became even more of a magnet for traders, merchants and settlers. It also put Kossoi and Songhay on the Moslem world map.

When Dia Kossoi became a Moslem, most of his other subjects were devoted to their traditional religions. Therefore he did not force Islam upon them, nor did he flaunt Moslem customs in his court. He retained the ways of his fathers at court, the histories tell us, and added Moslem observances to them. This began a transition to Islam among the Songhay leaders and a tradition that the king must be a Moslem. The religion did spread among the Songhay and, as we have seen, to other parts of the Western Sudan.

Over the years Gao extended its control over nearby areas. Because of its prosperity it was almost constantly under attack by raiding nomad tribes seeking plunder or by covetous kings hoping to annex it. The Songhay kings jealously and successfully defended their small but growing realm until the avalanche of Mansa Musa's legions in 1325. After Sunni Ali regained Gao's independence, the Songhay lands stayed free throughout sieges by the troops of Mali and attacks from the Mossi and Tuaregs.

The next "landmark" in Songhay history was a ferocious warrior named Ali the Great—Sunni Ali Ber. He came to the throne in 1464, at the time Prince Henry the Navigator was sending Portuguese ships down the west coast of Africa, opening a new world to Europe.

ALI THE GREAT

Sunni Ali Ber has become a legendary name in African history. It is as alive today in West Africa as that of Charlemagne in West Europe. The legends and romances of the people in the Niger-Senegal area keep Sunni Ali Ber's glory alive, and with good reason, for he was a remarkable man.

Mali was in decline when Sunni Ali came to the Songhay throne. The greatness of Mali had been dissipated by weak emperors and the hammer blows of invaders, the thrusts of raiders, and uprisings by rebellious kingdoms within the empire. It was a turbulent time, and Ali Ber came to power determined to make the most of it. Immediately he increased his army by conscripting the men of Songhay. Then, he plunged into battle after battle, crushing nomad terrorists, seizing tribal lands here, capturing caravan roadways there, taking market towns and trading villages and outposts, constantly thrusting outward and expanding the Songhay frontiers into Mali territory.

Ali Ber was truly a leader on horseback. The court was wherever he was, and he was almost constantly at the head of one army or another, leading his men to victory after victory. He first went after the Mossi, who had been raiding deep into Song-hay territory from the south. Hurling his warriors at the Mossi troops Sunni Ali Ber routed the enemy and chased them back to their homeland. Next he sent his soldiers against the Fulani and Dogon, rivals for land and loot, and beat them soundly. He quickly earned a reputation for fierce energy and ruthlessness.

At this time the famous city of Timbuktu was held by the Tuaregs, who had wrested it from Mali in 1433. Timbuktu was a city of merchants, tradesmen and, above all, scholars. Its great university, Sankoré, drew students and teachers from Moslem Africa and the far reaches of the Islamic world as well. (It was the city in which Mansa Musa directed the famous architect to build mosques and palaces.)

Located at the northern bend of the Niger River, Tim-buktu was an intersection point for trade between the Sahara and North Africa and the Western Sudan. Though it was an ugly, dusty, hot and crowded city, it was rich, and its leaders were Moslem sages. In fact, the *qadi*, or foremost Moslem religious leader of Timbuktu, considered the city an independent metropolis and himself its ruler. So, when the Tuaregs took the city from Mali, the people of Timbuktu resisted only half-heartedly because they expected that the conquerors, who were fellow-Moslems, would not upset their way of life and that the residents of the city might, in fact, benefit from the change of overlordship.

They were sadly mistaken, and soon the city leaders sent an appeal to Sunni Ali Ber to liberate them from their rapacious Tuareg masters. Such an invitation was all that Ali Ber needed. He sent his legions against Timbuktu and overwhelmed the Tuaregs, then pillaged the city and killed many of its leaders, whom he accused of disloyalty.

▷ *The Taking of Timbuktu* The sagas tell another story about the conquest of Timbuktu. They tell how the Tuareg chieftain, Akil, lived in the desert in the traditional way and appointed Ammar as his lieutenant to live in and govern Timbuktu. Ammar was an incautious man and in a moment of overweening pride, he sent a boastful message to Sunni Ali Ber. In it he taunted Ali Ber, saying that Timbuktu was invincible and that Sunni Ali could never capture it.

Now Ammar had responsibility for collecting taxes in Timbuktu and he was supposed to keep one-third of them and turn over the remainder to Akil, his chief. But after every tax collection was completed and Ammar was preparing to send Akil's portion to him, the Tuareg chief would sweep into the city with his warriors. Then Akil would take his tax money and seize Ammar's as well. In addition, the Tuaregs robbed the townspeople and raped their women.

Both the citizens and Ammar were more than a little bit upset by this pattern of behavior. Ammar was financially embarrassed—acutely so. Therefore he schemed to revenge himself upon Akil and sent another message to Sunni Ali Ber in great secrecy. Ammar invited Ali Ber to bring his troops and drive away Akil and his avaricious band. Ammar would do his part: He would turn over the city to the Songhay king. Hopefully, Ali Ber would reward Ammar for his assistance and forget that earlier, indiscreet communication.

This was the best offer Ali Ber had received in some time. He immediately put his army into the field and led his cavalry in the attack on Timbuktu. Moving along the Niger, Ali Ber's men reached the outskirts of the city. The clouds of dust from the horses' hooves nearly obscured the vast army. Akil, the Tuareg chief, turned tail and fled far away to Walata. At the Sankoré University there was consternation, for many of the hundreds of teachers and scholars there had been openly contemptuous of the Songhay and Sunni Ali Ber. The majority of the Songhay were still pagan infidels in the eyes of the Moslems, and most were illiterate as well. Thus the learned Mohammedan scholars had often heaped scorn on these "inferior" Songhays who now were at the door, about to capture Timbuktu and, of course, the University.

Ammar carried out his part of the bargain. He provided boats to bring Sunni Ali's warriors across the Niger River. But when Ammar's opportunity to meet the Songhay ruler arrived as Ali Ber stepped ashore in Timbuktu, Ammar had second thoughts. He too turned tail and fled. Timbuktu fell into Ali Ber's hands practically without a fight. Then the Songhay king sacked the city and killed hundreds of its people, among them many scholars. Since Ali Ber was a Moslem in name, if not in fact, Moslem historians condemned him bitterly for this treatment of brothers in religion. They labeled him a scoundrel and master tyrant and denounced his humiliation of the Sankoré scholars. Hundreds of Moslems fled the city, many of them taking refuge in Walata.

Cruel and ruthless he was, but Ali Ber had dealt a heavy blow to his arch rivals, the Tuaregs, and from this victory he went on to the next campaign—against the city of Jenne.

▷ *The Siege of Jenne* Jenne, some three hundred miles southwest of Timbuktu, was a trading center of major importance. However, its trade was mainly to the south—with the gold, kola nut and ivory producers of the forest areas and with the traders of Timbuktu and the Western Sudan. Unlike Timbuktu, Jenne was located in terrain easy to defend. Surrounded by swamps and waterways, it had foiled invaders for centuries and had been one of the few places able to withstand successfully the power of Mansa Musa. In fact, according to the legend, the Malians had tried ninety-nine times to take Jenne and finally had abandoned the effort. Jenne also had a famous university whose hundreds of teachers were known throughout the Moslem world, especially for their expertise in medicine and medical research. Surgery was a field in which they excelled and they were reported to have pioneered certain advanced surgical procedures. Architecture flourished at Jenne also and the combination of beautiful buildings and waterways made it a handsome city.

Ali Ber realized that he could not take Jenne by frontal attack, so he surrounded the city, cutting it off from the outside. His plan was to besiege it and starve it into submission. Because of the swamps, it was a difficult task. In the dry season the Songhay troops could camp on land around the city. But in the rainy season Jenne was surrounded by water and Ali Ber's troops had to move to high ground. A flotilla of four hundred war canoes was used to blockade the city also. It was a strange kind of siege, for there was little fighting. Yet the troops had to be there, and since they had to be fed, many of them tilled the fields in order to produce foodstuffs for the army. This siege was surely one of the longest in history. It went on not for a year or two, but for seven long years.

In fact, so long did it continue that Ali Ber's people became disheartened and his closest advisors counseled him to give up the attempt to take Jenne. The histories say that early in the seventh year Ali Ber decided that the struggle was not worth the prize. He was about to call off the siege when a secret message arrived from one of the captains in Jenne's army. The information was brief and grim: Jenne's people were starving; its army was about to collapse; the end was in sight—depending on whose endurance was greater. Resolved to take the city after this exhausting siege, Ali Ber ordered redoubled efforts to cut the suffering city off from any possible assistance or supplies.

It was on the seventh day of the seventh month of the seventh year of the siege—1473—that Jenne's leaders met, decided there was no hope and surrendered. Jenne's king then rode out of the city to meet Ali Ber in the Songhay camp. The king was young and the valor of the city in holding out so long impressed Sunni Ali Ber. Also, the people of Jenne had not "sold out" to Sunni Ali's enemies as had the leaders of Timbuktu in welcoming the Tuaregs.

Sunni Ali treated the Jenne king with great respect and invited him to sit at his side, thus launching a tradition which gave Jenne's kings this privilege in the future. It was symbolic of the mutual respect of the two leaders. Following this, Ali Ber led his troops into Jenne. But, far from repeating the plunder and slaughter of Timbuktu, the Songhay were well-disciplined and did not loot. Their regard for the courage of their adversaries was an important factor in this. In any case, Ali Ber demonstrated his attitude by taking the queen mother of Jenne as a wife, thus becoming stepfather of the king.

Conquest of Jenne made the Songhay dominant throughout the area of the old Mali empire. Within three years, Sunni Ali Ber had taken the middle Niger lake region west of Timbuktu. After that it was largely a matter of intermittent defense of Songhay territory: The Mossi sent cavalry raiders and were repulsed. The Dogons, Koromba, Fulani and Guaramantes attacked other Songhay towns and had to be driven off.

From this record it may seem that Sunni Ali Ber spent all his time in the saddle on one campaign or another. To a great extent this was true. He kept four palaces in operation simultaneously. Yet he saw the importance of governing his territory efficiently and appointed governors to oversee his provinces. And he recognized the strategic value of the Niger River, of the major cities of his realm (Jenne, Timbuktu, Gao), and of fast, mobile striking forces manned by professional soldiers. In his conquests and establishment of an invincible military force he was an African Napoleon.

He saw the inefficiency of drafting people into his armies for major campaigns. It took them from their fishing or farming and thereby caused a decline in crops and high prices for food, resulting in hunger and unrest. Sunni Ali solved this by instituting a full-time force of professional soldiers. He even separated the warriors from the rest of the population by keeping them in camps. Furthermore, he saw to it that they were well-equipped with the weapons and armor they needed—not equipment hastily corralled in frenzied preparation for an imminent battle (as had been the practice in the past). His camel and horse cavalry were protected by padded armor and carried swords and spears. His infantrymen also wore armor and carried spears or bows and arrows with poisoned tips. Most of his cavalrymen were from noble families and were men from the top of the social scale.

It was during the years of Sunni Ali Ber's reign that the Portuguese and other European nations were establishing trading stations on Africa's west coast. The records do not tell us of any major expeditions by the Europeans into Sunni Ali's domain. There is mention, however, of a request by the Portuguese for a mission to travel to Timbuktu and evidence that Sunni Ali approved it. Whether the mission was sent and what it may have accomplished are unknown. The Mandingoes were in contact with the Portuguese and at one time tried to bring them in as allies against the ever more powerful Songhay. This effort proved fruitless.

▷ *The Death of Sunni Ali* About 1480, the restless, fierce Mossi warriors struck from the south of the Songhay domain. Based in the Yatenga region around the Volta River, these intrepid people sent an armed column through Songhay territory and attacked the town of Walata, besieging it for a month and capturing it. They looted the town, slaughtered most of the men and rounded up the women and children as captive slaves.

Sunni Ali sent his troops after the Mossi. But the audacity of the Mossi thrust through the Songhay heartland stimulated Sunni Ali Ber to an extraordinary decision. He announced that a canal would be built from Lake Debo (a Songhay stronghold) to Walata. The canal would give him a firm supply route for reconquering and keeping Walata. The astonishing thing about this announcement is the fact that from Lake Debo to Walata is a distance of 150 miles. Sunni Ali was not one to think small!

He actually started this project, which would have taken tens of thousands of men perhaps a decade to complete. If completed, it would have been one of the wonders of the world. However, as the canal construction was getting under way, the Mossi abandoned Walata. Sunni Ali rushed his troops to face the Mossi threat, leaving the canal project to another time, a time that never came. The ferocity of the Mossi as warriors made them unconquerable, though the Songhay armies were able to hold them and press them back, containing them finally to their original area of Yatenga.

With a territory so vast it was all but impossible to prevent incursions and raids by tribes swift, skillful and daring enough to hit and run. Songhay lands and towns along the southern margin were particularly vulnerable to such strikes. Sunni Ali, until the end of his days, was plagued by raiding forays by the Fulani, Dogons, Koromba and Guaramantes from the ill-defined border areas. But the Mossi were by far the most persistent, audacious and dangerous.

Legend has it that Sunni Ali was returning from a punitive expedition against one of the tribes when he was swept from his horse while crossing a stream. He drowned. Thus, in 1492, ended the life of this seasoned campaigner whose relentless drive for nearly thirty years pushed the Songhay borders outward and established a solid base for further Songhay expansion.

Two months afterward, Sunni Ali's son Sunni Baru became the Songhay ruler. Sunni Baru, like his father before him, was a Moslem only for convenience. His primary religious allegiances were to the old, traditional deities and he had little time for the orthodox Moslem observances. His father, it was said, neither observed nor fulfilled the five daily prayer periods. Instead, he was known to wait until evening prayer call and recite at one time the prayers intended for all five times of day. Sometimes, when especially short of time, he was said to have compressed his religious observances to the absolute, irreducible minimum by merely reciting the *names* of the five daily prayers.

Sunni Ali Ber had been astute enough to see the importance of the Moslem traders and merchants and to encourage their participation in town life, trade, and government. But he had been merciless in his treatment of the Moslem leaders of Timbuktu after his conquest of that city. The Moslems were politically, economically, and socially strong in the cities and towns. In the countryside, the peasants were devoted to their traditional gods and timeless beliefs out of the past. Sunni Ali, like the most successful politicians of any age and place, managed to balance these two groups and their diverse, often diametrically-opposed needs and goals. His oppression of the Moslems was a key element in his political balancing act.

There was strong and bitter conflict between the native groups and the Moslems for many reasons. Moslem law, for instance, is written, and there is a large body of commentary and interpretation of the laws. These commentaries are based in the code of beliefs known as *sharia*, which come from the Koran's teachings and set forth the rules and observances for all devout Moslems. According to the *sharia* there is only one god (Allah), and superstition, witchcraft, sorcery and belief in spirits and gods other than Allah (the African's gods of the forest, the river, the sky, etc.) are abominations. Since the peoples of the Sudan had traditionally worshipped hosts of different gods and had deep-rooted faith in the powers of their medicine men, there was a fundamental conflict between Islam and the native views.

There were other factors that intensified the conflict. An important one was the difference in succession of leaders. In many African traditions when a leader died the elders met and elected a successor from among themselves or a field of candidates. In Moslem practice succession went automatically to the first-born son of the dead king or chief.

Finally, there was the fact that the Moslems had introduced a money economy; the Sudanese traditionally had used barter.

When Sunni Ali died, Moslem leaders in Songhay had hoped that Sunni Baru would turn his back on his father's oppressive policies. They called on the new ruler and urged him to embrace Islam wholeheartedly and, in so doing, to lift the oppression of his fellow Moslems. Sunni Baru refused repeated overtures of this sort. In fact, he clearly cast his lot with the countryfolk against the townspeople and their leaders, the Moslem traders. This was impolitic of him, for the townspeople were too powerful and too disturbed by this to accept it, with all its implications of continuing oppression, loss of power, influence, and trade, and increasing encroachment. Without hope of Sunni Baru's changing his mind and his policies, they therefore organized secretly to change rulers.

THE ASKIA

The Moslems were lucky. They found an unusually talented man to lead their revolt. He was a Soninke general, one of Sunni Ali's top commanders, a devout Moslem, named Muhammed Touré, whose title was Askia. Askia Muhammed gathered an army together, but before he could complete his preparations

Sunni Baru sent his forces against the rebels in early 1493. The regulars easily defeated the rebels and drove them across the land in one skirmish after another. Finally, on the very outskirts of Gao, Askia Muhammed's troops rallied and stood against the attack of Sunni Baru's army. This was the turning point, and Askia Muhammed's beleaguered forces rose and smashed Sunni Baru's army in a decisive victory that turned into a rout. The king ran before the rebel forces until at last he found refuge in a tiny village far to the south. And there Sunni Baru lived out his days in relative peace.

The victor, Askia Muhammed I, who founded the Askia dynasty, was quite different from his Sunni predecessors. First of all, he heeded the power and influence of the Moslem town dwellers and reckoned rightly that Islam was the wave of the future in West Africa. So he welcomed the scholars, doctors, poets, students and religious leaders and lawyers. They, in turn, rejoiced in his victory and once again Timbuktu and Jenne became great centers of learning. Their universities entered a golden age. Askia Muhammed surrounded himself with learned Moslems and the sound of the *Muezzin* was heard in the towns throughout the land. The king did, however, continue the most important traditional ceremonies and practices at court, adding to them the Moslem observances.

▷ *Askia's Hajj* As a devout Moslem, Askia Muhammed believed it necessary to make the holy pilgrimage to Mecca. Just two years after defeating Sunni Baru the new emperor set off on the *hajj*, leaving his brother in charge in his absence. We are told that the mighty ruler was accompanied by five hundred cavalrymen, a thousand foot soldiers and 300,000 pieces of gold. Askia's "budget director" calculated that one-third of this amount would be needed for expenses, one-third for distribution as alms in Mecca and Medina and to help pilgrims from the Sudan by underwriting the expenses of a shelter for their benefit. The final 100,000 gold pieces were for miscellaneous purchases.

With this heavy purse and a determination to be generous, Askia Muhammed's journey rivaled the Mansa Musa *hajj* of 250 years earlier. But the impact of Muhammed's trip was never as great on world opinion. Perhaps it was because in his time Mansa Musa was so unexpected; perhaps because he appeared more exotic in the narrower confines of that earlier time. By Askia Muhammed's day the world was fascinated with news about strange lands at the outer rim of knowledge, and word of a powerful potentate and his retinue showering gold on their *hajj* competed with word of the New World and new routes to the Indies.

In addition to his visits to the holy places, he had an audience with the *sharif* of Egypt, the spiritual leader of the Moslems of that land. This worthy appointed Askia Muhammed his lieutenant, or caliph, for all the Songhay lands. Thus the emperor returned after two years with his zeal for Islam renewed. Furthermore, he had taken on the official responsibilities of spiritual leader of all Moslems in the Songhay domains. He set out on his return to carry Islam to the benighted. He plunged into holy wars—*jihads*—against infidel tribes and nations.

▷ *War*   The Askia developed the Songhay cavalry into a striking force such as the Sudan had never before seen: disciplined and devastating, irresistible in war. He brought his infantry to a new peak of effectiveness. Then he turned this military might against the traditional enemy, the Mossi, with the sword of evangelical Islam. Thousands of the Mossi were captured and their youngsters raised as Moslems, later to become replacements in the Askia's armies. The remnants of Mali were taken

over toward the west, their peoples captured or driven almost to
the sea. Next the great king sent his legions east, storming
Hausaland. These kingdoms, between the Niger River and Lake
Chad, fell like dominoes—all except Kano.

The ancient mud-walled city of Kano held out stub-
bornly, fighting off the Askia's assaults. So determined was the
Kano defense that it threw the Songhay victory march out of
step. For nearly a year Kano resisted the besiegers. Defeat
finally came, however, and gave Askia Muhammed a chance to
display his magnanimity. Deferring to the bravery of his oppo-
nents, the Askia kept the king of Kano on his throne, and as a
mark of respect (or was it the desperation of a father of an ugly
girl?) gave one of his daughters to be married to the king.

These victories vastly enlarged the Songhay boundaries
and gave a single administration for the huge expanse of the
Western Sudan. It was now possible for traders to travel the
routes from Sahara to savanna in safety, except in the northeast,
where the caravan markets had been vulnerable for centuries to
the Tuaregs, those nomadic raiders to whom plunder was the
only way of life. They were ancient enemies of the Songhay. So
it was with particularly strong feelings that Askia Muhammed
flung his legions at the Tuaregs from the newly-conquered bases
in Hausaland.

Northward the armies swept, into the Sahara itself, about
the towns of Aïr and Taghaza. The Tuaregs, facing the armies
of Askia and especially his formidable cavalry, abandoned Aïr
and fled into the desert. They split up, settling at small oases far
enough distant to make pursuit costly, if not foolhardy. With his
troops firmly in command of the major Tuareg bases, Askia
Muhammed then settled colonies of Songhay in Aïr and the

market town of Agades to prevent the Tuaregs from retaking these places. Even today there are descendants of these settlers to be found in Agades (which was a Songhay-speaking town as late as 1850), surrounded by the Berber descendants of the Tuaregs.

During his thirty years of rule, Askia Muhammed only once experienced a military reverse. It came about when one of his allies in the expeditions against the Hausa, King Kanta of Kebbi, rebelled against the Askia and declared his land independent of Songhay. He was, he said, throwing off the yoke of vassaldom. Another report has it that he was unhappy about his share of the loot in the Hausa and Tuareg campaigns. At any rate, Kebbi was located in swampy territory that made it relatively easy to defend. King Kanta held off Askia Muhammed's armies successfully until the Songhay tired of the attack and concluded it was not worth continuing.

▷ *Askia's Achievements* It is not easy to rule an area as large as all of Western Europe, peopled with many tribes, nations and kingdoms. Yet, while the petty princes of Europe fought one another, Askia Muhammed had established a peaceful empire that stretched from the midst of the scorching desert on the north to the thick rain forest on the south, from Tekrur— near the Atlantic—to Agades, in the Sahara, and Hausaland, fourteen hundred miles to the east.

Askia Muhammed managed this vast land and the diverse peoples in it by building on the administrative structure developed by Sunni Ali Ber. Sunni Ali had left the much smaller Songhay empire with governors in charge of provinces, each with staffs of retainers to carry on the day-to-day work of government. Askia Muhammed refined this. He divided Songhay into five huge provinces, each with a governor who reported to him directly. The central government was in the hands of responsible officeholders, forerunners of civil service officials.

The emperor's armies were commanded by professional soldiers, headed by generals. And he also had a navy on the Niger River. It consisted of war canoes commanded by an admiral entitled the *Hi-koy*.

All of these military and civil leaders were members of the central government. There were also a chief tax collector, chief of woodcutters, of fishermen and so on. Also, the emperor appointed trusted lieutenants as administrators or "mayors" of towns and major villages. There was a system of justice in which Islamic judges were installed in every district. These men were administrators of Moslem law, not the traditional law. Of course, the Askia, as spiritual leader of the Songhay, was the judge of highest appeal and his court reviewed appeals from decisions of lower courts.

During his reign Askia Muhammed queried one of the outstanding Moslem sages about the traditional customs of his land. He asked this theologian for a legal ruling about the customs in the light of Moslem law. The Askia's purpose was to use the rulings as a basis for a program of social reform in line with Moslem beliefs. Here is one of his questions, put to the expert about 1495:

Among the people there are some who claim knowledge of the supernatural through sand divining and the like, or through the
disposition of the stars . . . [while] some assert that they can
write [talismans] to bring good fortune . . . or to ward off bad
fortune. . . Some defraud in weights and measures . . . others

adulterate gold and silver with copper, or do not extract the
sand from gold dust . . . others inflate meat and mix water
with milk. . . Others, when buying goods, take them and go
off with them before paying for them. . . . Some will sell a
slave-girl and then marry her to the purchaser without caring
whether or not she is already pregnant. Then, if it becomes
apparent that she is pregnant, they quarrel over the offspring.
This happens very frequently.

One of their evil practices is the free mixing of men and
women in the markets and streets and the failure of women to
veil themselves . . . [while] among the people of Jenne it is an
established custom for a girl not to cover any part of her body
as long as she remains a virgin . . . and all the most beautiful
girls walk about naked among people. . .

So give us legal ruling concerning these people and their
ilk, and may God Most High reward you.[2]

This veritable catalog of affronts to Moslem sensibilities was
answered by Muhammed ben Abd al Karim al Maghili, a
conservative North African Moslem theologian. Al Maghili's
response came to light only about thirty years ago in a book
called *The Obligations of Princes*, which was in many ways a
Moslem parallel to Nicolo Machiavelli's *The Prince*, written
about the same time. Here are portions of Al Maghili's reply:

The answer—and God it is who directs to the right course—is that
everything you have mentioned concerning people's behavior . . . is gross error. It is the bounden duty of the commander of the Moslems and all other believers who have the
power to change every one of these evil practices.[3]

Al Maghili's recommendations to rectify these evils were a bit extreme, to say the least. He suggested that those who refused to renounce their claims of "knowledge of the supernatural" be put to the sword. This drastic judgment could be changed: If the person simply "renounced" such beliefs he was then to be "left in peace." He recommended that standardized scales and measures and a chief of markets be appointed for each province to eliminate defrauding in weights and measures. Purchasers who refused to pay up should have their debts taken from them by force, if necessary. All slave-girls sold should be held in escrow, so to speak, by a responsible man until it was proven that they were not pregnant; then the delivery of the "merchandise" could be carried out.

The free mixing of men and women and women walking about naked are "the greatest abominations," cried Al Maghili. To prevent these things, the Moslem commander should exert himself and "appoint trustworthy men to watch over this by day and night, in secret and in the open." This is not spying, said the sage. "It is only a way of caring for them and curbing evildoers, especially when corruption becomes widespread in the land as it has done in Timbuktu and Jenne and so on. The correct and binding thing is that every woman should be taken away from the place where suspicion may arise. . . ."

"And, " continued the sage, "if no trustworthy man can be found to act as judge in such matters, nevertheless it will be better to appoint someone than merely neglect the evil. . . ."[5]

This puritanical approach must have grated against the accepted patterns of behavior in Songhay domains. Note that the sage is concerned with the way men live and with their salvation. The contrast with Machiavelli's ends-justify-the-means philosophy could not be greater.

Figure 22. Here is Taharqa, perhaps the greatest of the Kushite Pharaohs of Egypt. He ruled the Two Lands from 690 to 664 B.C. *and was a mighty builder who constructed temples throughout Egypt, and particularly in Kush. Note the cobra on his headdress and the animal head decoration at his throat.*

THE HERMITAGE, LENINGRAD.

Figure 23. Pyramids by the dozen are to be found in the royal burial grounds near Meroe. Here are a few of those that have survived for more than two thousand years.
INTERNATIONAL FILM FOUNDATION: THE ANCIENT AFRICANS.

Figure 24. This pyramid tomb at Meroe is typical of the fine stone construction used in many of the Kushite royal tombs. In the foreground to the right is the entrance to what was the chapel (its roof and walls have tumbled in) which served as an ante-chamber to the tomb inside the pyramid.
COURTESY OF THE ORIENTAL INSTITUTE, UNIVERSITY OF CHICAGO.

Figure 26. One of the king's retainers, sculpted in the wall of the Lion Temple at Naqa. Note the headband, earring, huge necklace—and the elaborate cuff and arm bracelets on the arm of the king (upper left).
INTERNATIONAL FILM FOUNDATION: THE ANCIENT AFRICANS.

Figure 25. A side view of the pylon entranceway to the Lion Temple at Naqa in Kush showing the extraordinary symbol of the god Apedemek. He has the body of a snake, the head of a lion, and wears a three-part crown as he emerges from a lotus flower. All of these symbols are important in Indian history and lead to conjecture that there was interchange of cultures between Kush and India. Note also the figures carved in the wall to the left. COURTESY OF THE ORIENTAL INSTITUTE, UNIVERSITY OF CHICAGO.

Figure 27. The ram, symbol of the god Ares, is found frequently in Kush and other African cultures. This granite ram is one of many at the royal gravesites in Naqa, Kush.
COURTESY OF THE ORIENTAL INSTITUTE, UNIVERSITY OF CHICAGO.

Figure 28. This pottery coffin, shown as it was excavated in the sand, tells much about the decline of Kush. This is thought to be from Kush's XXth Dynasty. It is a long way from the magnificent temples of Taharqa.
UNIVERSITY OF PENNSYLVANIA MUSEUM.

*Figure 29. This temple at Naqa in Kush was built
during the time of the Ptolemies, the Greek Pharaohs.
Kush's relations with Egypt were friendly, and the
Greek influences in this temple (the arches, capitals,
decoration) show that architects from the Egyptian
court must have had a hand in the design of this building.*
COURTESY OF THE ORIENTAL INSTITUTE,
UNIVERSITY OF CHICAGO.

Figure 30. Elephants were widely used in
the art and decorations of Kush. Here,
elephant heads decorate a bronze lamp
found at Meroe.
SUDAN ANTIQUITIES SERVICE.

Figure 31. The lotus motif is seen again
in these two gold and carnelian bracelets
from the tomb of a queen of Kush. Note
the delicate flower design in the clasps.
COURTESY, MUSEUM OF FINE ARTS, BOSTON.

Figure 32. This bronze head of the Emperor Augustus of Rome was taken by the Kushites in a raid into Egypt about 24 B.C., *when Rome ruled that land. The Roman military expedition sent to punish the Kushites looted major towns and destroyed Napata. The Kushites hid this head under the threshold of a small temple in Meroe where it rested for nineteen hundred years until excavated by archeologists.* BRITISH MUSEUM.

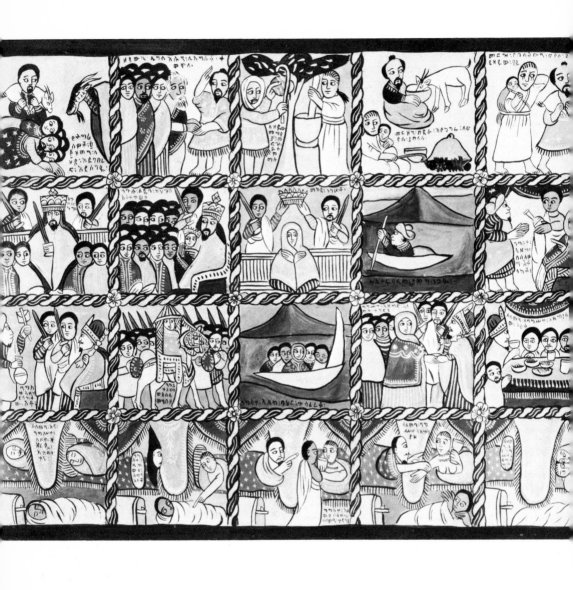

Figure 33. This painting depicting the legend of the Queen of Sheba is in traditional Ethiopian style although in fact it is relatively modern. The mural tells the following story:

For four hundred years, the natives of Axum worshipped a dragon and paid tribute to him. Agabos proposes to kill the dragon, and the people agree that if he is successful he will be crowned king. Agabos prepares a poison, which is then baked in bread and fed to a kid. The dragon eats the poisoned kid and dies, and Agabos is crowned. When his daughter Makeda is born, the King presents her to his people, and much later, she is crowned the Queen of Sheba.

One day a trader from Jerusalem visits the Queen. She gives him perfume to bring to King Solomon. The trader returns and gives the King Makeda's gift. Soon the Queen of Sheba decides to visit Solomon, and she and her party cross the Red Sea. The two great rulers meet. Solomon is quite attracted to the Queen, and he devises a plan to become her lover. He gives a banquet for her retainers, and he and the Queen dine together on a meal of highly spiced and salty foods. Solomon and Makeda make an agreement after she refuses him. In one version of the story, Makeda says, "When I ask you to grant me a favor, I will grant yours."

Solomon, Makeda, and her maid sleep in adjoining tents. By royal decree, all liquids have been removed from the camp except for one goatskin of water in Solomon's tent. The Queen of Sheba, parched with thirst, asks her maid to give her water, and Solomon grants the request. He watches the Queen drink the water and then insists on holding her to their agreement. Solomon and Makeda sleep together. (The Kings of Ethiopia claim direct descent from this union.) Later, Solomon gives the Queen a sign, and she returns to her home.

Figure 34. This huge stone church was excavated from the living rock during the reign of Lalibela (1150 A.D.). This one, Mehane Alem, is one of eleven such structures. ETHIOPIAN AIRLINES.

Figure 35. Two views of
St. George's church, one of those
excavated from the volcanic
rock of Ethiopia, illustrate how
the structure was cut away
from the surrounding stone.
ETHIOPIAN AIRLINES.

Figure 36. Carved from one piece of stone, this
is a typical obelisk from ancient Axum. Note the
false door at ground level, complete with false
lock, and the blind windows, tier on tier, above.
The tallest of these obelisks is still in Italy,
where it was taken by Mussolini's troops.
ETHIOPIAN AIRLINES.

Figure 37. This is the facade of St. Emanuel church, another of those excavated and carved from rock in one huge piece. These monumental engineering feats were accomplished nearly nine hundred years ago.
ETHIOPIAN AIRLINES.

Figure 38. The simplicity and strength of the design of the facade of St. Emanuel church give it a thoroughly contemporary appearance. The styling is thought to be derived from elements of Axumite art and architecture.
ETHIOPIAN AIRLINES.

Figure 39. Typical of monastic
art in the fourteenth century in
Ethiopia is this painting in
the Gabriel Monastery on the
island of Kebran, Lake Tana.
In the lower panel can be seen
the story of the expulsion from
the Garden of Eden. The
religious art of Ethiopia is a
treasure trove of the Coptic
Christian church.
ETHIOPIAN AIRLINES.

Figure 40. Pages from another
Ethiopian prayer book, showing
a strong and vivid style far
different from the Byzantine.
Note the treatment of the angels
and the decorative interlocking
of their wings. Details are stylized
and many (such as noses)
are omitted.

Figure 41. A page from a nineteenth century
prayer book from Axum, Ethiopia. The saints
have a strong Byzantine appearance and the
scripture is written in Ge'ez.

Figure 42. The four languages used in Ethiopian written works are old Greek (upper left), Arabic (upper right), Sabean (lower left) and Ge'ez (lower right). Ge'ez is an ancient form of writing, far older than either Arabic or our own script. It is a "dead" language.
ETHIOPIAN AIRLINES.

SLAVERY IN AFRICA

Al Maghili did not condemn slavery in his famous "answer." Slavery was then an accepted feature of Moslem as well as African living. In the Sudan there were basically two types of people, the "slaves" and the "free." The so-called free man was protected by a chieftain, and in exchange for such protection owed labor, taxes or tribute to that chieftain. The chief, in turn, owed tribute to a lord and the lord likewise owed allegiance and tribute to a king. Each was a vassal of the next in the hierarchy and owed service and allegiance in exchange for protection. Among the rights of these "free" men was that of selecting chieftains, in the old tradition.

If these "free" men were unlucky enough to be captured in battle, or if their town or kingdom was captured by an adversary, they then became "slaves"; that is, they were to live and work in a designated way, unable to change location or vocation at will. Other rules applied to them: Women who were slaves could not marry free men, for instance. This was modified by Askia Muhammed to allow such marriages but the children of such mixed marriages were to be "slaves," not "free."

Both free men and slaves worked, often side by side, at the same jobs or duties. The free men were paid not in money but in goods or share of crop. The slaves received only their food, clothing, and shelter. But both the social structure and necessity brought the slaves into the family unit and it was acceptable and common for a male slave to marry into the family. And there was considerable social mobility. Slaves did earn their freedom; even as slaves they could become traders and have free men working for them. In some cases they even made it to the top of the heap, becoming kings. The difference between this kind of slavery and the chattel slavery of the West was extreme. The African institution was milder, and more flexible, the distance between slave and master was narrower and could be bridged more easily; and the hazard of becoming a slave faced all masters if a battle or a war turned out unfavorably; and skin color—always a consideration in white racism—was not part of it.

From the *Tarikh al-Fettash*, that invaluable report on sixteenth century life in Africa, we learn how vassals served their masters. The *Tarikh* tells us that Askia Muhammed "inherited," as part of his estate, two dozen families or tribes. Each of these had a specialty, and owed to the Askia certain duties or products. One tribe, the Arbi, were royal bodyguards and men- and ladies-in-waiting at the royal household. Five tribes who specialized in ironworking had the specific responsibility of supplying the king with weapons. Each year every family of these armorers was required to deliver to the Askia one hundred spears and one hundred arrows with metal tips. And among the river folk, the vassal families were expected to supply the royal larder with ten packets per year of dried fish. In addition, they were obliged to man the canoes and carry the king and his emissaries whenever they needed water transportation. Another tribe was assigned to raise and harvest crops for the royal stables, to keep the emperor's horses fed.

▷ *Decline* By 1528 Askia Muhammed had ruled Songhay for nearly thirty-five years. He was in his mid-eighties and his eyesight had all but failed him. A palace revolt, sparked by one of his sons, swept the old man from his throne.

Askia called for his brother, Yahia, to help him against the *coup d'etat*, but the rebels intercepted Yahia and killed him. They took over the city of Gao, and Askia, old and tired, was forced to renounce his crown. Kept under house arrest in the royal place, Askia languished there while his son Musa took over the government.

Askia Musa counteracted his father's policies. He turned his back on Islam and by his cruelty and bloodthirsty actions rapidly became widely hated. His subjects rose up and assassinated him in 1531. He was succeeded by his brother Bengan Korei, notable for his defeat as head of the expedition against Kebbi.

Korei called himself Askia Muhammed II and bundled his aged father off to "exile" on an island in the Niger. There the old man suffered a plague of insects and complained of the torment by various animals that made his life miserable. These conditions he endured in his twilight for six years. Then another son—Ismail—unseated Muhammed II and came to power. Ismail brought the old Askia back from his degradation and misery, but a few months later the great man died.

In 1549 Askia Dawud came to power. He proved to be an energetic and wise leader who restored order to Songhay. During the preceding twenty years of his brothers' reigns, a number of major kingdoms had broken away from Songhay, taking advantage of the confusion and intrigue in the ruling circles. Dawud, however, ended these problems and for thirty-three years peace prevailed and Songhay prospered.

AFRICAN LION

We know a good deal about the people, places and conditions of Askia Muhammed's empire thanks to one of the peculiar quirks of fate. So significant was this event that a digression here may be permissible.

Piracy was a way of life in the Mediterranean at the time of Songhay's greatness. The Moslem pirates from Barbary and Turkey raided the northern coast of the Mediterranean and captured Christian vessels for slaves and loot; the Christian pirates of Spain, France and Italy returned the compliment. (Shakespeare's plays frequently and prominently mention the perils of sea voyages at this time.)

Fortunately for the Western world, in 1518 Christian pirates swooped down on a Moorish galley that was about to reach the shores of Tunis. They captured the ship, took its crew and passengers captive and headed for the major slave markets of Pisa and Genoa. However, among the passengers they discovered a young man named Al Hassan ibn Muhammed al Wazzani, of Fez, the cultural and religious capital of Morocco. This chap had with him the bulky manuscript in Arabic of a book: *The History and Description of Africa and the Notable Things Therein Contained*.

Al Wazzani, with considerable bravado, literally talked himself free of the slave block. He was articulate in several languages and told extraordinary stories. The pirates could not judge whether he was half-mad or completely sane. They only knew that in addition to very learned discourse he told strange tales of fabulous kingdoms, rulers, cities and people hidden away in the interior of Africa. The pirates decided that the Moor was harmless and that his vast store of "knowledge" was too valuable to sell through the usual slave market. Somehow (perhaps Al Wazzani suggested it?) they hit upon the idea of offering the captive to the Pope, who could not fail to be amused, if not impressed, by the great store of "information" the Moor possessed.

That a Moor, one of the hated and feared Moslems who

had been driven out of the European mainland only twenty-five years before should be welcomed by the chief of the Christian church may seem like one of Scheherezade's fanciful inventions, but it was true. Al Wazzani spoke Spanish fluently, and the Pope soon discovered his remarkable range of knowledge. In the best fairy tale fashion, the pontiff set the Moor free, took the young man under his wing, converted him to Christianity and baptized him with his own names—Giovanni Leone. Then he provided him with a pension and plenty of writing materials to translate his book about Africa into Italian. The young man, now known as Leo Africanus, completed the book in 1526.

It was the first report in a European tongue of the mysterious interior of Africa. Leo was widely traveled in spite of his youth. He had made his way from Morocco to Tartary, from Tripoli to the centers of Songhay at the height of its splendor under Askia Muhammed and he told about the way of life as well as the trade in these places.

On a mission for the sultan of Fez about 1510, Leo's uncle made the cross-Sahara trip via Sijilmasa-Taghaza to Timbuktu. Leo went along. Arriving in Walata, the northernmost Songhay town, after crossing the treacherous desert, Leo noted with relief, "the inhabitants are black people and most friendly unto strangers." On they went to Timbuktu:

Here are many shops of artificers and merchants, and especially of such as weave linnen and cotton cloth. And hither do the Barbary merchants bring cloth of Europe. All of the women of this region except the maid servants go with their faces covered, and sell all necessary victuals. The inhabitants, and especially strangers living there, are exceeding rich, insomuch that the king married both his daughters unto two rich merchants. Here are many wells containing most sweet water; and so often as the River Niger overfloweth they convey the water thereof by sluices into the town. Corn, cattle, milk and butter this region yields in great abundance: but salt is very scarce here, for it is brought hither by land from Taghaza which is five hundred miles distant. When I myself was here I saw one camel's load of salt sold for eighty ducats. . . .

The inhabitants are people of a gentle and cheerful disposition, and spend a great part of the night in singing and dancing through all the streets of the city: They keep great store of men and women-slaves, and their town is much in danger of fire: At my second being there half the town was burnt in five hours' space. Without the suburbs there are no gardens nor orchards at all.[6]

Leo found Timbuktu's appearance disappointing. Its houses, he said, were simply "cottages built of chalk and covered with thatch." No wonder the town burned so readily. Mansa Musa's famous buildings caught his eye: "There is a most stately temple to be seen, the walls whereof are made of stone and lime; and a princely palace also built by a most excellent workman of Granada [the Spanish city in which Leo and his family had once lived]."

The governor of Timbuktu entertained the mission and Leo observed:

The rich governor of Tombuto hath many plates and scepters of gold, some whereof weigh thirteen hundred pounds; and he keeps a magnificent and well-furnished court. When he travels anywhere he rides upon a camel which is led by some of his noblemen; and so he does likewise when he goes to war, and all his soldiers ride upon horses. Whosoever will speak unto this king must first fall down before his feet, and then taking up earth must sprinkle it upon his own head and shoulders; which custom is ordinarily observed by them that never saluted the king before, or come as ambassadors from other princes. He hath always three thousand horsemen and a great number of footmen that shoot poisoned arrows attending upon him. They have often skirmishes with those that refuse to pay tribute, and so many as they take they sell unto the merchants of Tombuto. Here are very few horses bred, and the merchants and courtiers keep certain little nags which they use to travel upon; but their best horses are brought out of Barbary. And the king so soon as he hears that any merchants are come to town with horses, he commandeth a certain number to be brought before him, and choosing the best horse for himself he pays a most liberal price for him.

Here are a great store of doctors, judges, priests and other learned men, that are bountifully maintained at the king's cost and charges. And hither are brought diverse manuscripts or written books out of Barbary, which are sold for more money than any other merchandise. The coin of Tombuto is of gold without any stamp or superscription; but in matters of small value they use certain [cowrie] shells brought hither out of the kingdom of Persia, four hundred of which are worth a ducat and six pieces of their gold coin with two third parts weighing an ounce.[7]

Continuing on, Leo visited Jenne where he saw a city prospering from its crops of rice, barley, fish, cattle and cotton. The cotton was a major crop, he discovered, sold "unto the merchants of

Barbary for cloth of Europe, for brass vessels, for armor and such other commodities."

When he arrived at Niani, or Mali, Leo found that Askia Muhammed's conquest of that city had impoverished the king of Mali to the point where he "was scarce able to maintain his family." The city was a place of six thousand families or more at this time.

> The region itself yields great abundance of corn, flesh and cotton. Here are many artificers and merchants in all places; and yet the king honorably entertains all strangers. The inhabitants are rich, and have plenty of wares. Here are great store of temples, priests and professors, who read their lectures only in the temples because they have no colleges at all. The people of this region excell all other Negroes in wit, civility and industry.[8]

On his journey three years later Leo apparently went overland from Timbuktu to Gao which was, of course, the capital of the great Askia. He found it a thriving unwalled city whose—

> houses are but mean, except those where in the king and his courtiers live. Here are exceeding rich merchants; and hither continually resort great store of Negroes which buy cloth here brought out of Barbary and Europe. . . . Here is likewise a certain place where slaves are to be sold, especially upon such days as the merchants use to assemble; and a young slave of fifteen years age is sold for six ducats, and so are children sold also. The king of this region hath a certain private palace wherein he maintains a great number of concubines and slaves, which are kept by eunuchs; and for the guard of his

own person he keeps a sufficient troup of horsemen and footmen. . . . It is a wonder to see what plenty of merchandise is daily brought hither, and how costly and sumptuous all things be. Horses bought in Europe for ten ducats are sold again for forty and sometimes for fifty ducates apiece. There is not any cloth of Europe so coarse, which will not here be sold for four ducats an ell and if it be anything fine they will give fifteen ducats for an ell; and an ell of the scarlet of Venice or of Turkey-cloth is here worth thirty ducats. A sword is here valued at three or four crowns and so likewise are spurs, bridles, with other like commodities, and spices also are sold at a high rate: but of all other commodities salt is most extremely dear.[9]

To his amazement, Leo discovered that gold was so plentiful in Gao that the market often would not absorb it. He reported that the natives were frequently forced to return with their gold because there was too much available at the time.

Following the victorious armies of the Askia into Hausa-land, Leo observed that the Songhay conquest had been crushing. To the kingdoms of Kano, Zaria, Katsina and Zamfara the Askia had "sent governors who mightily oppressed and impoverished the people that were before rich." Askia Muhammed's policy on conquest was described by Leo: "In my time [the king of Gobir] was slain by Askia and his sons were gelt and accounted among the number of the king's eunuchs . . . and most part of the inhabitants were carried and kept for slaves by the Askia." The kings of Zaria, Zamfara and Katsina were to also suffer a similar fate.

Nowhere does Leo say for certain that he met Askia Muhammed. He did meet his brother at a Niger River port called Kabara however, and found him to be "Black in color . . . most beautiful in mind and conditions."

THE GREEDY SULTAN

.The riches of Songhay had been reported for many generations by the merchants and caravans and had excited great interest in North Africa. In fact, in Morocco, the Sultan Mulay Ahmed developed an obsessive fascination with the wealth of Songhay. His fascination soon ripened into covetousness. About 1582 he dispatched an expedition of his soldiers to seize from the Songhay the town of Taghaza and its valuable salt mines.

Salt was the one essential material in the gold trade and Taghaza was the major source for it. There was no other reason for human beings to stay in what Ibn Battuta described about 1350 as:

an unattractive village, with the curious feature that its houses and
mosques are built of blocks of salt, roofed with camel skins.
There are no trees there, nothing but sand. In the sand is a
salt mine; they dig for the salt and find it in thick slabs. . . . No
one lives at Taghaza except the slaves of the Mesufa tribe,
who dig for the salt: they subsist on dates imported from
Dra'a and Sijilmasa, camel's flesh, and millet imported from
the Negro-lands. The Negroes come up from their country
and take away the salt from there. At Walata a load of salt
brings eight to ten *mitqals*. In the town of Mali it sells for

twenty to thirty, and sometimes as much as forty. The Negroes use salt as a medium of exchange, just as gold and silver is used [elsewhere]; they cut it up into pieces and buy and sell with it. The business done at Taghaza, for all its meanness, amounts to an enormous figure in terms of hundredweights of gold-dust.[10]

A century and a half later, Leo Africanus visited Taghaza and told of the perilous life led by the Negro slaves who were the miners then:

> The diggers of salt [have no] victuals but such as the merchants bring unto them; for they are distant from all inhabited places almost twenty days' journey, insomuch that oftentimes they perish for lack of food, when the merchants come not in due time unto them. Moreover, the south-east wind so often blinds them that they cannot live here without great danger. I myself continued three days amongst them, all which time I was constrained to drink salt-water drawn out of certain wells not far from the salt-pits.[11]

The living conditions in Taghaza did not concern Sultan Mulay Ahmed. Control of the key ingredient in the fabulous gold trade, however, was very much of interest to him. So the Sultan dispatched an expedition of two hundred soldiers armed with arquebuses, those primitive matchlock muskets, to seize the town and its valuable mines. The troops came to Taghaza only to discover a ghostly silence over the town, relieved only by the flapping in the desert wind of the camelskin roofs. The miners had fled; the town was practically empty. There was no one to work the mines. Furthermore, Askia Dawud had ordered that no Songhay must set foot in Taghaza.

Sultan Mulay Ahmed therefore found himself with a salt cellar he could not use. He abandoned it later, and it was never again worked, ending six centuries of salt mining at the desolate spot. Meanwhile, the Songhay developed another source at Taodeni, a hundred miles closer to Timbuktu. Mulay Ahmed pondered other approaches to the Songhay treasure trove and planned a daring, direct assault.

It took the Sultan of Morocco nine years to perfect and spring his plan on the Sudanese. The scheme was audacious: An attack would be launched by a small expedition of elite troops who would cross the Sahara and strike at the very heart of Songhay power. The Sahara desert had been the principal shield protecting the Sudan from northern invaders. Now Mulay Ahmed would use it as a highway.

Judar Pasha

The Sultan put together his very special striking force with infinite care. The leader he picked for the expedition was a blue-eyed Spanish eunuch who had been captured as a baby in the gypsy caves of Granada and reared as a Moslem in the royal palace at Marrakech. His name was Judar and he was a curious choice, for, so far as is known, he had no military experience. In fact, he was best known as a tax collector. Perhaps his honesty and organizing ability impressed the Sultan by their rarity. The contemporary account says Judar's youth was an important element in his selection. No doubt Mulay Ahmed chose him with an eye to his physical fitness because he knew the expedition would be grueling. At any rate, Judar was named *pasha*—general—and ten *kaids* were appointed under him. Four of these were also Europeans.

Judar led a band of four thousand men picked for tough-
ness, courage and discipline. Of these, two thousand were foot-
soldiers with arquebuses, almost all of them European renegades
or Spanish Moors; probably most of them were war prisoners
who could not ransom themselves. The mounted troops included
five hundred who carried arquebuses, and fifteen hundred Moors
with light lances. For good measure Judar had half a dozen
large and several small cannon. Special training and the finest
equipment available at that time were lavished on this special
corps. The Sultan assigned nine thousand animals to carry the
provisions for this force—eight thousand camels and one thousand pack horses with a thousand camel-drivers and six hundred sappers. It was a huge and precious gamble to cast across
seventeen hundred miles of murderous desert terrain.

Leo Africanus' description of the conditions faced by
Judar Pasha on his journey makes it clear that death was a
silent companion on every desert crossing:

In the way which leads from Fez to Timbuktu are certain pits en-
vironed either with the hides or bones of camels. Neither do
the merchants in summer time pass that way without great
danger of their lives: for oftentimes it happens that when the
south wind blows all those pits are stopped up with sand. And
so the merchants, when they can find neither those pits, nor
any sign thereof, must needs perish with extreme thirst; whose
carcasses are afterwards found lying scattered here and there,
and scorched with the heat of the sun. One remedy they have
in this case, which is very strange: for when they are so
grievously oppressed with thirst, they kill forthwith one of
their camels, out of whose bowels they wring and express
some quantity of water, which they drink and carry about

with them till they have either found some pit of water, or till they pine away for thirst.

In the desert which they call Azaoad there are as yet extant two monuments built of marble, upon which epitaphs are engraved signifying that one of the monuments represented a most rich merchant, and the other a carrier or transporter of wares. The wealthy merchant bought of the carrier a cup of water for ten thousand ducats, and yet this precious water could suffice neither of them; for both of them were consumed with thirst. . . . For some time being sore athirst we could not find one drop of water, partly because our guide strayed out of the direct course, and partly because our enemies had cut off the springs and channels of the foresaid pits and wells. Insomuch that the small quantity of water which we found was sparingly to be kept: for that which would scarce suffice us for five days, we were constrained to keep for ten.[12]

From Marrakech in Morocco the Sultan's army set out across the Sahara in October, 1590. How many died in the five months it took to reach the Niger River is unknown. A Sudanese observer estimated that when the invaders finally met the Songhay forces in battle only a thousand Moors were in the fight. That battle was a turning point in African history.

The Songhay were confident that the Sahara desert would shield them from invasion, as it had successfully done throughout the memory of man. No army, they were certain, could penetrate the sand sea. They knew that the invasion force was coming, of course. The movement of Judar Pasha's troops was scarcely a secret. Moving five thousand men and nine thousand animals along the caravan route kicked up a lot of dust, so to speak, and the caravans had brought word of the military force to Songhay centers.

As the Moors neared, Askia Ishak reckoned from their route that they would attack from the west and he sent troops there. When he heard that the invaders were moving south instead he pulled back his armies and called a war council. In this assembly there was much talk and no decision, except that all fighting men should be mobilized. What to do about the invaders remained undetermined, because the leaders could not agree on the Moors' intended targets or on how to counter them. Ishak dispatched messengers directing the desert tribes to harass the Moors and to cover the water holes they would need. This elementary decision, which might have ended the Moorish invasion if it had been carried out, was never executed. The messengers were waylaid by Tuaregs and shortly after were captured by the Moors with their orders still on them.

Moving toward the Songhay capital at Gao, Judar Pasha sighted the defending armies at a place called Tondibi. Askia Ishak put against the Moors about ninety-seven hundred infantry armed with bows and arrows, eighteen thousand cavalry with spears and an unspecified number of witch doctors equipped with assorted strong magical powers and a herd of cattle. The Moorish invaders fielded one thousand cavalrymen.

The Songhay drove the cattle into the Moorish ranks hoping to confuse them with the charging herd. But the Moors opened ranks and let the cattle pass through them, then attacked the Songhay forces from both flanks. Askia Ishak's advance guard of bowmen held its ground, their shins tied to their thighs so they could not run. They showered the Moors with poisoned arrows but were overrun by the invading cavalry and slaughtered to a man. Askia Ishak's main army was then routed by the

Moor's superior firepower and discipline. The Songhay troops fled, saved by the Niger, across which they escaped. The Moors had no boats. Technological superiority—firearms vs. hand weapons—had won the day.

Defeat

With this victory, the Songhay capital city finally fell to the invaders. At last, after all they had endured, the Moors thought they had within their grasp the fountainhead of the fabulous wealth that had made rich men out of hundreds of Mediterranean merchants. Here they would find the gold and other goods that made the Barbary coast cities great trading centers. With understandable haste and high expectations they marched into Gao, expecting to be dazzled by the splendor of its buildings, monuments and way of life.

Their incredulous eyes were greeted instead by a dusty city of mudbrick huts and buildings roofed with thatch. The palace of the Askia was simply another of the same, though larger and better furnished. Disappointment gave way to despair when the Moors searched the city for loot. Every item of value had been carried away by the fleeing people. There was no gold, no ivory, no cache of jewels and riches. The most extraordinary things the invaders found were a crucifix, a statue of the Virgin Mary and an unused Portuguese cannon.

The heart had gone out of Askia Ishak with the rout of his army and capture of his capital city. He offered to pay the Moors a thousand slaves and 100,000 *mitqals* (12,500 oz.) of gold if they would immediately leave the country. To Judar Pasha this sounded excellent, for he no longer believed in the myths of a Sudanese Eldorado and his soldiers were being racked by disease. Askia Ishak also offered to give the Moors control of the Songhay economy by letting them bring salt and cowrie shells into the land. Furthermore, the Askia promised to swear his loyalty to the Sultan.

Unfortunately, for all concerned, the Moorish general did not have the authority to accept or negotiate offers. Judar sent a message to the Sultan describing the terms and the condition of his troops, urging that the Askia's offers be accepted. Mulay Ahmed had schemed, planned and sacrificed for this victory. He had gambled his prestige with his own people, many of whom had opposed the invasion, and his international standing. So when he received Judar Pasha's intensely anticipated bulletin he was sent into jubilation by news of the victory, into incredulity by the report of the poverty of the Songhay capital and into a flaming rage by Judar's recommendation that the conquest be settled on Askia Ishak's terms.

One macabre footnote to the hollow victory was Sultan Mulay Ahmed's audience with the Turkish ambassador. Murad, the Turkish Sultan, was known to be jealous of the Moroccan chief, and Mulay Ahmed thoroughly detested Murad. The Turks and the Moors mutually despised one another. So Mulay Ahmed summoned Murad's ambassador and reported to him in fulsome detail the magnificence of the Moorish victory in the Sudan and the inestimable riches it had brought. Then, on a high dramatic note, he commanded that a container be brought him and from this he plucked the severed head of "Askia Ishak" and exhibited it to the Turk as proof of the Songhay conquest! This grisly scene was duly reported to Murad, whose reaction, unfortunately, is *not* recorded.

Sultan Mulay Ahmed announced the victory at Tondibi to his people, and promptly sent another general—Mahmud— to replace Judar. This pasha built boats and pursued Askia

Ishak's troops into a battle at Bamba that was a disaster for the Songhay. Ishak lost contact with his army during the rout and was killed, probably by Tuareg raiders. His successor offered to pledge his loyalty to the Sultan. When the new Askia and his followers arrived at the Moorish camp to do so, Mahmud Pasha had them slaughtered. The Moor then appointed a puppet Askia who was unacceptable to the majority of Songhay peoples outside the range of Moorish troops.

Meanwhile, a superlative guerrilla fighter and leader had become the legitimate Askia. This Askia Nuh bedevilled the Moors, luring them into ambush, drawing them into the Borgu forest area. Here, amidst tropical jungle, thick bush, malarial swamps and torrential rainfall the invaders were harassed incessantly. The tse-tse fly killed their horses, the bad water and food poisoned the men, and guerrilla attacks struck them from every direction, day and night. After two years of this, Mahmud Pasha sent a dispatch to the Sultan describing the exhaustion of his army and the impossibility of going on with the costly effort. Mulay Ahmed by 1593 was willing to accept this assessment from Mahmud which he had rejected from Judar. He sent Mahmud thirty-nine hundred men and some five hundred remounts to bolster his strength.

The Moors re-established their superiority along the Niger, occupied Timbuktu and Jenne, from which they exacted tribute amounting to scores of thousands of *mitqals* of gold. An example of their treachery was the Moorish method of wringing loot out of Timbuktu. It was announced that there would be a house-to-house search for weapons on the following day, but that the houses of descendants of one of the city's venerated former leaders would not be included. Knowing full well that in the search all objects of value would be stolen, everyone who could do so sought out a friend whose house would be exempt and deposited with him everything of value. So, on the appointed day the search was made and afterward the townspeople were assembled in the Sankoré mosque to swear their loyalty to the Sultan. Then they were dismissed and the descendants of the holy man were called to the mosque. As the doors of Sankoré swung shut behind them, Mahmud Pasha's troops looted their houses, filled with the treasure of the city, and raped their women. Many of the men in the mosque were murdered outright. From this venture alone Mahmud set aside 100,000 *mitqals* of gold for the Sultan, a calculation so stingy that it proved to be his undoing.

The Sultan was incensed that so rich a city as Timbuktu should yield him so little and he was further disturbed by Mahmud's cruelty and tyranny. The general was known for his statement "my sword is my sultan," indicating a somewhat diluted allegiance to Sultan Mulay Ahmed. The Sultan ordered Mahmud executed. Learning of the sentence, Mahmud threw himself into a final reckless attack on Askia Nuh's army which resulted in his death. Nuh was killed not long after in a battle with Mahmud's successor.

With Askia Nuh's death the back of Songhay resistance was broken. But the land had been disrupted and chaotic ever since the initial defeat of Askia Ishak by Judar Pasha. When the Moorish victory ripped the administrative skein that held the vast Songhay empire together, the result was anarchy. All the disaffected tribes and subdued but hostile kingdoms rose up, believing the time of liberation had dawned. Hordes of raiders from such groups as the Zagrana and Fulani descended on the peasants near Timbuktu and completely sacked the province of Jenne. The Tuaregs struck Timbuktu and the Sanhaja rose against a Moorish garrison. The Moors retaliated, and this became the pattern.

What had once been a peaceful and mighty empire was reduced to a host of armed camps. Al Sadi described it:

> ... Security gave place to danger, wealth to poverty, distress and calamities and violence succeeded tranquility. Everywhere men destroyed each other; in every place and in every direction there was plundering, and war spared neither life nor property nor persons. Disorder was general and spread everywhere, rising to the highest degree of intensity.

The results, for the Moors, were profitable but costly. They captured booty and squeezed out tribute, as we have seen. One eyewitness account of this is that of Jasper Tomson written July 4, 1599 in Marrakech as he watched the triumphal return of Judar Pasha:

> He brought with him thirty camels loaded with tibar [gold dust; Tomson estimated the value of the gold at £604,800] . . . also great store of pepper, unicorn's [probably rhinoceros] horns and a certain kind of wood for dyers, to some one hundred-twenty camel-loads; all of which he presented unto the king [Sultan] with fifty horse and great quantities of eunuchs, dwarfs and women and men slaves, beside fifteen virgins, the king's daughters of Gao, which he sendeth to be the king's concubines. You must note all these to be of the coal black hair, for that country yieldeth no other.

Thus Sultan Mulay Ahmed profited, though not so handsomely as he anticipated. His troops had discovered that when they took over the trading centers the flow of gold from the nether regions dried up. Furthermore, they found that the gold sources were in the rain forest and could not be captured. The Sultan's hopes for a vast and expanding traffic of gold and precious goods were thwarted. He had, in effect, killed the goose that laid golden eggs. For it was the peace and safety of the Songhay empire that had made it a thriving center through which riches flowed. The Moorish troops had destroyed the governing apparatus, the central authority of the Askias, and had failed to replace it.

Some reports state that the Moroccans lost twenty-three thousand men in war and to disease during their Songhay invasion. The merchants of Morocco who had carried on an ancient and profitable trade with the Sudan were apprehensive about Mulay Ahmed's expedition from the beginning. They feared it would upset their trade. In fact, it all but destroyed it. So they pressed for an end to the adventure without success until Sultan Mulay Ahmed died in 1603. But it was not until 1618 that the Moors finally decided the Sudan was not worth its cost. In that year Sultan Mulay Zidan officially withdrew his Sudanese expedition.

However, the mercenaries, renegades and other Moors who were in the territory had different ideas. They were beyond control of the Sultan and they had set themselves up as self-perpetuating military dictators who endured until 1780 in Gao, Jenne, Bamba and Timbuktu.

The greatness of the Songhay empire dwindled to but a memory and these people returned to the land of their ancestors, the country of the Dendi along the west bank of the Niger, where their descendants live to this day.

NOTES

1. Inscription at the City of Brass, C. thirteenth century, A.D., Anonymous Arabian; trans. by E. Powys Mathers in *A Little Treasury of World Poetry*. H. Creekmore (ed.), (New York: Scribner's Sons, 1952), pp. 145-146.
2. Basil, Davidson; *The African Past*, (Boston: Atlantic-Little Brown, 1964), pp. 86-88.
3. *Ibid.*
4. *Ibid.*
5. *Ibid.*
6. Leo Africanus, *History and Description of Africa;* trans. by Pory, (London: Hakluyt Society, 1897).
7. *Ibid.*
8. *Ibid.*
9. *Ibid.*
10. Ibn Battuta, *Travels in Asia and Africa;* trans. by H. A. R. Gibb, (New York: R.M. McBride & Comp., 1929).
11. Leo Africanus, *op. cit.*
12. *Ibid.*

It is man who counts.
I call upon gold:
It answers not.
I call upon rich fabric:
It answers not.
It is man who counts.

EVALUATION
Traditional Akan poem

◁▷ ◁▷ ◁▷ ◁▷ ◁▷ ◁▷ ◁▷ ◁▷ ◁▷ ◁▷ ◁▷ ◁▷ ◁▷ ◁▷

SONS OF GIANTS

◁▷ ◁▷ ◁▷ ◁▷ ◁▷ ◁▷ ◁▷ ◁▷ ◁▷ ◁▷ ◁▷ ◁▷ ◁▷ ◁▷

VII

ONE OF THE FIRST DESCRIPTIONS OF THE
kingdom of Kanem is by Al Muhallabi, a tenth century Moslem
writer:

> The kingdom of the Zaghawa [the ruling tribe] is said to be a great
> kingdom among the kings of the Sudan. On their eastern
> boundary is the kingdom of Nubia which is above upper
> Egypt. Between them there is a distance of ten days' journey.
> They are many tribes. The length of their land is a fifteen

days' journey through habitations and cultivations all the way. Their houses are all of gypsum and so is the castle of their king. Him they respect and worship to the neglect of Allah the most High; and they falsely imagine that he does not eat food. His food is taken into his house secretly and if any one of his subjects happens to meet the camels carrying it, he is immediately killed on the spot. He has absolute power over his subjects and takes what he will of their belongings. Their cattle are goats and cows and camels and horses. Millet chiefly is cultivated in their land, and beans; also wheat. Most of the ordinary people are naked, covering themselves with skins. They spend their time cultivating and looking after their cattle; and their religion is the worship of their kings, for they believe that it is they who bring life and death and sickness and health.[1]

According to legend, the So, the people who originally settled in the wide, grassy plains around Lake Chad, (the area of Kanem), were superhuman. They were a people who appear in the legends as:

giants of prodigious force, and surprising feats are celebrated in their name. With one hand they dammed the rivers; their voices were so great that they could call from one town to another, and birds took flight in panic whenever one of them should cough. Their hunting expeditions drew them far from their dwellings; in a single day they would go hundreds of miles, and the animals they killed, hippopotamus and elephant, were carried easily on the shoulders of these fortunate hunters . . . Their weapons were bows from the trunk of the palm tree. . . . Even the earth bore their weight with difficulty. . . . [2]

Unfortunately, neither archeology nor rock drawings have yet given us substantial proof to verify this legend, impressive though it is. What we do know is that the So were extremely industrious: They built towns, they were accomplished craftsmen in pottery (and made many pots in the ram's head shape reminiscent of Meroe and the worship of Ares) and they used the "lost wax" technique to produce bronze pieces of artistic value. They also brought new ideas in social organization. Women, for example, had a new, higher status in So life and actually participated in government.

But the question of the origin of the So is a mystery. The giants arrived and had no difficulty whatsoever in conquering the "little men" who lived there. At any rate, these legendary people have disappeared and three expeditions of French archeologists have been assiduously attempting to sift fact from fancy about them. They have found near Lake Chad pottery and metal objects that prove the So were proficient in bronze, copper and ironworking at an early date—probably the eighth century— and that their society was elaborate enough to require accomplished artists who made intricate ceramics and decorative animals, toys and religious figures of clay.

The French archeologist Lantier says, "such of their works as we know already witness to a mastery which presumes a long industrial past."[3] In other words, their skills with various materials were too great to have developed overnight. Where did they perfect their craftmanship? Conjecture points to Meroe-Nubia—either through teachers or through migrants who may have fled from the Axumite invasion. But as this point it remains conjecture and will until archeology gives us more information about who these people were and where they came from.

The Growth of Kanem

After the So people came the Kotoko, who left records written in Arabic. Then the empire of Kanem developed, reaching its peak in the thirteenth century. It was primarily a grain-growing, cattle-, goat-, horse-raising land that had no gold mines but did control valuable caravan trails over which the gold traveled to the Nile and to Tripoli. To coordinate the activities of this increasingly prosperous and populous land, one family or tribe, the Sefuwa, emerged as the rulers. And they instituted a strong central government which had as its core a council of twelve men who represented the empire, advised the ruler and were responsible for executing his decisions. The council began, says one expert, as a family meeting in which the elders got together to discuss important matters and to take appropriate action. From this evolved a council of men who had inherited their right to belong and over which right there were frequent dynastic battles. But internal battles or not, the strong central government and astute rulers managed to keep Kanem independent and vital well into the late sixteenth century.

The Bornu Chronicle (a compilation of the origin, legends and oral histories of Bornu) reports that Kanem was at its zenith under a sultan named Dunama Dibbalemi in the period 1210–1224, about the time of the Magna Carta. At this time Kanem had pushed its borders to the middle Nile on the east, colonized the Bornu area on the south and west of Lake Chad and reached up across the Sahara to the Fezzan on the north, capturing Tibesti and Kauwar as outposts against nomad raiders. Kanem at this time was in a truly strategic position, located directly in the path of the caravans from Mali to the Nile and Somali coast to the east and perfectly capable and willing to "tax" each well-laden camel and pack.

All went smoothly—relatively—until Mai (Sultan) Dunama's reign when, as the Chronicle puts it, "a civil war broke out that was due to the greed of his children." Each prince, it reports, went with his family and followers back to his home territory and from these strongholds they battled for their rights and privileges. Mai Dunama managed to put down these challenges to his authority. Meanwhile, the Bulala, nomadic cousins of the Kanem tribes, were developing into a powerful people. Two or three reigns after Dunama, feuds broke out that went on for nearly two hundred years. And these were complicated by wars of conquest. But it was the growing strength of the Bulala and their encroachments that set off the serious war, the conflict that by 1400 A.D. drove the Kanem rulers out of their land to the west side of Lake Chad.

Though it may appear that there was constant upheaval in the land, all indications point to relative peace and calm, with—above all—safe passage for the caravans during these times. The trails north to Libya and south and west into the Hausa states were deliberately policed with care. The trade that passed through was much too valuable as a source of revenue to risk losing because of unsettled conditions or banditry. Along these routes the flow of hoof-and-foot traffic was vital, bearing as it did leather goods, cottonstuffs and kola nuts from Hausa, salt and precious stones and ore and the luxuries of Europe and the Maghreb from the north. And from south to north moved that seemingly ceaseless flow of ivory, slaves, and goods such as ostrich feathers and horn.

So, though Kanem declined, the area west of Chad, called Bornu by this time, developed and prospered under the leadership of Kanem's exiled Sefuwa family. It dominated the routes to Tripoli and Libya via the oases of the Libyan desert.

As the caravans funneled through Bornu it expanded into a trading center even larger and wealthier than its venerable rival, Kanem. Furthermore, with the traders came the teachers and students, the businessmen and scribes and lawyers and religious leaders until Bornu blossomed into a center for culture as well as commerce of the Sudan and Libya.

Children of Noah

There is a time-veiled tradition that the name Bornu refers to the Biblical Noah. Supposedly, Noah was born in this part of what is now Nigeria, and Bornu means "Country of Noah" (Ber-Noh). A tradition in an area of what is now Chad, to the north and east of the lake, has it that after the Flood, Noah, his ark and its contents, landed there. Tradition has it that the passengers—Noah's family—were the ancestors of the ruling tribe.

The land of Bornu is a vast table-like countryside sloping eastward to Lake Chad. It is blessed with plentiful water, found by sinking deep wells through the black soil to a depth of sixty-eight feet—the level generally maintained by Lake Chad. It is an area rich in beans, grains and other edible crops including some grain such as rice and wheat. There is much honey in the land, from vast quantities of bees. Familiar features of the countryside include figs, palms, tamarind, wild cotton and indigo (resulting in the production of much blue-striped cloth). The heat in the summer months hovers above the 100° mark, day and night. In spite of this, it is an indication of high status to wear many robes and turbans made of multiple scarves; in fact, the more the better! Today, leading citizens live in modest, individual compounds with a separate house for each wife. Polyg-

amy is a way of life, though few households number more than
two or three wives.

The country has been a natural home for centuries for
abundant wildlife, including lions, giraffes, elephants, crocodiles,
hippopotami, hyenas, gazelles, ostriches and antelopes. Horses,
camels and oxen have been the traditional domestic helpers in
the area and the Bornuese have a great reputation as horsemen.
In the past they proved to be fierce warriors on horseback,
dashing into battle wearing light armor made of iron, which
they also used to protect their steeds. They were great builders
as well, and the huge walls they erected about their towns were
twenty feet thick and from thirty-five to forty feet high. The
chief's quarters were a series of towers or turrets with sloping
terraces filling the spaces between them. The early capital, called
Jima, was on the shore of Lake Chad, and the first dynasty of
record, the Sefuwa, were "the people descended from Sef."

Emperor Mai Idris Alooma III

We know, from the Chronicle, more about Bornu's greatest hero
than we do about all of Kanem's rulers, however. The most
famous of Bornu's emperors was Mai Idris Alooma II. As a
boy, when his father died, the young prince was kept from the
throne while his cousin ruled. The cousin's son succeeded him;
meanwhile there were plots against Idris' life and his mother
spirited him away, heavily disguised, to his grandfather who
was living east of Lake Chad with the Bulala. These people,
though cousins, were traditional enemies of the Bornu. In 1580,
about the time Philip of Spain was building his Armada to
attack England, Idris Alooma's second cousin died and the
young man asserted his claim to Bornu's throne.

Now the years previous had been filled with raids by plundering bands and the new Sultan's first duty was to rid the land of this problem. Mai Idris became, like Sunni Ali Ber, a leader on horseback. He put down the rebellious tribes on every side and re-established peace and order in the Bornu countryside.

Idris' years of "exile" with his grandfather, living among the Bulala, had convinced him that it would be a tragedy for Bornu and the Bulala to go to war. He brought his council together and announced to them that he planned to try to establish peace between the two peoples. As undisputed ruler by divine right, his decision was unalterable and had the force of law. Nevertheless, some of his counselors, perhaps disappointed at the prospect of a negotiated settlement between the two peoples rather than a war in which booty and slaves might be won, asked the Sultan why he was avoiding battle with Bulala enemy. Mai Idris reply was, in effect, "Why fight if it is not necessary? I believe we can be friends. However I intend to make Bornu strong and will attack other villages if I must." Fortunately his forbearance proved wise and he did work out a peaceful arrangement with the Bulala that developed into a closer and closer relationship which eventually resulted in a joint realm.

Though he had been on the throne only a short time, Mai Idris decided to make the *hajj*, against the advice of his counselors. They feared that he had not fully consolidated his power and that once he left the empire it would fall to pieces with jealous, warring princes struggling for power. The Sultan was determined, and argued that as a true Moslem he must make the *hajj* and that it was wiser to go sooner because the plans he had for the country were too elaborate to be interrupted at some later time by the trip to Mecca. That was his response to his questioners. But there is reason to believe that he wished to make the *hajj* in part, at least, so that he could strengthen his army. He made a thorough inspection of the latest in arms and armament on his way back from Mecca.

We know that he stopped in Egypt on his return and was shown muskets and artillery. After he first witnessed the firing of a musket he said that he had not believed it possible that one gun could make such a blast. The Egyptian demonstration was convincing evidence that the new weapons could make a tremendous difference in Bornu's relations with its neighbors, to put it mildly.

Mai Idris made arrangements to strengthen his army by adding firearms. He contracted for a contingent of the musketeers to train his officers and crack troops in using these weapons and ordered shipments of the guns to be delivered in Bornu. Further, he hired a group of Turkish musketeers to come and train his personal bodyguard in using them. Then he added the power of these well-equipped soldiers to his corps of camel and horse cavalry and his archers and shield-carriers.

This powerful new combination overwhelmed the opposition of the pagan tribes to the south, who, of course, had never been face-to-face with firearms before. The general plan of the Sultan's officers was to take the enemy with quick marches and surprise attacks. These campaigns were more or less annual in nature, but in case the results of the battles were inconclusive, Mai Idris left bands of guerrilla fighters in the area to ravage the enemy countryside and keep him off balance until the next major effort could be mounted.

We read that year after year he had to campaign against one tribe or another. The Chronicle tells how he attacked the Ngafata in their fortified town of Damasak. They had been

particularly destructive—looting and burning Bornu towns. He
ordered a siege of Damasak but the barrage of poisoned arrows
from the defenders dampened his troops' enthusiasm. He con-
trived to have a wall of shields carried in front of his soldiers
and his armor-clad horsemen. The shields turned aside the archers' best efforts to slaughter Idris' troops, the battle was soon
won, the Ngafata surrendered or fled.

Many of the southern tribes were ripe targets for Mai
Idris. They had desirable lands, and besides, they were pagans,
which justified the missionary zeal of the Sultan to convert them
to Islam, which he did with a passion.

Another of his major victories was against the fortress
town of Amsaka in the south. It was an interesting place. The
Chronicle says that for a century or more the town had been a
magnet for outlaws and adventurers. Naturally such people had
little love for tax collectors and authorities from a strong central
government such as Mai Idris'. The Sultan decided to capture
this town and quietly brought together a contingent of cavalry
and launched a surprise attack against the Amsakans. To his
chagrin and to the shame of the Sultan's army, they were repulsed and severely beaten by the free-wheeling Amsakans. Mai
Idris took the defeat but resolved to prepare more thoroughly the
next time.

Distracted by other more pressing matters, he was not
ready to spring his second attack for several years. This time
when the Sultan's soldiers reached the town they discovered that
a deep, dry moat had been dug encircling the entire village.
Then began an interlude in which Mai Idris ordered his troops
to fill the ditch with stalks of grain gathered in the nearby
fields. The troops dutifully obeyed, but the villagers came out at
night and emptied the stalks from the ditch. The next morning

Mai Idris' troops put them back again. This went on for several days until the Sultan called a halt to this absurd process. He ordered a concerted effort in which one group of soldiers filled the ditch with stalks and another troop of warriors were poised to rush across the improvised "bridge" as soon as possible. But the Amsakans, watching this procedure from behind their walls, had an answer. They tossed flaming torches into the stalks and brought the project to a roaring finish.

This setback simply doubled Mai Idris' determination and he ordered his troops to fill in the moat with earth instead of flammable materials. At the same time he had his engineers build towers tall enough to give his marksmen platforms from which they could fire over the walls into the town. With these preparations complete, he ordered a mighty attack, with thunderous beating of drums and blood-curdling battle yells and the roar of muskets as the marksmen set about their deadly business. According to the Chronicle, the noise terrified the Amsakans and they fled from the town after dark. However, they were not successful in escaping. Mai Idris' troops completely ringed the town and they captured most of the Amsakans and executed them.

At a later time, relations between Bornu and the Bulala deteriorated. A new Bulala ruler was decidedly unfriendly and war erupted. Idris led his legions into battle and, after much heavy fighting, the Bulala were vanquished. This decisive event meant that Bornu finally had complete power over Kanem at last. Idris appointed his cousin Muhammed as viceroy and the Bulala were forced to swear allegiance to him. Then war prisoners were set free, since it had been a conflict over political and not religious matters.

Mai Idris Alooma is remembered by his people as one who

brought Moslem law to the land, replacing the previous, limited tribal law. He installed Moslem judges, built a refuge at Mecca for Sudanese pilgrims, and constructed a famous mosque in Bornu, the first built with bricks.

It was a strong, relatively peaceful and vastly enlarged land that Mai Idris Alooma left to his successor Muhammed V when he died in battle in 1617—a year after Shakespeare's death. So well did Idris Alooma and Muhammed V set the pattern of sound government and wise rule that Bornu endured with little change until the mid-eighteenth century.

NOTES

1. Al Muhallabi, quoted by R. Oliver and J. D. Fage; *A Short History of Africa*, (New York: Penguin Books, 1962), p. 47.
2. Margaret Shinnie, *Ancient African Kingdoms*, (New York: St. Martin's Press, 1965), p. 67.
3. R. Lantier, "Les Bronzes Sao," 1953.

△
▽
△
▽
△
▽
△
▽
△
▽
△
▽
△
▽
△
▽
△
▽
△
▽
△
▽
△
▽
△
▽
△
▽
△
▽
△
▽
△
▽
△
▽
△
▽
△
▽
△
▽
△
▽
△
▽
△
▽
△
▽
△
▽
△
▽
△
▽
△
▽

"Through wisdom I have dived down into the great sea, and have seized in the place of her depths a pearl whereby I am rich. I went down like the great iron anchor, whereby men anchor ships for the night on the high seas, and I received a lamp which lighteth me, and I came up by the ropes of the boat of understanding."

THE QUEEN OF SHEBA
from the *Kebra Nagast*[1]

◁▷ ◁▷ ◁▷ ◁▷ ◁▷ ◁▷ ◁▷ ◁▷ ◁▷ ◁▷ ◁▷ ◁▷ ◁▷ ◁▷

FROM AXUM
TO ADDIS ABABA
◁▷ ◁▷ ◁▷ ◁▷ ◁▷ ◁▷ ◁▷ ◁▷ ◁▷ ◁▷ ◁▷ ◁▷ ◁▷ ◁▷
VIII

ETHIOPIA TAKES ITS NAME FROM *AETHIOPS*—
"burnt faces"—the name the ancient Greeks gave the people
living in the areas along the Red Sea and inland south and west
of Egypt.

The other widely-used name for Ethiopia, Abyssinia,
comes from a tribe called Habashat or Habashan. These people
are said to have come from Arabia via the Red Sea sometime
before 500 B.C. (The name "Habesh" is still used for Ethiopia

in Arabic countries and the German—*Abessinien*—is closer to this than our English spelling.)

SOLOMON AND MAKEDA

Ethiopian annals go back at least to 1000 B.C. and the country begins its "history" with the incomparably romantic episode of Solomon and the Queen of Sheba. And that tale begins with Solomon's decision to build a temple, as described in the Bible. He sent forth to the four corners of the world notices to all merchants that the temple was under construction and that those who brought goods for the building would be paid by the great king in gold and silver.

Now Makeda (c. 1005–955 B.C.) the queen of Axum (as Ethiopia was known in that day) or Sheba, as it was also called, had among her subjects an important merchant named Tamrin. Tamrin decided to respond to Solomon's call and he packed up stores of valuables including ebony, sapphires and red gold, which he took to Jerusalem to sell to the king. During his stay in Solomon's capital he was greatly impressed by the magnificence of the buildings and richness of the people's clothing and way of life. Tamrin was even more impressed with the wisdom of Solomon. So, when the merchant came back to Sheba, he reported to Queen Makeda on these wonders. So enthusiastic was Tamrin that he aroused the interest of the Queen who was, after all, a lonely young woman, reigning by herself over Sheba. Because of the merchant's description, Queen Makeda decided to see for herself this paragon of a ruler and the wonders of his realm.

The Queen assembled a caravan for the journey and it numbered no fewer than 797 camels plus so many donkeys and mules that no count was kept of them. These beasts were heavily laden with Makeda's gifts for the great king, not to mention her own foodstuffs, water, gold, wardrobe and cosmetics. When Makeda's caravan arrived at Solomon's palace the great king welcomed her royally and, according to the Chronicle, "entertained her honorably, lodging her and her retinue, seeing to it that she was fed generously and giving her eleven changes of garments daily." Makeda, it is reported, stayed many months at Solomon's court, observing the king as he directed the building of the great temple and as he ruled over his thriving domain. She was so impressed in her discussions with him that she renounced the religion of her fathers, that is to say, astrology and the worship of the heavens, the stars, sun and moon. Solomon converted her to the religion of Israel and she accepted Yahveh, or Jehovah.

The time came, after half a year, that the Queen decided she must return to her homeland. Now Solomon had also been much impressed by this beautiful woman and though he had many women in his harem and several wives of importance, including the Pharaoh's daughter, he desired the Queen of Sheba. The chronicle tells of Solomon's driving passion to have many sons who would carry the faith of Israel and destroy heathen images. Thus he considered Queen Makeda: "A woman of such splendid beauty has come to me from the end of the earth. Will God give me seed in her?"[2] He was determined to find out, and devised a shrewd, if not scrupulously honorable, scheme.

The Queen was invited to a magnificent farewell feast at Solomon's sumptuous palace. The banquet was a long one that went on for hours and hours. There were special hot soups, peppery condiments, vegetables with vinegar, broiled meats and salty delicacies, sugared and preserved desserts and spiced wines. In short, by the time the feast ended, very late in the night, all were thirsty (as the king had planned) as well as sleepy. Since it was so late, Solomon invited Queen Makeda to stay in his palace. She was not at all sure that she should, but finally secured Solomon's promise not to take her by force since she was a virgin and could only keep her throne if she remained so. The king asked her to promise not to take by force anything in his palace. She pouted at this and said with some heat that the Queen of Sheba was not a thief—and then promised as requested. Beds were then drawn up on opposite sides of the royal sleeping chamber and the two retired.

It was not long before the Queen, dying of thirst, sought a drink. Now the servants were nowhere to be found and she did not dare to call them for it might awaken Solomon. She looked about and saw, in the center of the room, midway between the royal beds, a large water jar. She left her bed, tiptoed to it and filled a cup with water. Just as she put it to her lips and sipped, Solomon leaped from his bed, rushed to her and seized her arm, saying, "You have broken your oath that *Figure 33* you would not take anything by force that is in my palace." The Queen protested, of course, that surely the promise did not cover something so insignificant and plentiful as water, but Solomon argued that there was nothing in the world more valuable than water, for without it nothing could live. Makeda reluctantly admitted the truth of this and apologized for her mistake, begging for water for her parched throat. Solomon, now released from his promise, assuaged her thirst and his own, immediately taking the queen as his lover.

The following day, as the Queen prepared to leave on her return to Ethiopia, Solomon came out to bid her farewell. From his hand he took a ring and placed it in the Queen's hands. "If you have a son, give this to him and send him to me," he said. With that the Queen returned to the land of Sheba and, sure enough! she did bear a son. She named him Son-of-the-Wise-Man and raised him as prince and heir apparent to the throne. When he was grown, he wanted to see his father. So the Queen outfitted another caravan which she sent with her son, under the leadership of the merchant Tamrin, to Jerusalem. To Tamrin, Makeda gave a message for Solomon, that the great king should anoint their son as king of Ethiopia and proclaim a law that from that time on only the males descended from their son should rule Sheba. Before this, as in Makeda's case, queens had been the rulers of Ethiopia.

As this great caravan came to the land of Solomon, far from Jerusalem in the Gaza area, the Israelites saw the prince and bowed and saluted him. "Hail," they cried, "the king lives!" Others, however, remembered that the king was still in Jerusalem. They sent messengers to Jerusalem, therefore, to find out which was the real king. When they were shown into Solomon's presence, the messengers cried out and said, "Behold, one has come to our land who resembles you in every feature." Solomon asked about the stranger and the messengers admitted that they had not asked where he came from, "for he seemed to be one of great authority, but his followers said they were of Ethiopia."[3]

Then, says the chronicle, Solomon rejoiced in his heart, for here was his first-born son. Though he had many wives, the king had been unsuccessful in begetting sons and had at that time only one, Rehoboam, a boy of seven. So, when the prince arrived at the royal palace he gave the ring to Solomon. But the king, embracing him, exulted, "What need is there of the ring? Without a sign I know you, that you are my son."

Tamrin the merchant gave Solomon the message from Makeda and the king arranged to honor her requests. With the holy oil Solomon anointed the young man and renamed him Menelik, meaning, "how handsome he is." He proclaimed that only his male descendants should rule in Ethiopia. The high priest, Zadok, then explained the laws of Israel, pronouncing blessings on Menelik so long as he should uphold the laws and curses if he should forsake them. Though Solomon entreated Menelik to stay in Israel and reign as his first-born son, the boy would not and insisted upon returning to Ethiopia. Solomon therefore called his nobles and leaders and told them, "I am sending my first-born son to rule in Sheba. Do you also send your first-born sons to be his counselors and officers."[4] And, according to the chronicle, they did as Solomon commanded.

▷ *Menelik's Ark* Menelik asked Solomon for a piece of the fringe of the covering of the Ark of the Covenant so that the Ethiopians might have a relic to revere. Solomon granted this. But without his knowledge the sons of his counselors, angry at having to go to Sheba, decided to take the Ark of the Covenant in secret. They had a substitute built, which they surreptitiously placed under the three sacred covers when they removed the real Ark. The following day Solomon sent Zadok to bring him the outer covering of the Ark and this he gave to Menelik for the temple in Ethiopia. Full of joy, Menelik rounded up his caravan with the first-born sons of the nobles and started out on the return trip. Divine intercession lifted the entire caravan one cubit above the earth and they "sped like eagles," covering in one day what normally would have required thirteen days' journey. When they were across the border in Egypt, the sons of the nobles told Menelik that they had brought the true Ark with them. Far from being shocked and determined to return the relic, Menelik, says the chronicle, "skipped like a young ram before the Ark."[5] They continued their trek, arriving safely in Sheba.

In Jerusalem, meanwhile, Zadok, the high priest, suddenly suspicious, removed the second and third coverings of the Ark and discovered the substitution perpetrated by his son and the other nobles. The news of the catastrophe was told to Solomon, who rose up in wrath and sent an army after Menelik. When the troops arrived in Egypt, however, they learned that the Ethiopians had preceded them long before. Filled with sorrow and lamentations, the king was comforted by a prophecy that came to him saying, "the Ark of the Covenant has not been given to an alien but to thine own first-born son." With this consolation Solomon called off the expedition and all hope of recovering the true Ark.

And so Menelik returned to Sheba, triumphant, with the sons of the nobility of Israel. And, goes the chronicle, he ruled in Ethiopia for many years wisely and well. And after Menelik, his sons ruled and their sons after them, and so on until the latest time when, even now, the ruler of the land is the "conquering lion of Judah," descended directly from Solomon and the Queen of Sheba. (Curiously, there has been a "sea change" and the current rulers of Ethiopia claim to be descended from Solomon, but through the female line—via the queens instead of the kings!)

So goes the legend. And, though it is almost completely without foundation, this romance has had a profound influence on the history of Ethiopia and this whole area of the Middle

East and Africa. The "official" version of the legend is to be found in a fourteenth century book entitled the *Kebra Nagast*, or *Glory of Kings*. This in turn traces its antecedents to an Arabic original of 1225 A.D. and it refers mainly to events in the general time period 650 to 1150 A.D. The *Kebra Nagast* itself was considered so important that upon it depended the legitimacy of Ethiopian sovereigns. In 1872 the king of Ethiopia wrote the British, who had taken the *Kebra Nagast* to England in 1868. "There is a book," wrote the king, "called *Kebra Nagast* which contains the law of the whole of Ethiopia and the names of the princes and churches and provinces. . . . I pray you will find out who has this book and send it to me, for in my country my people will not obey my orders without it." The trustees of the British Museum, where the book was on display, met and voted to return the *Kebra Nagast*. They sent it back, thereby restoring the king's authority.

But true or not, the legend of Solomon and the Queen of Sheba gave to Ethiopians certain priceless things. They were, they believed, chosen people, guardians of the true Ark of the Covenant and heirs to the promises made by God to Abraham. With such a heritage, the descendants of Menelik could not fail to uphold the faith and to resist the onslaught of the Moslems and pagans. The belief of Ethiopians in their descent from the house of Judah has provided a continuous rallying point and has helped Ethiopia maintain its unity.

(Though Judaism has never been the predominant religion of Ethiopia, it has had profound effects. All of the major celebrations of the country show mixed elements deriving from Christian, Jewish and pagan sources, for example. And the Falashas—known as the "black Jews" of Ethiopia—are today about twenty-five thousand strong, far below their numbers before wars with the Amhara kings and forced conversions to Christianity. Though most Ethiopians consider themselves direct decendants of the tribe of Judah, the country was pagan until the acceptance of Christianity in the fourth century when it took on the Byzantine type of evangelical religion and carried out religious warfare against both Moslems and Jews at home and across the Red Sea. †)

HISTORICAL ETHIOPIA

It is a fact that Ethiopia was known to the ancient Greeks and Romans. Pliny the Elder's *Natural History* and Pomponius Mela's *Geography*, which cited Ethiopia, were reasonably well-known works in antiquity although they dropped out of sight during the Dark Ages. Pliny stated that Ethiopia was a "famous and power- ful country as early as the Trojan War." The Egyptian rulers

†The roots of the legend, of course, went back to the Scriptures. In the Sep- tuagint, the early Greek translation of the Old Testament, "Ethiops" is the rendering of Kush, the son of Ham. The Ethiopians, delighted to find some mention in the text, embraced this as evidence of their own ancestry, in spite of the inescapable curse of Noah that Ham and all his descendants, including the Ethiops, "shall be slaves."

One of the scholars of the thirteenth century, Abu Salih, wrote a history of Egypt's monasteries and churches and refers to the legend in the *Kebra Nagast*. He says that the Ethiopians have the Ark of the Covenant and says their kings are descended from Moses, not from the house of David. This connection with Moses was based on the scriptural reference in Numbers xii, I, where Moses, it is stated, took a Kushite wife. In the Septuagint, "Kushite" is written "Ethiopian." The son of Kush (Ethiops) is written "Seba," which is the same spelling as is used for Sheba and may explain why Sheba was thought to be in Africa—near Kush—instead of lower Arabia.

Ptolemy II and III sent out Greek sea expeditions in the third century B.C. to the Ethiopian shore. They were military expeditions seeking African elephants to train for battle. So they explored the Red Sea and established hunting and trading posts along the coast of what is now Ethiopia. One of these posts became the town of Adulis, port of the kingdom of Axum at a later time.

Ethiopian scholars believed—and said so in their histories—that their land was the oldest civilized country on earth, that their remote ancestors had established the foundations on which were built every later civilization, including Egypt. Such was the claim, and the supporting evidence reported in the Latin edition of *Bibliotheca Historica* by the ancient historian Diodorus Siculus. Herodotus, of course, mentions the "long-lived Aithiopes" frequently and calls them the "tallest, the handsomest and most just of men."

In the last half of the first century A.D., a famous description of the Red Sea and Indian Ocean entitled the *Periplus of the Erythraean Sea* was written. In it Adulis is described and the author has a note about the life of the Ethiopia of that time. Eight days' journey inland from Adulis was the capital of the Axumites. It was through this city that all of the ivory from beyond the Nile was channeled and from it to the port of Adulis and on to the cities of Rome. Zoscales, "a covetous and grasping man but otherwise noble and imbued with Greek education," is mentioned as the king of Axum—the first historical king of the region.

It is true that Ethiopia is the oldest continuously Christian nation on earth, second only to Rome. It became so in 333, about a decade after Christianity was declared the state religion of the Roman Empire.

By the sixth century A.D., Ethiopia is mentioned in the *Christian Topography* by a merchant, Cosmas. He tells us that when he visited Adulis, the king of Axum sent orders to the governor of the town to copy two ancient Greek inscriptions that existed there. Cosmas was asked to do this and made two copies, one of which he published in his *Topography*. One of them related to Ptolemy III's exploits; the other told of the conquests of an Ethiopian king—how he subdued the country of Semien, the people of Danakil, penetrated to the straits of Aden, conquered the Bejas, the Tangaites and built a road from Axum to Egypt. He crossed the sea and conquered the Arrabites and peoples occupying the Hejjaz, winding up his saga with this paean of self-praise:

Of the kings that went before me I am the first and only one to have subdued all these peoples by the grace granted to me by my mighty god Ares, who also begat me. It is through him that I have subdued all the peoples that border upon my empire, to the east as far as the land of perfumes, to the west as far as the land of Ethiopia [by which he meant Nubia] and Sasu. Some I fought myself, against others I sent my armies. When I had established peace in the lands subject to me I came to Adulis to sacrifice on behalf of those who voyage on the sea to Zeus, Ares and Poseidon. Having assembled all my armies I have set up here this throne and have consecrated it to Ares in the twenty-seventh year of my reign.[6]

This great conqueror king was active about the third century A.D. Unfortunately for the everlasting pride of the king, his name has not survived: Cosmas failed to note it—or it was missing in the inscription he was copying.

The next known king was Ezana, who called himself

simply, "king of Axum, Himyar, Raidan, Saba, Salhin, Siamo, Bega and Kasu, king of kings, son of the unconquered Mahrem [which translates as *Ares* in Greek]." It was Ezana who sent the expedition which smashed the Noba, as we noted in Chapter III. Ezana's inscription is a milestone in another direction: It is the first Christian record in Ethiopia. In it, Ezana shifts from his previous style of commemorating his victories as "son of the unconquered Mahrem" and simply calls himself the "son of Ella Amida, the unconquered." And his victory now is attributed to "the Lord of the Heavens who has power over all beings in heaven and earth," instead of to Mahrem. And it is during Ezana's reign that the pagan crescent and disk appear on the coins for the last time, to be superseded by the Christian cross.

▷ *The Brothers* Ezana, then, was the first Christian king of Ethiopia, and we know something of the background of his conversion. The story goes back to the time when Meropius, a philosopher of Tyre, the city on the Mediterranean coast in what is now Lebanon, decided to visit "India" (the term used in those days for the Red Sea coast of Ethiopia and Somalia). He took with him two small boys whom he was educating. On the return, the ship put in at a dangerous port for water. Barbarians seized the ship and massacred all aboard except the boys, who were found preparing their lessons under a tree. They were taken to the king who was delighted with them and made one, Aedesius, his cupbearer, and the other, Frumentius, his secretary and treasurer.

After many years, the monarch became mortally ill. Before dying, he released the young men whom he held in great affection and honor. The queen, however, begged them to stay and help her administer the kingdom until her son should come of age. The two brothers discussed this between them and decided that they owed it to the king's family and to the stability of the country to help as requested. They stayed, and Frumentius, who was a gifted administrator, ran the kingdom as regent.

Now during this period Frumentius carefully sought out the Christian Romans who were in the country—merchants, traders, scholars, teachers and artists. To these he gave responsible positions and encouraged them to Christian worship. Furthermore, he promoted Christianity in the kingdom among the native population.

When the young prince finally came of age, Frumentius and Aedesius did a remarkable thing: They handed the reins of government over to the rightful king as promised. The queen mother begged them to stay on, but this time they did leave—Aedesius to their parents in Tyre; Frumentius to the Patriarch in Alexandria. He told this bishop of the modest Christian movement in Ethiopia and urged him to send some qualified man to lead the flock. To Frumentius' surprise, he was appointed to the work. He returned to "India" as first bishop of Axum where he ministered with such fervor and success that thousands of "barbarians" were converted to the faith. And after what must have been many years of proselytizing, Frumentius succeeded in bringing the young king, for whom he had been regent, to accept Christianity. This ruler's name, of course, was Ezana.

Christianity in Ethiopia

In the two centuries that followed, Christianity gained quite a solid foothold in Ethiopia. By about 525 A.D. there was a king of the country called Ella Atsbeha or Ellesbaas and known also as Kaleb. The Jews had control of Yemen, across the Red Sea, and their king was persecuting and slaughtering Christians in the region of Himyar, the southwestern Arabian area once dominated by Axum. So Ellesbaas sent an army to Himyar and defeated the Jewish king. Thus Solomon's descendant struck a powerful blow at the kingdom of Judea in a clash that was inevitable from the time Ethiopia's leaders adopted Christianity.

Now Ellesbaas set up in the Himyar a viceroy named Abraham who built a colossal church at his capital city. So remarkable was this church that it attracted Arabs from the entire area and actually competed with Mecca and the holy places as an attraction to pilgrims. The legend goes that Abraham rallied around him a great army and marched to assault Mecca and demolish the Ka'aba, which was to become the holy of Moslem holies. Then, as the warriors approached Mecca a swarm of birds swooped down on them, dropping tiny pebbles on the invaders. These miraculous stones caused pustules to break out wherever they touched the skin of Abraham's soldiers, causing them to become sick and die. Thus was the invasion defeated and the Ka'aba spared in the Year of the Elephant— the year of the birth of the prophet Mohammed.

In the legends of Ethiopia, Ellesbaas and Abraham are spoken of as twin brothers who accomplished mighty feats, the greatest of which, say the stories, was the introduction of Christianity into the country. Though they did much to further it, as we have noted above, Ezana and Frumentius are the two who deserve credit for this two centuries before.

Christianity in Ethiopia had (and has) a number of elements that differentiate it from the religion as practiced elsewhere. In its observances and ritual it follows the Coptic church (the native Christian church which used Coptic—the extinct language of ancient Egypt), under the Patriarch at Alexandria. Its bishop was, until 1950, always an Egyptian Copt who generally did not read or understand Ge'ez, the written language of the Ethiopian church, or Amharic, the spoken language of the country. Its calendar is Coptic too, with the ancient Egyptian system of twelve months of thirty days each, plus an extra five days to balance out, plus an extra day every Leap Year. The Ethiopians celebrate, as do the Copts, the Lord's Baptism (Epiphany) by mass ritual bathing and their Lent has ten more days than that of the Western church.

Special aspects of the Ethiopian Christian observances include vigorous dances and highly sophisticated drumming as central features of the liturgy on some of the high holy days. They celebrate the feasts of the Nativity, St. Michael, Abraham, Isaac, Jacob and Our Lady every month. And when a new church is dedicated it is customary to sacrifice animals—a ewe, an ox and a she-goat. Also, the Ethiopian Christians, like the Jews, do not eat "unclean" meat, by which they mean the flesh of animals that do not have cloven hoofs, don't chew their cuds, or have been choked or ripped in slaughter. They also observe a Sabbath and a Sunday, with the liturgy given on both days and fasting not required. Another peculiarity is the belief that those who have had sexual relations are impure the following day and must be turned away from the churches. As in Jewish life, baby boys are baptized on the fortieth day, girls on the eightieth (in Jewish practice, the children are presented at the Temple on those days.) Among the practices permitted, if not encouraged, is simple and easy divorce. Concubinage and polygamy have been widespread at various times in Ethiopian history, in spite of Church condemnation of them.

In the sixth century, Byzantium was at war with Persia. This practically halted Byzantine trade with India (the Asian India), so Justinian, the Byzantine emperor, conceived the idea that by developing official relations with Ethiopia, perhaps the second greatest Christian power at that time, he could circumvent the Persians. Justinian sent an ambassador to Ellesbaas, emperor of Ethiopia. Though the scheme foundered because the Ethiopian seamen were short-distance sailors and limited their trips to the Persian Gulf, the ambassador's report to Justinian on Ellesbaas' court is valuable:

> The king wore a linen skirt richly embroidered with gold and held by suspenders inlaid with pearls. His linen turban was also embroidered with gold and from it four gold ribbons danced as the king shook his head. About his neck was a collar of gold and on his arms were heavy gold bracelets. He surveyed his court from a high, gold-encased, four-wheeled chariot pulled by a team of four elephants. Ellesbaas carried two small spears of gold and a gilded shield. The king's counselors stood by, carrying gilded spears and shields. The music of flutes dominated the court.[7]

Figure 36

Unfortunately the relics of the Axumite culture are few. The major ones are the mysterious obelisks of stone. Flat, rather than square, and tapered to a rounded top, they are carved of a single, huge block of granite and are taller than those of Egypt. On the face they have low-relief sculpture which appears to represent a tower. At the base a door is depicted (complete with ring or lock) and above it, tier on tier, are sculpted blind windows with what seem to be log floors separating them. At the top are the familiar Axumite disc and crescent, symbols of Ares. None of these bears any inscriptions, so their purpose is unknown, but they are tremendously impressive. In fact, so impressed were Mussolini's Italian invaders of 1936–1941 that they packed the largest (110 feet tall) and shipped it to Rome where, at this writing, it remains, despite continued official Ethiopian protests.

The upsurge of Islam in the seventh century had a profound effect on Ethiopia. According to tradition, when Mohammed wrote the kings of the earth telling them his mission on this planet, he received only one reply. (Actually the Chinese also replied.) It was from the king of Ethiopia and it was friendly. This friendliness was demonstrated when Mohammed's first attempts to overcome the existing government at Mecca were crushed and his followers fled the land. Many of them went to Ethiopia where they were given asylum. Because of these actions the Moslem attitude toward the Ethiopians was different from that toward other Christians. Officially, the Ethiopians were exempt from the *jihad* aimed at all other Christians and unbelievers.

Unofficially, however, there was warfare, raiding, destruction and looting back and forth on both sides. The Ethiopians in the seventh and early eighth centuries took to the Red Sea as pirates and captured ships and raided Arabian coastal towns. In 702 they shocked the Moslem world by actually landing in force and sacking the town of Jedda, the port for Mecca, through which hundreds of thousands of pilgrims pass annually going to the holy city. This electrified the Moslems and they put together forces that assaulted the Ethiopian coastline, occupying towns and islands that controlled the strip along the sea and snuffing out completely Adulis, the port for the Axumite capital. Adulis passed into history, never to revive.

Ethiopia was then isolated from all other Christian lands by the Moslem grip on Egypt and control of the Red Sea coast. It was two centuries before the Ethiopians recaptured enough of the coastline to become a sea power again.

▷ *Shangri-La?* Tongues in Europe and the Middle East were set wagging in the late ninth century by the fabulous report of Eldad the Danite. According to this detailed, impressive story, there was somewhere in East Africa an unconquered Jewish empire dating back to a time long before the fall of Jerusalem. At that time the Jews had come in two groups to the land called Havilah—the first after Eden mentioned in the Creation. The Jews who settled in "the land of Havilah where there is gold" were of the tribe of Dan and three other tribes, and it seemed that their entire lives were spent in fighting outsiders. They had neatly parceled out the burden, however, and each tribe battled and plundered neighboring lands for three months then turned the duty over to the next in rotation. They rushed into battle 120,000 strong, bearing a huge banner of white with the legend, "Hear, O Israel, the Lord Our God is One God." Each of the soldiers carried a miniature white banner with him.

Now just across the miraculous Sabbation River from the Danites and their fellow tribes was the other half of this Jewish empire. It was peopled by Levites who had arrived three centuries later, during Nebuchadnezzar's time. The whole group had been transported on a cloud at night from their exile in Babylon. These Levites now lived in luxury in "glorious houses and fine buildings and castles and they trained elephants for themselves in their times of joy." Fortunately for their safety, their domain was completely surrounded by the river Sabbation which was unnavigable. "They see no man and no man sees them except those four tribes [the Danites and their associates]," but these were forced to shout across the river—a somewhat unsatisfactory method of communication.

The Levite land was a paradise. It had no dogs, foxes, flies, fleas, scorpions or serpents. There all men were equal, with none doomed to be servants and others masters. As a matter of course they lived to a hundred years of age, and most reached one hundred twenty years. Gold, silver and jewels were (naturally) abundant. And the river Sabbation was truly remarkable. It was governed by the Ten Commandments and flowed only six days a week. "On the seventh day it rests and is tranquil until the end of the Sabbath." On its day of rest, however, the river was shrouded in heavy fog, thus protecting the Levites.

Lest anyone doubt the truth of this glowing report (of which this is only the barest outline) its author Eldad the Danite identified himself fully. This report bears his signature and full name—a provenance that includes thirty-eight forefathers and requires a dozen lines of print to complete.[8]

Eldad's report was believed widely in Europe, and not by Jews alone. More and more "evidence" pointed to Ethiopia as the location of this Jewish empire and when word came to Europe of the "black Jews of Ethiopia," Eldad's concoction seemed about to be confirmed.

The truth of the matter is that a group known as the Falashas (exiles) who are black Jews, have been in Ethiopia at least since the fourth century. They are an enigma in many ways. They live in the mountains north of Lake Tsana and were ruled by their own kings for centuries. They are not Semites, but are native African stock and they speak a Hamitic language and know no Hebrew. They do not observe Purim nor do they have the Talmud or Mishna, and their customs are said to be archaic, though some of their observances are clearly derived from the Talmud. Though they claim descent from the original band of nobles who accompanied Menelik from Jerusalem, it is more likely that they were converted to Judaism by

Jewish emigrants who fled to Arabia via the Red Sea.

By the tenth century the Falashas were so powerful and their leader so fanatical that they went on the rampage and devastated Ethiopia. In 975 the king of Ethiopia wrote the king of Nubia imploring him to send help. The Ethiopian monarch was forced to scuttle about from one hiding place to the next in a most un-regal fashion, fleeing before the warriors of a Jewish amazon named Judith *The Fire*. She literally overran the country and practically destroyed Christianity in the land, burning churches, enslaving Christians, killing priests, looting and plundering. The king sent another desperate plea, this time to the Patriarch in Alexandria, asking for a new *abuna* (Ethiopian bishop). This time he received a quick and favorable response and, according to the *History of the Patriarchs of Alexandria*, shortly after the *abuna's* arrival the tide turned. Judith was defeated, *The Fire* was quenched and her followers suppressed.

The net effect of this internal uproar was the loss of Ethiopia's remote possessions and the growth of Moslem dynasties controlling parts of what is now Somaliland. These Moslem centers were from that time on serious threats to Ethiopia.

▷ *Lalibala*   It was sometime after 1150 A.D. that one king, Lalibala by name, set his people working on an extraordinary project. Nowhere else on earth is there parallel for Lalibala's

Figures 34-35-37-38   incredible monuments: Ten huge churches were built, completely cut from the living rock. These were not mere caves. They were full-scale churches built by excavating into the rock itself a broad, dry "moat" to separate the walls of the edifice from the surrounding stone. Then the engineers cut into the stone itself to form the buildings. All ten survive today. The largest church, called "The Redeemer of the World," is more than one hundred feet long, seventy-five feet wide and more than twenty feet deep. Inside are five aisles with twenty-eight columns and eight bays. There are dozens of windows, at two levels, and a colonnade about the building, consisting of massive, rectangular columns.

The smaller churches have carvings of the ruler and the saints. Many of their architectural touches seem to be Byzantine or Arabic in origin, leading to speculation that perhaps some of the masons who executed these unique, monumental buildings may have been imported from Egypt.

Lalibala was unusually pious and is remembered as a founder of monasteries and churches throughout the kingdom. But his claim to immortality rests on the ten rock churches which are Ethiopia's equivalent of Egypt's pyramids. Though Lalibala was one of a dynasty of usurper kings of Ethiopia and his name is therefore not to be found in the official chronology of its rulers, he is a saint of the Ethiopian church and is memorialized for his support of the church and for his achievements on its behalf.

▷ *John the Priest-King* It was during this period—the twelfth century—that the legend of Prester John circulated in Europe. It developed from rumors of a powerful Christian monarch ruling a vast empire somewhere in the East. But the legend took on new force when, in 1165, a letter was delivered to the Byzantine emperor supposedly from Prester John, describing his kingdom: the three Indias under his control; the seventy-two kings who were his vassals; the Amazons; the Bragmans; the unclean races shut up by Alexander in the north. There were, he said, twenty bishops and twelve archbishops in his realm, plus the protopope of Samargantia and the archprotopope of

Susa and the patriarch of the Indies. So modest was Prester John, however, that he called himself priest, nothing more.

His palace was a marvel: Built to the designs of St. Thomas, it featured a miraculous mirror on a pedestal several stories tall. In this mirror the four corners of his land and all within it were visible, making it easy for him to "detect conspiracies." His daily guests included thirty thousand courtiers who ate from tables of gold, amethyst and emeralds. There must have been much competition for seats at the emerald tables with the amethyst legs, for these had magic powers. The guests could drink to their heart's content (far beyond the bounds of good sense) and yet "no person sitting at the table can become inebriated!"

When he traveled, Prester John was preceded by four lions bound with chains. He took with him, as his holiest relics, two Tabots, or miniature reproductions of the sacred Ark of the Covenant. These were borne by priests who followed pages carrying a huge cross and ringing bells.

Each month, seven kings in rotation served the great monarch. Prester John, by his own description, was easily one of the greatest of the great. His power could be reckoned—"if you can number the stars of heaven and sands of the sea, then you can calculate the extent of our dominion."[9]

As for power, when this mighty ruler took to the field in war "we have carried before us fourteen golden crosses ornamented with precious stones in the place of banners and each of these is followed by ten thousand mounted troops and a hundred thousand infantry." A hasty calculation from these figures would set Prester John's military strength at more than 1.5 million troops! And it was his burning desire, he confessed, to lead his armies to Jerusalem to liberate the Holy Land from the infidels.

Although it may seem surprising to us that Europeans of this period could swallow this airy concoction, we must remember that they had it on good authority. In 1122, a "John, patriarch of the Indians" appeared in Rome and told of miracles at the shrine of St. Thomas in India. Otto, bishop of Freisingen, reported that he had met a bishop from Syria at the Vatican in 1145 who told of the great and powerful King John beyond the Tigris River. This king, after defeating the Medes and Persians, had marched west to fight for the church at Jerusalem but had been turned back by his inability to cross the Tigris. Then, in 1165, came the letter we have just quoted, a letter widely copied and circulated throughout Europe (at least one hundred copies exist in libraries and museums even today). And in 1177 the Pope himself wrote a widely-copied letter to Prester John warning against overweening pride. With the intelligent leaders of medieval Europe so convinced of the existence of Prester John it is little wonder that there was such widespread belief in him.

So, across the continent there was a swelling of renewed enthusiasm for the Crusades, which had been inconclusive and extremely costly. The *next* Crusade, it was believed, would enlist Prester John and his vast legions attacking the Moslems from their rear while the European troops struck from the fore.

It was all very pretty indeed. But, of course, the whole business was a mixture of shameless fakery, fable and wishful thinking. The specific origins of the legend are shrouded in mystery. One theory has it that Prester John is a corruption of the title of a Turkish leader who, about 1145, defeated the Persian Moslems in what Moslem historians consider a great disaster. Others believe that Mongol tribes were reported by European travelers to be led by Khans who were vassals of Prester John. Marco Polo reported that Unc Khan, the lord of the Tatars, was "the same we call Prester John."

However, as more accurate information about the poverty-stricken nomadic tribes of the steppes came in, it was clear that Prester John's wealthy realm lay elsewhere. Thus the reports of a Christian kingdom beyond Egypt somewhere in the interior of Africa excited hopes anew that the true land of Prester John was Ethiopia. By the fourteenth century this hope had been solidified into a certainty in the minds of Europeans. They apparently gave little thought to the fact that the legendary monarch would have been more than two hundred years old by that time.

The Prester John legend received a new lease on life when the Portuguese explorers returned in the fifteenth century with reports of a mighty Christian ruler somewhere in Africa's interior. When Vasco de Gama reached Mozambique on his first voyage he was told "Prester John resided not far from this place . . . in the interior, and could be reached on the backs of camels." This information, confessed the hard-bitten de Gama, "rendered us so happy that we cried with joy."[22]

As a result of such information, Portugal's king decided to try to reach Prester John. One of the official efforts made use of specially-trained and equipped ambassadors. Over the years a number of Negro women had been brought to Portugal by various expeditions returning from Africa and it was decided to groom some of these as Ambassadors to the Great Potentate. Their message to Prester John would be a description of Portugal's wealth and strength, its religious fervor and desire to ally itself with the great king. To carry out this mission, the ladies were outfitted in elegant finery representative of the splendors of the Portuguese court and given gold, silver and spices to present to Prester John to impress him with the goodwill and wealth of the sponsoring country.

They then sailed down the west coast of Africa to what is believed to be the present Angolan coast and there the first was put ashore, alone, unescorted and completely on her own! This procedure was repeated in several more spots along the coast. The women were bade "Godspeed" and left to make their way through unknown terrain, via people who might be hostile or friendly, who spoke no Portuguese and did not know the ambassadors' language either, carrying valuable gifts and clad in European court dresses. Their fates are unknown.

This exercise in futility proved little, except, perhaps, that one can carry out mad schemes if one is king. Of course, in the Europe of that day the Portuguese king's project seemed reasonable. It was a time of religious fanaticism, and the king and his advisers of both church and state were piously convinced that the Lord would protect these ambassadors in the purity of their mission. What the women thought of all this we are not told. It seems implausible that they could have been forced to go on such an expedition against their will. More likely they were converts to Christianity and, in the strength of their faith, willingly accepted the hazardous assignments in the spirit of religious missionaries throughout the ages.

In 1487, Portugal's King John II (known as "the Perfect") sent two other missions to seek and find the great king. The first was an expedition by sea around the African coast, under Bartholomew Diaz in 1487. Simultaneously the King dispatched an ambassador via land. This envoy, Peter de Covilham, succeeded in reaching the Ethiopian court. He made his way from the Levant to Ethiopia and actually presented himself to the king. But he was kept at the court, prevented from leaving and so was considered dead by the Portuguese. He was discovered some thirty years later when an official embassy from Portugal did arrive at the Ethiopian court. It stayed six years in the land and was finally allowed to return, whereupon Fr. Francisco Alvarez, its chaplain, published his observations. His report made it sadly but indisputably clear for all time that Prester John was *not* alive and well in Ethiopia.

Ethiopian Culture

It was about 1270 A.D. that a usurping dynasty in Ethiopia was cast out and a king claiming the all-important descent from Solomon and the Queen of Sheba seized the throne. With the stimulus of royal patronage there was a vast literary flowering which continued for fully five centuries.

As in the past, much of the literature was religious, but now there were, in addition, popular histories, chronicles, collections of homilies—some in rhyme—and translations of significant works from other cultures.

The lives of the saints, stories of Christ, the Virgin and the Apostles and fabulous miracles attributed to them make up a great portion of this literature. For the most part, these were original works. There were, however, translations of religious works from Moslem and Coptic originals, including collections of hymns, litanies and prayers with titles such as *Praises of Mary*. Also popular was a calendar of saints for the entire year, known as the *Synaxar of the Church of Alexandria*, and compilations such as the *Faith of the Fathers* and *Book of Light*.

Popular history flourished, with chronicles reminiscent of

Shakespeare's *Henry V*. One of these, the earliest, tells of 'Amda Seyon (Column or Pillar of Zion) whose reign was from 1314 to 1344, about the time of Dante's death. 'Amda Seyon begins his rule as a mad tyrant and with a miraculous change of character becomes an Ethiopian El Cid, the scourge of the small Moslem kingdoms and rebellious vassal states on Ethiopia's borders.

Other rulers who received literary treatment were Zar'a Yakob (Seed of Jacob), Ba'eda Maryam (By the Hand of Mary), Alexander, and Na'od.

The chronicle of Zar'a Yakob tells not only of his military might but of his reforming zeal. He resolved to stamp out paganism in the kingdom, and organized a veritable secret police that spied on people and reported pagans and idol worshippers to the grand inquisitor, the Keeper of the Hour. This inquisitor had such vast and frightful power that his excesses soon made him deeply hated and feared. People of the realm became so indignant about the inquisition that a popular revolt was narrowly averted only by the removal of the Keeper from office. Actually, in addition to persecuting the unbelievers, Zar'a Yakob did much to spread the faith by making priests give instruction in religion from published books of the customs, laws and doctrine of the Church, which the king ordered distributed.

Among the translations which were popular were the *History of the Jews*, the *Universal History* by John of Nikiu, and a *History of Alexander The Great*. John of Nikiu was an Egyptian bishop who tells in the *Universal History* of the Arab conquest, an event that occurred only shortly before he was born. It is one of the few reliable accounts of that historic event. Also of this period was the *Kebra Nagast*, which we have mentioned before, with its "official" version of the beginnings of the kingdom and the Solomon-Makeda romance.

Figure 42

The language used in Ethiopian writing is Ge'ez, a blocky, strong calligraphy in which words are separated by dots placed like the colon in our usage. Ge'ez is an ancient form, older than Arabic or our own writing. It is now a "dead" language, like Latin, and has a similar function in that is used only for written works and the church liturgy. Ethiopia's official spoken language is Amharic, from the province of Amhara.

One European traveler to Ethiopia, Giacome Baretti, in 1655 told the outside world something about the literature of the country. He was shown the royal library of more than ten thousand manuscript volumes. The Ethiopians boasted that some of these were the oldest works in the world, claiming that they had been written by sages during Moses' time. Baretti reported that twenty-three copyists were working full time to transcribe deteriorating manuscripts. And another reporter noted that for the longer, more elaborate works, from a hundred to a hundred-fifty goats were required, just to provide the necessary number of parchment pages.

Most of the works were religious. They stemmed from the monumental translation of the Bible into Ge'ez which took over two hundred years, beginning in the fifth century. It should be noted that the Ethiopian Bible consists of the usual Epistles, Acts, Testaments, etc., plus a number of works not to be found in Western Bibles. These are the "Apocrypha," books taken from the Septuagint but not found in the Hebrew.

From 1508, with the accession of Lebna Dengel ("Incense of the Virgin"), Ethiopia's history is written by contemporaries in chronicles that have been continued up to the present day. Thus the literary tradition of the country is a long and illustrious one.

In art, Ethiopian churches and monasteries abound in

paintings of saints, scenes from the lives of the saints, of Christ, the Virgin, the Old Testament stories, of kings of the country and, inevitably, the love affair of Solomon and the Queen of Sheba. Such themes are also found as illuminations in the books produced over the centuries and in calendars and pictures painted for wall decoration. Sculpture is relatively rare, for the attitude toward it was that likenesses of the human form bordered on idolatry and its use was discouraged if not actually proscribed.

Figure 39

Sometime in the last half of the fifteenth century Nicholas Brancaleone, a Venetian painter, came to the Ethiopian court. The king hired him to paint church walls in many parts of the land. Prevented from leaving Ethiopia, Brancaleone painted for more than forty years and his style influenced his contemporaries and the later art of the country. Even in the Ethiopian manuscript illuminations there are Italian influences noticeable in details such as clothing and flora and fauna.

Early in his career Brancaleone caused a tremendous scandal when he painted a Virgin and Child in a major church. The Venetian painted it in the European tradition, with Mary holding Jesus in her left arm. That was enough! In the Middle East, the right hand is used for eating, work and all good things; the left hand is for dirty chores, and thus to show Christ held in the left hand was a blasphemy. Priests and commoners alike raised a commotion, claiming that this was dishonor to the Lord and demanding destruction of the picture. Fortunately for Brancaleone, the king backed him and the picture remained on view in the church until 1709 when it was destroyed in a raid by pagan Galla tribesmen. Pictures of the Virgin and her many marvelous miracles have been the major stock-in-trade of Ethiopian artists throughout the country's history.

▷ *Sixteenth Century Ethiopia* Fr. Alvarez reported to the king of Portugal that Ethiopia's king at the time of his visit (1517–1523) was Lebna Dengel. He ruled over a group of vassal chiefs and kings and was having some difficulty keeping order in the realm. According to Alvarez the reasons were several, and not the least was the fact that Lebna Dengel had spurned the daughter of the king of Hadya. She could not be returned to her Moslem father because she had converted to Christianity for the wedding. Lebna Dengel married the girl to one of the court nobles, but the girl's father considered this an insult and took up arms against the king.

The riches of the realm were fabulous and Alvarez described the tribute paid from the kingdom of Gojjam: Three thousand horses were followed by three thousand mules, followed by three thousand men, each bringing a cotton cloth heavy enough to use as a blanket. These were followed by yet another three thousand men, each with a lighter-weight cotton cloth. Bringing up the rear of this procession, which took ten days to pass, were three men, each with a tray laden with ten thousand gold *ouquias*. If this tribute-paying parade was especially arranged to impress the Portuguese delegation, it succeeded then, as it undoubtedly would today.

Ethiopia at this time was a land without a capital city. To be sure, the kings went to Axum, the venerable capital of the former empire, for coronation ceremonies. However, the king maintained a royal camp the size of a small town and this was his movable capital. Alvarez tells us about this: Five tents were the king's own. They were set upon the highest point of ground, and surrounded by a curtain wall or stockade if the camp was to remain in the place for some time. The camp faced west and on that side there was an open ground with the church of the

Holy Cross on one side and that of St. Mary on the other. Each of these had two tents attached, one for vestments and furniture, the other for a bakery for communion bread. The king's valuables were guarded in an enclosure beyond the churches.

The pages had their quarters north of the king's pavilion; the queen was directly south; the kitchen tents were adjacent to the king's quarters to the west and "two crossbow shots" further west was the court of justice pavilion flanked by two tents for the pair of chief justices, two for prisons and a third serving as church for the court. Beyond this to the west was a sizable open space with four lions chained in it—the royal mascots who accompanied the king everywhere. Futher on was the church of the marketplace, the market itself and the camps of the tradesmen, merchants and *hoi poloi*. Clustered about the king's pavilion were the tents of the *abuna*, the Keeper of the Hour (the king's chaplain), the king's two chief ministers, ranking officers and beyond these the tents of the nobles.

Now when this traveling city actually arose and betook itself elsewhere it was a gloriously moving spectacle, to say the least. Leading the procession were six saddled mules and six saddled horses, each led by four men. Behind them were twenty pages and then six more leading the king's mule. The king was completely surrounded by red curtains on poles as he rode, and thus was invisible to all but the highest officials and his pages. The royal lions, each on two chains, came next, followed by a hundred men carrying as many jars of meat and a hundred more with burdens of bread.

Next came the stately splendors of the church: One deacon bore a silver cross and censer; another sounding a bell preceded eight priests, four of whom carried the richly ornamented platform on which the altar was fixed. A parasol was held over the head of the ranking prelate as a sign of his venerability. Since there were a number of churches in the entourage, the procession was a solemn and impressive passage. The sequence of the procession was predetermined, just as was the location of each element of the capital when at rest.

Traditionally, the king had been completely secluded from his people, Alvarez tells us. However, in more recent times (*circa* 1520) the king appeared to his people on a high dais on three occasions annually: at Christmas, Easter and Holy Cross Day. This was instituted, says Alvarez, because the courtiers had concealed the death of a previous king for three years and had run the domain to suit themselves!

The system of circumventing palace revolts was direct and effective. Only males could claim the throne. Therefore, when a new king was crowned, every one of his brothers and their families were sent off to house arrest in an *amba*—a heavily guarded mountain-top fortress, completely cut off from the outside world. Here, well cared for, they lived and died. On at least two occasions, invaders, by capturing the *amba* and its royal families, were able to all but snuff out the collateral heirs to the throne by liquidating everyone they found in the fortress.

The system of justice in Ethiopia at this time was highly developed and remarkable in many respects. It was oral throughout, with no written records taken or kept. In the justice tent the judges sat on the ground in two groups. The plaintiff and defendant were brought in and each first stated his case to the judges and then made a reply to the other. The bailiff then summarized the arguments and stated his judgment. Each judge in turn did likewise, followed by the chief justice who summarized all the statements and announced the decision. In case a question of fact came up, the court adjourned until the necessary information came in. When a case was of extreme importance, it was heard before the two chief ministers and the judges of appeal in the open area in front of the king's compound. Their function, however, was not to decide, but to carry the summary of the case to the king and ask whatever questions he raised and finally to render the king's decision.

Penalties varied; many required mutilation; political offenders were banished to remote *ambas;* flogging was the most common punishment and, according to Alvarez, appeared to be savage but was not all that it seemed to be. Prisoners, naked to the waist, were staked to the ground and beaten by four executioners with whips. However, the executioners beat the convicted man only as instructed by the judges: Generally they struck the ground rather than the guilty one, perhaps only giving him three or four—or no—lashes in the process. Miscarriages of justice were not uncommon, and Alvarez witnessed several floggings of the chief justices for such "lapses." They were apparently neither hurt nor lacking in prestige as a result.

The good Father Alvarez took a lively professional interest in the Ethiopian church and was astonished at the number of basilicas, chapels, monasteries and churches in the land. It *Figures 40-41* abounded in them and in clerics. Everywhere he went he saw churches and monasteries. On the hills and mountains of the countryside monasteries were perched; in every town he visited there were half a dozen churches.

He wrote admiringly of the architecture and decoration, the paintings and trappings of the holy places. Stone was the usual building material, whether in the extraordinary hewn-rock churches of Lalibala or those built in a more conventional manner.

Alvarez was awed by the wonders of the Lalibala rock

churches and feared "that they will not believe me if I write
more, and because as to what I have already written they may
accuse me of untruth, therefore I swear by God, in whose
power I am, that all that is written is the truth, and there is
much more than what I have written, and I have left it that
they may not tax me with its being falsehood."

In addition to the rock churches there are many elabo-
rately built chapels and churches in caves. Many of these date
back to the twelfth century and are stunning works of original
architecture, often covered inside and out with frescoes of Biblical
scenes, martyrs, saints and royal patrons. The definitive catalog
of Ethiopia's riches in this department has yet to be made,
though in recent years there have been published books of
photographs of some of the religious art treasures.

Alvarez at first was startled by the shouting, singing and
dancing at the major religious services. However, he soon saw
in such observances much goodness, since they were aimed at
the glorification of God and were in no way disrespectful. He
noted that some customs accepted in Roman Catholic churches
shocked the Ethiopians: spitting in church was one.

▷ *Ethiopians and Europeans* The Portuguese mission returned
to Lisbon in 1527 and within months Ethiopia became the
target of *jihad* led by Ahmed ibn Ibrahim el Ghazi, called El
Gran ("the left-handed"). With a nucleus of two hundred Turks
equipped with matchlocks, Gran invaded Ethiopia. He destroyed
the king's troops wherever and whenever he met them and the
religious fanaticism of his men drove them to extremes. They
burned and ruined churches, killed priests in droves, looted all
the treasure they could find and converted the people to Islam
at gun- or sword-point. The invaders ranged from one end of
Ethiopia to the other. The king was in hiding and barely man-

aged to send a message to the Portuguese imploring for help.

The Portuguese in 1541 managed to send a task force of four hundred men under Christopher de Gama, son of the famous Vasco. They landed at Suez and made their way to the coastal province of Ethiopia, meeting Gran's forces in several inconclusive skirmishes. Gran managed to obtain nine hundred musketeers from the Turkish garrison across the Red Sea in Yemen and with these reinforcements he descended on the Portuguese camp near Lake Ashangi. Crashing through the Europeans, the Moslems killed more than half of them, including de Gama, and seized their arms and ammunition.

Convinced that there would be no further resistance, Gran was over-confident and let down his guard. The Portuguese, intent on vengeance, re-armed from a secret cache of weapons. King Claudius (who had succeeded his late father in 1540) was determined to smite the invaders, and assembled eight thousand soldiers and five hundred cavalrymen. This combined force struck Gran's ill-guarded encampment. By a stroke of fortune, Gran was shot in the fighting and the Somali troops fled. The Turks fought on, but were overwhelmed by the Portuguese-Ethiopian assault.

King Claudius reconquered his kingdom with the help of the surviving Portuguese. The king of Portugal, continuing the special relationship which had linked the two countries, ordered this formidable band of seasoned troops to serve the Ethiopian ruler. They did so, and their descendants continued to do so after them. Claudius, meanwhile, rebuilt churches and set the monks to restoring the destroyed books. He extended the borders of the kingdom and subdued the rebellious tribes.

Thanks to the important part played by the Portuguese, the country was restored. But the next European contacts were nearly disastrous. In the latter part of the sixteenth century, Jesuit missionaries established themselves in Ethiopia and by the middle of the next century were to be found in many parts of the country. These missioners were Portuguese, Spanish and Italian and among them were some unusual men. One of these priests, Pedro Paez of Castile, converted two of the Ethiopian rulers to Roman Catholicism. The second of these, Sisinnius, set out to make this the faith of the people.

On Sisinnius' invitation the Pope sent to Ethiopia a Spanish prelate named Mendez to be patriarch. This man was a supreme example of bigotry and narrowness, completely barren of tact or understanding. Fr. Mendez began by suspending all of Ethiopia's priests until they could be reordained by him. He then declared that all baptisms up to that time were invalid, meaning that the entire Christian population must be rebaptized. The liturgy was rewritten; the calendar was changed to conform to the Roman. Statues—"graven images" to the Ethiopians— were introduced into the churches, a move that scandalized the populace. Churches were reconsecrated and altars of the Roman type were installed. Little wonder that popular revolts broke out throughout the land, rising in pace and seriousness to the level of civil war. This went on without respite for years, until one bloody encounter in 1632 filled the king with revulsion. He proclaimed to his people:

Hear ye! Hear ye! We first gave you this faith believing that it was good. But innumerable people have been slain: Julius, Gabriel, Takla, Giorgis, Sarsa Kristos and now these peasants. For which reason we restore to you the faith of your forefathers. Let the former clergy return to the churches, let them put in their altars, let them say their own liturgy. And do ye rejoice.[10]

Sisinnius then abdicated and died not long after. His son, Basilides, succeeded him and immediately expelled the Jesuits and executed those who refused to leave. In addition, he banished Ethiopians who continued their Roman faith and confiscated their property. Basilides then took his court to Gondar and built a group of massive castles there. He also rebuilt the cathedral at Axum which had been destroyed by Ahmed el Gran years before.

The rest of the story is one of declining power of the emperor and more and more assertion of independence by local chiefs and petty kings. Eventually the emperor was ruler in name only, acting as puppet for others who held the real power. More and more the provincial governors gathered power to themselves, setting up their own individual dynasties until the mid-nineteenth century. Then a remarkable bandit named Theodore graduated from leading his robber band in the west to increasing dominance over section after section of the country until he conquered whole provinces. By 1855 he was strong enough to cause the *abuna* to install him as king of kings at a formal coronation.

Though he began his reign as an enlightened ruler, seeking greatness for his country and Christian piety for his people, Theodore's later years were characterized by fierce repression and terrorism employed to maintain his power. This course, not surprisingly, had much the opposite effect. But it was the British who ultimately brought him down, in an ironic twist of history.

Theodore, anxious to link his reign with that of the most powerful empire on earth, wrote to Queen Victoria of Britain proposing that diplomatic relations be opened between the two countries. Through an incredible oversight not altogether unique in the history of Britain's Foreign Office, this letter was pigeonholed. Two years later, when dispatches arrived from England and there was no response to his suggestion, Theodore flew into a rage, taking this silence as a personal insult. He instantly threw a number of important Englishmen into prison. In 1866, a British agent arrived to secure release of the prisoners. Theodore seized him and rounded up sixty additional Europeans whom he put in irons and, with the previous prisoners, cast into jail in a remote fortress.

The British organized a military expedition under Sir Robert Napier in 1867 and, with elephants, camels, oxen and mules carrying artillery, men and supplies, invaded Ethiopia to liberate the prisoners. The 325-mile trip to Magdala, Theodore's fortress, took the expedition nearly one year. Napier's modern weapons mowed down Theodore's cavalry and troops in the pitched battle of April 10, 1868. The following day Theodore shot himself in his fortress. Napier freed the prisoners and ignored the claims to the throne of the several contenders. He took the crowns of Theodore, and the *abuna*, a gold chalice, the royal copy of the *Kebra Nagast* and a trove of priceless old manuscripts. (The latter became the foundation of Britain's program of Ethiopian studies.) Then he turned around and left Ethiopia to stew in the struggle of various factions for control of the country.

John IV emerged from the smoke and gunfire as the next king of kings. During his rule he managed to throw back Italian and Egyptian attacks but was killed in a battle with Dervishes in 1889. Menelik II then came to power and soon displayed the astuteness that brought modern Ethiopia into being. As the rest of Africa was cut up and parceled out by the colonial powers, Ethiopia, under Menelik's shrewd guidance, fended off the Europeans. The king willingly received military missions, counsel and armaments from European countries. He granted concessions for many necessary developments—railroads, electric lights, telephone and telegraph.

As he moved to extend his control by subduing the one-time provinces, he pushed the borders outward with the help of modern arms and military advisers. He also established a new capital, Addis Ababa, in the geographical center of the nation. He secured an outlet on the Red Sea and defeated the Italians in 1896.

Menelik controlled the land until 1908 when he was incapacitated. After a period of upheaval, his daughter Zauditu was proclaimed empress and was succeeded by the present emperor, Haile Selassie I, in 1930. He has displayed steadfast determination to defend Ethiopia's independence while bringing about reform and modernization—without losing sight of the great elements of Ethiopia's heritage.

NOTES

1. Queen of Sheba, from the *Kebra Nagast* (*The Glory of Kings*), trans. by Sir E. A. Wallis Budge; P. Rutherfoord (ed.), (New York: Vanguard Press, 1958), p. 66.
2. *Ibid.*
3. *Ibid.*
4. *Ibid.*
5. *Ibid.*
6. Cosmos Indicopleustes, *Christian Topography:* trans. by J. W. McCrindle, (London: Hakluyt Society, 1897).
7. Account given by unnamed ambassador of Justinian, Byzantine emperor.
8. A. H. M. Jones and E. Monroe, *A History of Ethiopia*, (London: Oxford University Press, 1955).
·9. J. Doresse, *L'Empire du Pretre Jean*, (Paris: Plon, 1957).
10. Wm. L. Hansberry, "Ancient Kush, Old Aethiopia and the Balad Es Sudan," in *Journal of Human Relations*, (Wilberforce, Ohio: Central State College, Vol. VIII, No. 3 & 4, 1960).

He who knows not the Oba
  let me show him.
He has mounted the throne,
  he has piled a throne upon a throne.
Plentiful as grains of sand on the earth
  are those in front of him.
Plentiful as grains of sand on the earth
  are those behind him.
There are two thousand people
  to fan him.
He who owns you
  is among you here.
He who owns you
  has piled a throne upon a throne.
He has lived to do it this year;
  even so he will live to do it again.

THE OBA OF BENIN
Traditional Bini poem

◁▷ ◁▷ ◁▷ ◁▷ ◁▷ ◁▷ ◁▷ ◁▷ ◁▷ ◁▷ ◁▷ ◁▷ ◁▷ ◁▷ ◁▷ ◁▷ ◁▷

LOOKING BACKWARD: OTHER CULTURES

◁▷ ◁▷ ◁▷ ◁▷ ◁▷ ◁▷ ◁▷ ◁▷ ◁▷ ◁▷ ◁▷ ◁▷ ◁▷ ◁▷ ◁▷ ◁▷ ◁▷

IX

IN THE CHAPTERS UP TO NOW WE HAVE CON-
centrated on one empire at a time in some detail. Now, however,
we move on to take a quick look at several cultures. Unfortunately we do not have time and space to look at all of the cultures
and peoples of Africa—that would require a huge encyclopedia.
Our purpose here is to cover briefly a number of different,
widely-scattered peoples to see the range, the richness and di-
versity of ancient African cultures.

Our solid knowledge of the civilizations and achievements of many of Africa's peoples is in its infancy. For the past two or three millennia world attention has focused on Egypt. Since the Napoleonic expedition to the land of the Pharaohs, far more time and money for archeology and scholarship in Africa have been invested in Egypt than in the balance of the continent.

Fortunately there has been a change in this century, and today there is increasing interest in the cultures we know about only through oral history and legends, pieces of sculpture, castings, metal weapons, sophisticated pottery and building ruins. But the fact remains that in most parts of Africa scientific efforts to uncover the archeological evidence about little-known cultures is only beginning. True, there was a concentrated task-force approach to examining as much of Nubia–Kush as possible before the sites were covered with water by the new Aswan high dam. But such forced-draft urgency and activity is rare, if not unique, in African archeology.

For the most part, major archeological discoveries in Africa have come about by accident and by report of travelers.

The following are some examples of the information we have today about a few of the better-known ancient centers in Africa. These will indicate how recent our knowledge is and, by the absence of detailed information, how far we have to go to find answers to the questions that persistently come up, such as "who were these people and how did they live?"

THE NOK MYSTERY

In what is modern-day Nigeria, in an area north of the Benue and Niger Rivers, there is a dusty village of the Japa people.

It is called Nok, and there in 1931 two pottery heads were found. The heads were slightly under life size. They were thought to be "sports"—unique and unrelated to other works—because they were so unlike any art known in the region.

Figure 43

How completely wrong this view was became clear when, in 1944, a small treasure trove was uncovered. Three more heads, some pots, one of them for cooking, plus a ceramic human foot and leg were found. That same year, in a tin-mine shaft, some twenty-five feet below the surface, "an exceptionally fine head in terra cotta" was found in the hills near Jemaa, about twenty-four miles from Nok. The specialists might have dismissed this last discovery as unrelated to the others, but one sharp-eyed observer noted that the Jemaa head looked like a pottery monkey head found in Nok years before. Comparing the two, the authorities found there were striking resemblances.[1]

This was only the beginning. From that time on, more and more ceramic pieces from what has been dubbed the "Nok Culture" have turned up over an area extending about one hundred miles north, and some three hundred miles east-west along the Benue and Niger river valleys. Hundreds and thousands of objects have now been found, ranging from heads to feet, and from the size of a fist to life-size portrait heads. There is a considerable—and fascinating—range of styles and this adds to the mystery of the Nok people.

Usually a certain artistic style is characteristic of a people and time, and the artists of that time work within the existing conventions. Egyptian art—except during the Amarna period—is a case in point, with the highly-stylized figures that are so familiar: heads, feet, legs, and pelvis in profile, but shoulders in front-view. We recognize vases painted in black or red on a light background as Greek by the freedom and naturalness of the figures, their dress (or lack of it) and the geometrical decorative motifs. In a similar way we can identify European paintings of particular times and places as Sienese, Flemish, or Venetian according to stylistic evidence and subject matter. The same is true in Oriental art. The techniques, shapes, colors and clays used in Sung pottery, for instance, are so well established that finding such pottery in an archeological dig is an invaluable clue to the time period of the culture being investigated, and a T'ang horse (ceramic or bronze) would never be mistaken for another. In Japanese court painting, the use of gold leaf, perspective, and color easily distinguish the Edo from Heian period. And further examples could be cited endlessly.

The interesting fact in the Nok discoveries is that *both* realistic and highly-stylized human sculptures are found and apparently they were made *at the same time*. To find both approaches in the same time and place is unusual enough to stir speculation. What kind of culture and/or religion would have tolerated if not stimulated such diametrically different styles? At this point it is simply one more fascinating question challenging us.

One expert says that the area in which the sculpture and pottery have been found so far "may be only a fraction of the actual distribution."[2] According to Carbon-14 dating, the earliest figurines were produced about 900 B.C.; the latest seem to have been done about 200 A.D. The experts now say that the Nok culture flourished at least during the period from about 500 B.C. to 200 A.D. They are undecided or unwilling to estimate how much beyond that date the Nok style persisted. However, they grant that the evidence that is accumulating indicates the Nok art style very probably survived much, much longer.

Conjecture at this point is that the Nok peoples ranged

far and wide and that their art influenced many other peoples over a broad area. The bases for this supposition are as follows. The Nok peoples are known to have had a sophisticated agricultural society and to have been ironworkers. With this background and knowledge and the ability to produce weapons of iron at this early time they undoubtedly must have had relations— peaceful or otherwise—with other peoples over a wide expanse of the African interior along both sides of the Niger and Benue Rivers, and downstream toward the coast from the point where the two join.

But the truth of the matter at present is that we just do not know who the Nok peoples were or how they lived. We have no written records, we have no legends or myths that explain them. As of now, and until archeology gives us more to work with, we can only ponder the mute testimony of the Nok figures.

IFE AND THE ONI

Shortly after the turn of the twentieth century, a German adventurer-explorer-ethnologist named Leo Frobenius was "poking about" in what today is Nigeria. The people of the Yoruba area offered him many terra cotta heads, life-size, of men and *Figures 44, 46-47* women long vanished. The pieces were excellent sculptures done in a completely naturalistic style, and showing great dignity and strength.

Surprised at first by the authority with which the heads were executed, and then increasingly impressed at the quantities of them that he came across, Frobenius was convinced that neither the Yorubas nor their ancestors could have produced anything so fine. They were, he announced to the world, the work of the artists of Atlantis, the legendary lost continent! And the world, impressed with the extraordinary quality of the work and having been told that the Yorubas today do not produce anything of this sort, swallowed the judgment of this ethnocentric, white European. Those who doubted the Atlantis theory concluded simply that the works had really been done by Portuguese artists of four or five centuries ago or by native artists trained by the Portuguese.

This "alien artists" theory stood for thirty years, and then it began to crack wide open. In the first place, there was the link between the Ife sculpture and the Nok pieces turned up in the 1930s and 1940s. Students of sculpture pointed out the obvious similarity in techniques, tending to support the conclusion that the Ife peoples of some prior time might well have learned their craft from the Noks.

Then in 1938 and 1939 a huge cache of cast brass works of art was discovered at the palace of the Oni (king) of Ife, linking Ife with the great bronze-brasses of Benin, found by the *Figures 45, 48* British in their expedition of 1897. This tended to confuse the issue thoroughly, and it was not until after World War II, when the Carbon-14 dating process was developed from atomic research, that the whole time sequence was unraveled.

The atomic analysis revealed that the Ife terra cottas had been done about 1200 A.D., nearly three hundred years before the Portuguese activity in Africa. That took care of the Europeans. (As for Atlantis, evidence now points to an "O" shaped island in the Aegean as the site of the fabled island—but that's another story!)

Experts believe that as time goes on more excavations

and finds in the major areas of the African west coast—from
Benin to Yorubaland—will explain the relationships between
them. The theory is that the art and artifacts of Ife and Benin,
with their common base, actually stem from a tradition that has
its roots in Nok culture—not in any European or other source
outside Africa itself. The brass and terra cotta sculptures of the
Yoruba clearly show their descent from the artistic styles of
Nok.[3]

The technique used to produce the terra cotta sculptures
is one of "building up." The sculptor starts with a core and
adds to it, putting on the basic head shape the nose, ears, hair
style, etc. The Nok pieces are hollow and are "high-fired," that
is, placed in an intensely hot fire, which gives them greater
strength. (Low-fired pieces are weak and easily broken—a flower
pot is a good modern-day example.) Firing pottery requires
great skill, especially when the figure being worked on is the
size of a teenager.

It is important to note that the technique used in pro-
ducing the Nok terra cottas is similar to the early stages of the
process of making castings by the "lost wax" technique. In this
system, the artist starts with a core, then carefully builds upon
it a wax model of his subject. When he finishes the wax sculpture
he then covers it with many layers of mud. When the mud is
thoroughly dry, the whole thing is heated until the wax melts
and runs out. The molten metal is then poured in. When the
metal has cooled, the mud cast is broken off, exposing the
finished art work.

It is perfectly plausible that there is an unbroken tradition
in the art of the Ife-Nok-Benin area. And new finds tend to confirm this. In 1953 and 1957 the Nigerian Antiquities Service dug

one hundred shafts near Ife and turned up some thirty thousand pieces of pottery. The emphasis so far has been on rescuing the Ife art objects rather than attempting to figure out the chronology of the pottery. However, with the vast number of pieces to work with, it should be possible to develop a theory to explain the beginning, evolution and flowering of the art and relate it to present-day Yoruba work.[4]

The beginnings of the Ife culture and the Yoruba people are dimly seen through traditions, legends and oral histories. Sultan Mohammed Bello, a distinguished scholar and statesman of the Sudan in the early nineteenth century, wrote that:

The people of Yoruba are descended from the Bani Kan'an and the kindred of Nimrod. Now the reason of their having settled in the west according to what we are told is that Ya'rub ibn Qahtan drove them out of Iraq to westwards and they traveled between Misr and Habash [Ethiopia] until they reached Yoruba. It happened that they left a portion of their people in every country they passed. It is said that the Sudanese who live up on the hills are all kindred; so also the people of Yauri are their kindred.[5]

Another view was given in 1897 by a distinguished historian who found no mystery whatever:

The origin of the Yoruba nation is involved in obscurity. Like the early history of most nations, the commonly received accounts are for the most part purely legendary. The people being unlettered, and the language unwritten, all that is known is from traditions carefully handed down.

The National Historians are certain families retained by the King at Oyo whose office is hereditary; they also act as the king's bards, drummers and cymbalists. It is on them we depend as far as possible for any reliable information we now possess; but, as may be expected, their accounts often vary in several important particulars. We can do no more than relate the traditions which have been universally accepted.

The Yorubas are said to have sprung from Lamurudu, one of the Kings of Mecca whose offspring were Oduduwa, the ancestor of the Yorubas, the Kings of Gogobiri and of the Kukawa, two tribes in the Hausa country. It is worthy of remark that these two nations, notwithstanding the lapse of time since their separation and in spite of the distance from each other of their respective localities, still have the same distinctive tribal marks on their faces; and Yoruba travelers are free amongst them and vice versa, each recognizing each other as of one blood.

At what period of time Lamurudu reigned is unknown, but, from the accounts given of the revolution among his descendants and their despersion, it appears to have been a considerable time after Mahomet. . . .

That the Yorubas came originally from the East there cannot be the slightest doubt, as their habits, manners and customs, etc., all go to prove. With them the East is Mecca and Mecca is the East. Having strong affinities with the East, and Mecca in the East looming so largely in their imagination, everything that comes from the East, with them, comes from Mecca; and hence it is natural to represent themselves as having hailed originally from that city.[6]

An updating of this view is given by a modern Nigerian historian who put it this way in 1955:

In our search for the origins of the Yoruba we ought to glance at the
Kingdom of Meroe . . . .

> The modern Yoruba themselves usually confused the Near
> East with Arabia and owing to the prestige of Islam located
> their origin in Mecca. The probable place is Upper Egypt
> rather than the Yemen. . . .
>
> It is almost certain . . . that the Yoruba migrations from
> the Near East occurred between 600 and 1000 A.D. The
> Yoruba did not emigrate from their original homes in one
> mass exodus . . . [but] in successive waves which may be
> grouped into two major waves with an interval of about three
> hundred years in between. . . .[7]

The Yoruba must have migrated to their present homes from a
region or regions where they may have been influenced by
ancient Egyptian, Etruscan and Jewish cultures. When circum-
stantial evidence is considered, the links with ancient Meroe
seem strong. The national god of the Yorubas is Shango, who is
worshipped with a ram's mask strongly reminiscent of Kush or
Old Egypt. And in a grave at Abiri, ten miles from Ife, a ram's
head and a coiled serpent were found, both popular in Egypt
and Kush. The Meroitic temple at Naqa, built between 100 B.C.
and 100 A.D., has a coiled serpent prominently displayed on its
facade.

According to tradition, Ife was the first Yoruba state and
it was there that the father of them all, Oduduwa, the god
figure from whom all Yoruba dynasties stem, settled. His descendants went forth to start other independent states. They
were independent, but their kings acknowledged as their spiritual leader the king of Ife, the Oni. One of these states earned
for itself, with the assistance of European and American slavers,
the most frightening title ever given a place.

THE "CITY OF BLOOD"

The city-state of Benin on the Gulf of Guinea in modern Nigeria is the place named "City of Blood" by the British expedition of 1897. But Benin's beginnings stretch back beyond the written word, into the tribal memory through its oral history, back more than one thousand years. That memory, that oral history, has been set down by the curator of the Benin Museum and it tells of a land far different from that which shocked the Victorian world some seventy years ago.

The people of Benin, the Binis, came to their location near the mouth of the Niger from Egypt. The empire of that first dynasty was founded about 900 A.D. and the rulers were called Ogiso (king) before Oduduwa and his party arrived at Ife about the twelfth century. Some time before 1170, one ruler named Owodo was banished for misrule by his angry subjects. They appointed as administrator of the country, a certain Evian, and when he "was stricken by old age he nominated his son as his successor." The Bini people refused to allow this, however, because, as they quickly pointed out, it had been agreed that a republican form of government would be set up and he was trying to change this.

In the midst of this dispute, the Binis sent to Oduduwa, the Oni of Ife, asking him to send one of his princes to rule them, since Benin was rapidly deteriorating.

Oduduwa shrewdly decided to test the Binis before sending his son to govern them. So he sent seven lice to the chiefs of Benin with instructions to care for them for three years and return them to him. When the time was up, the lice were returned, sleek and fat. Impressed, the Oni remarked "people who can take care of such minute creatures can undoubtedly take care of my son." And so he sent Prince Oranmiyan, accompanied by an impressive retinue of courtiers and native doctors, in the year 1170.

Now Oranmiyan's arrival was opposed by the son of Evian, but the people ignored his objections. The prince took up residence in a newly-built palace, married a beautiful princess and soon had a son. Then, after some years he did a remarkable thing. He called the people together and announced that he was going to abdicate. The land was a country of vexation (*ile Ibinu*—from which it henceforth took its name), and he was convinced that only a person born, trained and educated in the arts and mysteries of the place could reign over such a people. He then named his son to succeed him as Oba (king) and returned to Ife, leaving trusted advisers as regents.

He wisely withdrew from the country in stages, spending three years at a place called Okha where he could be reached for decisions. Then he went on to another town where he stayed for two more years before finally returning to Ife. Apparently Oranmiyan was incapable of staying put. After three years in Ife he went to Oyo where again he left a son to become ruler, thus starting another dynasty. Oranmiyan returned to Ife again and ruled there until death and thus is explained the close relationship between the royal houses of these three places.

Now at a later time the Oba of Benin wanted to produce art works similar to those he recieved from Ife which were greatly admired. He therefore entreated the Oni of Ife to send a brass-smith. The Oni complied, sending one of his finest workmen, a man named Iguegha. This artist was so splendid that he left many excellent works, so much appreciated that Iguegha was deified and is worshipped to this day by brass-smiths of Benin. It was during this time that the practice began of making brass-castings to memorialize important events. (There seems to be a discrepancy in the history at this point, for this Oba is traditionally supposed to have acceded in 1280, but brass-casting is thought to date after 1400.)

We skip in the oral history to Ogun, a great magician, traveler, warrior and doctor. He was powerful, courageous and wise. "After the murder of Uwaifiokun, Ogun," says the curator of the Benin Museum, "was crowned Oba of Benin with the title Ewuare, meaning 'it is cool' or 'the trouble has ceased.' " This was about the year 1440. Though "cool" may have been the hope, the facts of Ewuare's reign were quite different.

He began even before his enthronement by causing a "great conflagration in the city which lasted two days and nights as a revenge for his banishment." Then, after becoming Oba, "he fought against and captured 201 towns and villages...on this side of the river Niger. He took their petty rulers captive and caused the people to pay tribute to him."

Oba Ewuare "made good roads in Benin City and especially the streets known as Akpakpava and Utantan. In fact, the town rose to importance and gained the name 'city' during his reign . . . Ewuare was the first Oba of Benin to come in contact with Europeans, for Ruey de Segueira visited the Benin area in 1472. . . ."[8] At this point the history of Benin becomes available as part of the European record also.

In 1485, a Portuguese explorer named John Affonso d'Aveiro arrived at Benin City, bringing with him coconuts and guns. D'Aveiro came again shortly after 1504 and recommended to the Oba (a new one, named Esigie) that he accept Christianity, which would improve his country by bringing the benefits of learning, contact with the great outside world and salvation through religion. Esigie thereupon sent one of the Bini priests as an ambassador to Portugal to study this proposal. The king of Portugal was requested to send priests to teach the Oba and the Binis the faith and this was done. The king also sent traders who set up establishments at the port and traded in ivory, Benin cloth, pepper and other items. The climate and unfamiliar diseases soon discouraged them, however, and they left.

The indefatigable John Affonso d'Aveiro and the flock of missionaries remained, and churches and schools were established. The missionaries made great progress and "thousands of people were baptized before the death of the great explorer John Affonso, who was buried with great lamentations by the Oba and the Christians of Benin City."

The European record of the earliest contact with Benin was a chronicle written for Portugal's John II about 1486. In it, the beginning of the pepper trade and the "great quantity" produced in Benin and the Guinea coast is described. Samples of pepper were sent to various European cities by the Portuguese and in this way they built up a large market for the spice. The king of Benin sent an ambassador to the Portuguese court to find out about the lands from which the curious white men were coming.[9]

It is notable that there is *no* mention in this report of taking or buying or even of observing slaves. This is an important point, for it indicates that whatever slavery existed at this time was not a prominent feature of Bini life.

A report nearly seventy years later gives us an idea of the court and commerce of that time: The court itself was located some ten leagues from the river in a huge building with earthen walls. It had no windows, but the roof was of louvered boards, to let in air and light. When his subjects approached the king they cowered, covering their faces, not daring to look up until he commanded them to do so, and in leaving the royal presence, his subjects crept out, faces down, not turning their backs.

According to the report, the king at this time had been to Portugal as a boy and knew the language. When the English merchants told him they were seeking goods to purchase and trade, the monarch told them to take a look at the pepper in the local warehouses and to show him their wares. With an escort of nobles the merchants went back to their ship and fetched their trade goods to put before the king. He liked the merchandise, and offered to round up all the available pepper in exchange. In the space of a month some eighty tons of pepper were collected. However, this was worth more than the British trade goods, so the king promised to credit them for the merchandise they had with them, and to trust them to return with goods to make up the balance! There was no mention of slavery or the purchase of slaves in this report.[11]

In 1602, a Dutchman who visited Benin described it in terms very much like those he might have used for one of the cities in his own country. Benin town, he remarked, seemed very large as one came into it via the main street, which was seven or eight times as broad as Warmoes Street in Amsterdam. Though it was not paved, the street was straight and ran for about four miles through the city, continuing on into the suburbs. Entering the city gate through thick earthen walls, one could see street after street and on them, shoulder to shoulder, were the houses of the citizens. They stood in good order, said the Dutchman, close and even, like the ones in Holland, and consisted of kitchen, dining and other rooms covered by a roof open in the middle to let the breeze and light in.

The Oba's court was in a building surrounded by square

plazas which were walled and had galleries surrounding them on which guards were posted. Our observer noted that he passed four such plazas and wherever he looked he saw "gates upon gates to go into other places." There were many courtiers on horseback and many male slaves in the town, carrying water, yams and palm-wine "which they say is for their horses."[11]

It is worth emphasizing the fact that this observer from one of the most advanced nations of Europe found much of Benin not only admirable, but so understandable in terms of his own experience.

Another report on the king and customs comes from a British merchant, 124 years later. There had been significant changes. At this time three "great lords" attended the king, told him what the people were requesting and relayed his answers and commands. This technique was necessary because it was now forbidden to approach nearer than thirty paces. According to the British merchant, the Oba went out in public only once a year on the occasion of the Coral-Feast. Dressed in all his finery, accompanied by his covey of wives, his state ministers and court nobles, he conducted the sacrifices to his gods and so launched the great feast. It was a time for the "honors list" in which the king promoted or honored worthy subjects by bestowing on them a string of coral. Everyone entered into the spirit of the great celebration—the nobles followed the Oba's example and sacrificed to the gods and then everybody concentrated on drinking, dancing and merrymaking.

The Extraordinary Benin Bronzes

Now in Benin at this time, as for many centuries before, the religion of the people, sponsored by the Oba, had as an important element not only sacrifice of animals, but the production of art. The bronze-brass castings that have inspired world admiration were made over the years by craft guilds of metalworkers, well organized and dedicated to making elaborate pieces for altars and decorations for the palace and houses of the nobles.

Religious sacrifices were made to insure salvation, to induce fertility and birth of many healthy children, and as a kind of insurance, to bring safety. Altarpieces cast in bronze were made for the places of worship and generally these powerful works of art consisted of many human figures, each of which had a socket in its head for insertion of a length of elephant tusk, finely carved. Thus an altar would have perhaps fifteen figures of bronze with curved ivory arcs several feet long sweeping upward and back from their heads.

The bronze plaques made by these same master artists were carefully placed on pillars of houses and in the walls surrounding the compounds. Shown on these beautiful sculptures are more prosaic scenes of people at work and play. Some of the plaques give us historical insights, for they show contemporary activities. For example, on a number of them are men in European armor, armed with crossbows and arquebuses. Knowing the dates of such armor and weapons, we can place these in time and see the way of dress and life in the city at that time.

▷ *Life in Benin* A rare insight into the life-style of the people themselves, written by one of them, is the memoir of Gustavus Vassa, whose real name was Olaudah Equiano. Equiano was born about 1745 in the interior, north of Benin city. Here is his description of that place and time from his autobiography, a work written with freshness and keen observation:

This kingdom is divided into many provinces or districts; in one of the most remote and fertile of which I was born . . . . The distance of this province from the capital of Benin and the sea coast must be very considerable, for I had never heard of white men or Europeans, nor of the sea; and our subjection to the king of Benin was little more than nominal.

. . . . As our manners [there] are simple, our luxuries are few. The dress of both sexes are nearly the same. It generally consists of a long piece of calico, or muslin, wrapped loosely round the body . . . . This is usually dyed blue, which is our favorite color. It is extracted from a berry and is brighter and richer than any I have seen in Europe.

. . . . Our manner of living is entirely plain . . . bullocks, goats, and poultry supply the greatest part of [our] food. These constitute likewise the principal wealth of the country, and the chief articles of commerce . . . . In our buildings we study convenience rather than ornament. Each master of a family has a large, square piece of ground, surrounded with a moat or fence, or enclosed with a wall made of red earth tempered, which, when dry is as hard as brick. Within this are his houses to accommodate his family and slaves which, if numerous, frequently present the appearance of a village.

. . . . These houses never exceed one story in height; they are always built of wood, of stakes driven into the ground, crossed with wattles and neatly plastered within and without. The roof is thatched with reeds . . . . Houses so constructed and furnished require but little skill to erect them. Every man is a sufficient architect for the purpose. The whole neighborhood afford their unanimous assistance in building them and in return receive and expect no other recompense than a feast.

As we live in a country where nature is prodigal of her favors, our wants are few and easily supplied. Of course we

Figure 43. More than two thousand years ago in what is now central Nigeria, artists of a lost civilization were sculpting superb figures in clay. Many of these were life-size. This powerful head is fourteen inches tall, was done in terra cotta between 500 B.C. and 200 A.D. and was found near the village of Nok, where the first of hundreds of pieces was discovered and from which the unknown Nok culture has taken its name.
COURTESY OF THE NIGERIAN FEDERAL DEPARTMENT OF ANTIQUITIES, LAGOS. PHOTOGRAPH BY ELIOT ELISOFON.

Figure 45. This hunter triumphantly carries an antelope home from the hunt. Slung across his chest is the quiver for his arrows, and rubbing his right leg is his trusty hunting dog. This late nineteenth century bronze is in the great Ife-Benin tradition, and is thought to be Yoruba work.
BRITISH MUSEUM.

Figure 44. Here a small chameleon crawls over a rock in this tiny terra cotta executed by a skilled artist of Ife centuries ago. The mastery of form is typical of Ife art.
NIGERIAN MUSEUM.

Figure 46. In the Ife region of Nigeria are found some of the great masterpieces of world art. The Ife worked in stone, terra cotta, clay, wood, ivory, and metal. This life-size terra cotta head of a queen is dated between the twelfth and fifteenth centuries. The fine detail and sensitive expression are typical of the naturalistic portraits done by Ife artists.
BRITISH MUSEUM.

Figure 47. Calm dignity is the hallmark of the portrait heads of Ife. This handsome terra cotta is typical of the many superb sculptures discovered (and still being unearthed) in that region. Compare it with the bronze portrait of the same period, and the Nok terra cotta from some fifteen hundred years earlier.
COURTESY OF THE BROOKLYN MUSEUM.

Figure 48. This portrait bronze of an Ife king is about half life-size, though the head is nearly full-size. In his left hand the Oni carries a horn; in his right he held an axe; both of these are symbols of power to the people of this region even today. Note also the headdress, necklaces and bracelets and compare them with those of Kush and Benin. This bronze is a treasure of the Nigerian government. Europeans believed that superb sculptures like this were made by foreign artists. (This is a photograph of a cast of the original made by the British Museum.)

*Figure 49. It was the British military expedition to the
city of Benin in 1897 that brought to world attention
the magnificent bronze art of that city-state. This
life-size portrait head was cast in bronze about
1550-1680. The hat, pendants and necklaces in real life
were made of coral beads. The remarkable detail in
this and other Benin bronzes proves that the artists
were masters of the lost-wax process of metal casting,
as well as of sculpture.*
COURTESY OF THE MUSEUM OF PRIMITIVE ART, NEW YORK.

Figure 50. Here is a king of Benin (c. 1550-1680) with his retainers. He wears a coral crown, anklets, necklaces and necklet, rides side-saddle and is flanked by a sword-bearer and retainers who shield him from the sun. This is one of the many bronze plaques that were mounted on the walls in the city of Benin.
COURTESY OF THE MUSEUM OF PRIMITIVE ART, NEW YORK.

Figure 51. In this bronze, a royal dignitary (perhaps a king) of Benin carries a double-edged ceremonial sword and, under his left hand, a small animal, possibly a leopard. His attendant carries a sculpture of an animal head that may be a ram. Note the coral necklet, loops of coral beads across the chest, and the anklets. There is also a necklace with wild boar tusks. This plaque was made between 1550 and 1680. The hundreds of plaques found show scenes of animals, Binis and Europeans.
COURTESY OF THE MUSEUM OF PRIMITIVE ART, NEW YORK.

Figure 52. Here a Benin horseman of the late seventeenth century halts momentarily for his portrait. He wears a lavish hat of coral beads and feathers, carries a woven shield and guides his bedecked steed with a chain bridle. The horse collar is decorated with bells. Note the woven motif on the base of the work; it is a characteristic theme in Islamic art. BRITISH MUSEUM.

Figure 53. This inlaid ivory bracelet-cuff also comes from the Benin court and was carved about the same time as the one to the right. In this, an intricate design interlocks human faces, helmets, hair and mustaches with tail-biting snakes.
COURTESY OF THE MUSEUM OF PRIMITIVE ART, NEW YORK.

Figure 54. The Binis were also masters at sculpture in other media, such as wood and ivory. This bracelet from the court of Benin was carved in the seventeenth or eighteenth century. Note the leopard above the warrior on the right and the human figure upside-down on the left.
COURTESY OF THE MUSEUM OF PRIMITIVE ART, NEW YORK.

Figure 55. This Benin court musician stands more than two feet tall, and dates back between 1550 and 1680. He seems to be wearing a leopard-skin skirt edged with feathers. That the Binis could cast complicated, free-standing figures such as this is evidence that they had prodigious technical skill with metals as well as highly-developed artistic sensitivity.
COURTESY OF THE MUSEUM OF
PRIMITIVE ART, NEW YORK.

Figure 56. This is the conical tower in the Zimbabwe Great Enclosure. The tower now reaches thirty-four feet skyward. The walls nearby are up to twenty feet thick, built of expertly cut and fitted granite blocks held together for centuries, through the care and skill of the original craftsmen, without mortar. These are the largest of more than three hundred stone ruins in Rhodesia and nearby countries.
BRITISH INFORMATION SERVICE.

Figure 57. At this point the wall of the "Temple" of Great Zimbabwe is thirty-one feet tall. The masonry compares with the finest work to be found anywhere. The double chevron pattern at the top of the wall is found in many ruins in the area of the Monomotapa empire, and signifies the residence of the king.
RHODESIA NATIONAL TOURIST BOARD.

Figure 58. Great Zimbabwe, located inland in Rhodesia, is the mysterious ruin that has stimulated the imagination of men for a century. H. Rider Haggard wrote the novel King Solomon's Mines *about the site. There are signs of man's having lived in the area for fifteen hundred years. This, called the Acropolis, is a site that may have been finished by about 1750 A.D., with most of the construction carried out during the preceding three hundred years. In addition to this complex, set high on a hill, there are two other vast stone complexes—the Valley of Ruins and the Temple or Great Enclosure.*

RHODESIA DEPARTMENT OF TOURISM.

Figure 59. These walls, extremely well preserved, are at Nalatale, another site in the Monomotapa-Zimbabwe area. This was occupied in the seventeenth-eighteenth centuries and the wall is an ellipse some one hundred fifty feet across. Note the characteristic stone patterns of the chevron, rope, and herringbone.
SOUTHERN RHODESIA DEPARTMENT OF TOURISM.

Figure 60. This stonework is part of the ruins at Dhlo-Dhlo, near the Khami site. Built in a similar manner, it shows the extraordinary skill and sophistication of the masons who worked without mortar.
RHODESIA NATIONAL TOURIST BOARD.

Figure 61. Detail of the stone masonry in the walls of Nalatale.
RHODESIA NATIONAL TOURIST BOARD.

Figure 62. Here is part of the fortress and settlement complex of Khami, near Bulawayo, believed to have been built after 1600 A.D.
RHODESIA NATIONAL TOURIST BOARD.

Figure 63. These views show a Carthaginian ten-drachma piece used during 241-146 B.C., *the period when Hannibal challenged Roman power. The Punic goddess Tanit is on one side; Pegasus on the reverse.*
PHOTOGRAPH BY WILLIAM R. DEVINE,
THE CHASE MANHATTAN BANK
MONEY MUSEUM.

Figure 64. Queen Dido, according to legend, fled Asia Minor and established the Phoenician settlement of Carthage on the shore of North Africa. It was there that she welcomed the fugitive Trojans who fled Troy after their defeat at the hands of the Achaeans. Dido fell in love with the Trojan leader, Prince Aeneas, giving the world one of the great tragic love stories of all time. In this fifteenth century painting by Francesco De Giorgio, Dido meets Aeneas.
FROM THE COLLECTION OF THE PORTLAND
ART MUSEUM, PORTLAND, OREGON.

Figure 65. There was nothing legendary about the wealth of Carthage. The city flourished and was a major rival of Rome. To the left is a silver tetradrachm issued by Carthage from 410-310 B.C., with a lion under a date palm.
PHOTOGRAPHED BY ARTHUR LAVINE, THE CHASE MANHATTAN BANK MONEY MUSEUM.

Figure 66. Leptis Magna was one of the oldest and most prosperous cities on the North African shore. This picture shows the amphitheater with the Mediterranean Sea in the background. The original settlement was established by the Phoenicians and the city was part of the Carthaginian empire. It became a major Roman city on the African coast and was the birthplace of Septimus Severus, one of Rome's emperors, who sponsored construction of many buildings and improvements in the metropolis. The ruins of Leptis have yet to be completely revealed, though archeologists have been working on the site since 1911. Wealthy and powerful, Leptis was but one of many Roman cities of importance that declined after the fall of Rome.
INTERNATIONAL FILM FOUNDATION.

have few manufactures. They consist for the most part of calicoes, earthenware, ornaments, and instruments of war and husbandry . . . . We have also markets . . . . These are sometimes visited by stout, mahogany-colored men from the southwest of us: We call them Oye-Ibo, which term signifies red men living at a distance. They generally bring us firearms, gunpowder, hats, beads and dried fish . . . . They always carry slaves through our land; but the strictest account is exacted of the manner of procuring them before they are suffered to pass. Sometimes indeed we sold slaves to them, but they were only prisoners of war, or such among us as had been convicted of kidnapping, or adultery, and some other crimes which we esteemed heinous. This practice of kidnapping induces me to think that, notwithstanding all our strictness, their principal business among us was to deceive and snare our people. . . .

From what I can recollect of these battles [between Equiano's rural tribe and the Ibos] they appear to have been eruptions of one little state or district on the other, to obtain prisoners or booty. Perhaps they were incited to this by those traders who brought the European goods mentioned amongst us . . . . When a trader wants slaves, he applies to a chief for them and tempts him with his wares. . . .[12]

Equiano himself was kidnapped in 1756 and herded along with other prisoners to be sold at the port on the Niger delta. By this time he had heard about white men and, along with his fellow-captives, understood that they were cannibals and would purchase the lot of them for food. At the auction, he saw:

. . . white men with horrible looks, red faces and long hair . . . . When I looked around the ship and saw a large furnace of copper boiling and a multitude of black people of every description

chained together, every one of their countenances expressing
dejection and sorrow, I no longer doubted of my fate . . . .[13]

Equiano's fate was extraordinary, however. He was taken to
Virginia by a slaver and there sold and resold. With the aid of
his master, a Philadelphia merchant, in 1777 he bought his
freedom and became a sailor. Known as Gustavus Vassa, he
was one of the black leaders of the early Abolitionist movement.

Though Benin at this time was a territory slightly larger
than Wales, its influence extended over a much wider area.
From the Congo River on the south to what is now Sierra Leone
on the west there was widespread belief that the strongest spirit
in West Africa was the chief spirit of Benin. This spirit lived in
Benin City, tended by a corps of priests, the leaders of which
exercised the true governing power, with the king as a figure-
head. In later times the worship of the chief spirit developed a
bloodthirsty character, for, according to the priests, he demanded
human sacrifices.

Benin deteriorated swiftly, largely because of the slave
trade. Through the profits from the trade the merchants and
rulers of Benin had the motivation and the power—from the
firearms they secured—to push their boundaries outward and
capture more human "merchandise." Benin's armies were kept
constantly on the move, rounding up captives and taking over
small tribes in the Niger delta. By 1650 the limits of Benin's
power were Bonny in the east and Lagos in the west and the
capital city of the Oba was flourishing.

However, the constant turmoil caused by the warfare
and the insecurity caused by the slave roundups severely affected
Benin's fortunes by the beginning of the eighteenth century.
Sections of the countryside had been scoured for slaves and

people had fled, leaving large areas deserted. In many places the farmland went back to jungle. The raiding armies found it increasingly difficult to find slaves and had to travel farther and farther. It got so bad that they actually turned against one another, fighting over what spoils they could collect. The large, highly-developed capital city was affected also and many parts of it crumbled as its citizens fled or were sold to the slavers.

Eventually Benin's slave trade dwindled to the point that the European slave ships seldom called. And because the countryside had been so depopulated and demoralized that agriculture could scarcely be carried on, pepper and other crops declined also. The European merchants found less and less reason to put ashore at Benin. The Oba's warriors continued their slave raids. But now their purpose was to secure victims for human sacrifice. The greatness of Benin washed away in the bloody traffic in slaves and religious supplication.[14]

The final chapter of independent Benin's story began with the killing of nine Europeans traveling from Gwato, the second city, to Benin in 1897. The British immediately sent a punitive expedition of twelve hundred men. The column had to fight its way into the capital. After five days, the troops, equipped with the most modern arms of that time, forced their way into the city. This is what they found, as described by their leader, commander Bacon:

Truly has Benin been called the city of blood. . . . Blood was everywhere. . . . On the right [of the main compound of the king] was a crucifixion tree with a double crucifixion on it, the two poor wretches stretched out facing west, with their arms bound together in the middle. . . . At the base were skulls and bones, literally strewn about, the debris of former sacrifices, and down every main road were two or more human sacrifices. . . . [15]

Bacon did not know, and perhaps would not have cared to know, that these excesses were the frantic, last-minute sacrifices of the priests to the chief spirit, an attempt to stave off the defeat that overwhelmed them as the British blasted their way into the city.

It should be noted that the British took an enormous number of Benin bronzes back home, and as a result, have an incomparable collection in the British Museum. These are recognized today as rare treasures of African art.

Figures 49-50-51-52-53   Soon after these magnificent sculptures were brought to world attention by the British, the pundits, amazed at the sophistication, the quality of craftsmanship, and expressiveness of the pieces, dismissed the possibility that the Binis could have been their creators. "The bronze art of Benin is almost entirely due to the inspiration of the Portuguese," trumpeted Sir Harry Johnston in 1910. As we have noted, Leo Frobenius stamped them as produce of the lost Atlantis or the descendants of its survivors. Other experts came up with convenient theories—the bronzes had really been made by some lost European who encamped at Benin and forthwith produced these masterpieces of "un-African" design. Some "experts" said there must have been some wandering Greeks or an ancient Greek colony somewhere in the background of these exquisite pieces. No, said others, these were masterworks in the great tradition of the European Renaissance. None of the "experts" was willing to make himself the target of ridicule by suggesting that these art works were made by the Binis themselves.

There were reasons for this, of course, and among them

was ignorance of Africa and its traditions. Another was the
inability to believe that these black men could have an art so
sublime, or that they had centuries of expertise and experience,
and that they had developed the technology of smelting and
casting the metal, not to mention the aesthetic sensitivity and
skill to create such wonders. The doubts, as recorded above,
were dispelled when atomic dating techniques proved the works
to have originated three centuries earlier than the arrival of
the Portuguese. The lost Atlantis continued to be lost. Thanks to
modern science, the greatness of African artistic genius at Benin
has been verified beyond doubt.

Figures 54-55

FROM AZANIA TO ZIMBABWE

From the Bight of Benin to the Indian Ocean is a large jump
of more than twenty-six hundred miles, nearly the span of the
U.S.A. from California to Carolina. The mysteries of this coast
and the interior behind it are intriguing. We have evidence of
skilled people, active traders, merchants, artisans, builders and
farmers. Some of the mysteries may be unlocked as more and
more of the records of coastal traders—Portuguese, Arabian,
Indian and Chinese—are revealed to the world and translated.
Some of the questions—how the people lived, what their customs
and cultures were, to what other peoples were they related, who
their gods and demons were—can be answered by the tools of
archeology.

   We have one fascinating report by Ibn Battuta, an Arabian traveler, about some of these peoples. But concerning most
of them we must rely on the ruins of their civilizations and the
story they tell.

About two hundred fifty miles inland and some three hundred miles south of the Zambezi River are the awesome stone ruins of Zimbabwe. They are close by the road from Salisbury, Southern Rhodesia, to Johannesburg. The ruins are of many buildings, built by skilled hands all long departed. But the greatest of these structures are the so-called "Acropolis" and the "elliptical temple." On a hillside, raised more than two hundred feet above its surroundings, clutching as an anchor a huge outcropping of granite, are the sweeping walls of a great *Figures 56-57-58* enclosure. Hugging the land and following the terrain, built with infinite pains from the very stone of the hillside itself, the castle is an architectural triumph. It embodies those principles dear to modern architectural leaders such as the late Frank Lloyd Wright—the importance of functional simplicity, the use of local materials, and the need to capitalize on the setting and "lay of the land."

In the valley nearby is an egg-shaped enclosure built by these people—granite stone walls solidly planted in the lush plain. This huge structure measures two hundred twenty feet by three hundred feet and its graceful, strong walls reach skyward thirty feet and are up to twenty feet thick. The entire construction is of flat granite blocks expertly cut out of the stone of the region, which tends naturally to "flake" in slabs a few inches thick. The blocks have been so beautifully cut and fitted that the walls are extremely solid, though no cement is used in them. Scientists have established that some of the earliest construction at Zimbabwe was done about fifteen hundred years ago and that the most recent building activity at the great fortress was about 1700–1750 A.D. Unlike most Western fortresses, these extraordinary structures built at Zimbabwe have gracefully curving walls.

Zimbabwe Discovered

The first reports of Zimbabwe to western Europe came back only a century ago when a hunter named Adam Renders mentioned that he had seen some large stone-fortified places in the interior. A German geologist named Karl Mauch visited the area in 1871 and brought back his judgment: These had been built by a highly civilized people in antiquity. The elliptical building in the valley, he reported, was obviously patterned directly on the palace in Jerusalem in which the Queen of Sheba sojourned about 1000 B.C. And the plan for the hill fortress was no less distinguished in history, said Mauch. It was the very image of King Solomon's great temple on Mount Moriah!

From this imaginative launching pad Europeans zoomed to the conclusion that here, at last, were solid proofs of the fabled land of Ophir. Ophir! Famed from the Biblical descriptions of Solomon's expeditions to it for gold, silver, peacocks, apes and ivory, this rich, exotic place—now located—beckoned. And, as always at the mention of the magic word "gold," the response was immediate. Thousands of Europeans rushed to the area, and by 1900, some 114,000 gold claims had been registered in the section surrounding the great Zimbabwe. Most of them were placed at sites that had once been digs for gold or minerals, ancient open mine shafts from ten to a hundred feet in depth. Other "prospectors" went after the actual building ruins hammer and claw, tearing them apart in the frantic search for gold—raw or in ornaments, it made no difference.

By 1902 the government of Southern Rhodesia ruled out such devastating exploitation of the ruins, but, as one observer commented, "the damage done was immense, for everything except the gold was treated in a most reckless manner." One prospector (and there were hundreds) whose company was systematically breaking and raking its way through the ruins, admitted in 1902 that in the previous seven years he had personally examined forty-three sites out of 141 that he knew of himself. His company managed to find five hundred ounces of gold in five years — how much of it in priceless works of art by prehistoric peoples we never will know. Nor will we ever have accurate information about the other prospectors who swarmed over the area like beetles, destroying everything in their path.

Much of the valuable record of these peoples was irretrievably lost. The romantics and racists denied that these vast stone dwellings and forts could have been built by the ancestors of today's Africans who were being driven off the Mashona and Matabele tribal lands. Some credited the Sabaeans and Phoenicians with building this inland empire between 2000 B.C. and early Christian times. De Gama and other Portuguese who first traversed the east coast of Africa believed the inland empire was that of Prester John, as we have already noted.

The archeologists and other researchers began their serious inspection of Zimbabwe only in 1905. From the truly prodigious number of stone ruins, the terrace agriculture, the mines, the quantities of beads from India and Indonesia and porcelain from China, the soapstone sculptures of birds found in the ruins and the reports of the Portuguese plus the oral traditions of the peoples now living in the area, they developed a tentative history of the people.

(Actually, the term *zimbabwe* comes from the Bantu language, that tongue common to the peoples of Africa below the equator. It derives from *zimba*: "houses," and *mabgi:* "stones," and was used by the Portuguese for the main dwelling of a tribal chief. However, after 1550, the term was centered on one group of ruins, the two largest of which we described above, now called Great Zimbabwe.)

A Highly Civilized People

Radio-carbon dating of materials taken from the Great Zimbabwe ruins tell us that there were people living there at least as early as the sixth or seventh century. There were, apparently, three periods in Zimbabwe's active life. The first period may have begun as early as the fourth century and ended in the twelfth. The people of this lengthy period knew how to smelt iron and make tools and weapons from it. The traditions state that these people came into the area from the north.

This group, in turn, was forced out by another wave of peoples from the north in the twelfth century, the Monomotapa people. The word is Bantu, interpreted by some as "lord of the water-elephants," i.e., the hippopotamus—which is a sacred animal to the Karange people of this area to the present day. *Monomotapa* actually is the title of the ruler, but has been applied to the whole group. These people stayed in this area until the middle of the fifteenth century when, it is believed, they abandoned the site.

Another group is thought to have come to the area about 1400, and taken over the Zimbabwe site. The Portuguese recorded the name of the Monomotapa of that time—he was Mokomba Menamotapam—and said his empire extended to the coast and included the town of Sofala with the capital at Great Zimbabwe.

About 1600, two other peoples of related stock are known to have built many villages and forts to the south as far as the area beyond the Limpopo River. They were energetic and strong and by 1700 challenged the Monomotapa. We know, from oral history and the archeological evidence, the story of these people.

The lower part of Southern Rhodesia was taken over in the early years of the fifteenth century by Bantu-speaking Karanga peoples. For the most part they were farmers and herdsmen, raising cattle. They grouped their huts in small clusters consisting of silos for grain and huts for farm animals and themselves and enclosed the entire group with a stockade of mud and thatch. From the cities of the coast Arab and Indian traders carried goods to exchange there for the precious metals—gold, iron and copper—and ivory that originated in the Zimbabwe area.

Near the middle of the fifteenth century, a skillful leader arose among these people. He was called Mutota Mwanamutapa and he expanded his territory rapidly so that in ten years he governed the entire region. His son, Matope, ruled for the next thirty years, continually extending his power and rule until his domain covered the area from the Zambezi and Indian Ocean throughout what is now called southern Mozambique, with the exception of the coastal trading cities. This vast domain flourished and was at peace as he ruled until 1480 through a system of governors, kin and vassals.[16]

Changamire's Challenge

There were, however, many intrigues among the ruling barons and vassal governors. One of these, Changamire, who ruled one of the remote southern provinces, challenged Matope's successor openly and by 1490 there was a showdown between challenger and the reigning Monomotapa. This is the story of that confrontation as it was described to the king of Portugal in 1506:

When Changamire learned that Mokomba, the king, wished to kill him, he decided to beat him to it. He took a sizable troop of courtiers and soldiers with him and trekked to the capital city, Zimbabwe. Nearing the capital, he was met by a group of the king's nobles who had received advance notice of Changamire's expedition. They deserted the Monomotapa and joined Changamire, accompanying him to the palace. The challenger's troops surrounded the palace and Changamire entered with his trusted lieutenants. The king was in the throne room with a number of his slaves and courtiers. Changamire addressed him and, before there could be any organized resistance, whipped out his sword and cut the Monomotapa's head off with one slashing blow. Thus he made himself king and all obeyed him.

Mokomba was survived—but not for long—by twenty-two children. Changamire, to prevent dynastic challenges to his authority, killed them all, whatever their sex or age. All, that is, except one—the eldest—who escaped just in time to the kingdom of his uncle.

Now Changamire ruled as the Monomotapa for four years in peace. But by that time the young prince, Mokomba's son, was twenty-two years of age and assembled an army to help him retake his realm from the usurper. Changamire, warned of the advancing liberation army, marched out from the palace to battle the prince's troops. The two forces met in a field near the capital city.

As the enemy approached, Changamire saw that the prince had rallied many of his subjects to the challenger's banner. The Monomotapa ordered his troops to attack, but their assault was repulsed. The prince's army stood fast and counterattacked. There were many casualties, on both sides. The fighting increased in intensity and it became a see-saw battle that raged for three and a half days, with much slaughter and many casualties. At length, the prince managed to isolate Changamire and, in hand-to-hand combat, he killed him, thus avenging his father.

Now the rightful Monomotapa assumed his place as ruler. However, the territories of Changamire would not submit to the new Monomotapa and resisted all efforts to subdue them. The war between these two factions continued not for days or weeks, but stretched on for months and even years. Because of this, the gold mining was disrupted and the flow of the precious metal to the port of Sofala was reduced to a trickle, much to the dismay and concern of the Portuguese who found themselves powerless to do anything about it.[17]

Gold, of course, was the primary interest of the Portuguese and the Africans knew it. With harsh laws they tried to prevent the Europeans from finding the sources of the yellow metal. So, if by some chance the Swahili Moslem traders from the coastal towns happened upon a gold mine, they were supposed to shout until one of the citizens heard him and came to the place. Both of them were then supposed to cover the mine, camouflage it, and set a great tree limb on the site to warn other Africans to avoid the place. If the Monomotapa's subjects did come to the place, they were to be summarily executed, even though they did not attempt to take any gold. With such extreme penalties, the Monomotapa attempted to keep the Portuguese from finding out about the "digs," to prevent them from trying to seize the country.[18]

We have a description of the Monomotapa, his court and their relations with the Portuguese: When the king went forth from his palace he carried in his hand a bow and arrows as did his nobles and bodyguards. He was preceded by a man carrying a huge "cushion" which he beat with his hand. It gave a deep rumbling sound that notified the people of the realm that the king was at hand. There were times when the Mono-motapa carried an *assegai*, or spear, made of black wood with a point of pure gold, in one hand, and three wooden *fimbos* in the other. These were symbolic of his power and when he was judging persons accused of crimes he listened to the evidence and, if he decided that the subject was guilty and deserved punishment, the king dropped one of the *fimbos* on the ground. This signified that the prisoner was guilty and the king's execu-tioners would then seize the man and execute him with an *assegai*.

The Monomotapa had a sizable harem, but his principal wife was his "sister," Mazarira, who was highly respected. She was also a great friend of the Portuguese. When they gave the king his gifts, she would also receive from them handsome clothes. No man was allowed to speak with either the Monomotapa or his chief wife unless he brought a gift of some kind. The Portu-guese gave beads, but the Africans gave cattle, goats or clothes. However, if they were too poor to give such gifts, they brought a sack of earth to acknowledge their allegiance or a bundle of straw to thatch the king's houses (for all the houses in the land were thatched).[19]

By the time the Monomotapas consolidated their empire they were rulers of a domain that stretched some seven hundred miles along the Zambezi Valley upwater from the ocean, from the Zambezi to the Limpopo. It was at this time of Portuguese penetration of the Zambezi and the coastal areas that the Changamire and Monomotapa peoples were most active in build-ing their stone structures, including the extensive additions and

Figures 59-60-61-62

strengthening of Great Zimbabwe and the elliptical temple, and elaborate "palaces" for chiefs at many places, including Dhlo-Dhlo, Matendere, and Naletale. Also installed at this time were hill-top locations in various places.

The Changamires were shrewd enough to control the sources of gold and to keep the Portuguese at arm's length. They dealt with the white men by bringing their products and the precious metal to trading posts in the Monomotapa area or through coastal traders. The net result was that the Portuguese did not penetrate into Changamire territory as they did—with fatal results to the independence of the dynasty—in the Mono-motapa region. In 1565, the Monomotapa ruler signed a treaty of trade and friendship with the Portuguese. Before seventy years more passed, the threat of Changamire military power forced the Monomotapa to plead for Portuguese protection, declaring himself a vassal of the Europeans in return.

The Portuguese moved in and all but took over. They established many settlements and trading stations, using slave labor. As they encroached further and further, the Monomotapa's people fled and deserted to the Changamire. Finally, in a bitter two-year campaign, the Changamires defeated the Monomotapas and the Europeans and pushed them out of the territory, confining them to a small area where the master-puppet relationship between the Portuguese and the Monomotapa was continued. What happened to the Changamires after that is not clear until the middle of the eighteenth century when they went down to defeat before the great Zulu warriors in a wave of immigration from Natal.

There is one important event thought to be related to the Changamire-Monomotapa-Zimbabwe cultures. Its full significance is not yet clear, but its implications are fascinating.

The Site at Mapungubwe

Imagine the year is 1932. The place is just south of the Limpopo River, that boundary between Southern Rhodesia and the Transvaal. The land is wild and sparsely settled, and in one particular area there are many sandstone hills, a number of them with steep sides and flat tops, like small aircraft carriers anchored eternally in the countryside and overgrown with trees and thick shrubbery. Among the hills, forest animals, including lions and elephants, still forage. The Africans of the region have talked for generations about a "sacred hill" where their ancestors are buried among the treasures of a long lost-culture.

A hunting and prospecting party of five white men has ventured into this out-of-the-way region nearly four hundred miles up the Limpopo from the ocean. They are searching for the taboo place, the place of fear sacred to the Great Ones, ancestors of the local Venda peoples, who refuse to face the spot and tremble at the thought of it. However, the leader of the expedition finally succeeds in locating a Venda who points out one particular hill which measures somewhat less than a quarter-mile in length and rises perhaps a hundred feet, with sides too steep to climb. Their African guide shows the white men an accessway to the top, screened by underbrush. The whites hack their way to an opening in the cliff and there, leading upward, is a narrow, vertical shaft long unused, with notches on either side, for the ends of ladder rungs.

Emerging at the top after an arduous climb, the men find themselves on a narrow tableland cluttered with bits and pieces of pottery, beads, scraps of metal. Walking about the place and scuffing away the loose topsoil here and there, one of the men suddenly spies a dull gleam in the dust. He plucks it out of its earth setting. It is gold. With a shout, he and his fellows dig and scratch, scrape and shovel. The yield is beyond their dreams: beads, plates in various shapes, ornaments, exquisitely-fashioned wooden rhinoceroses with gold ears and tails, and perhaps seventy-five ounces of the precious metal. Even more precious than the gold, though they do not realize it, are the human skeletons they find. However, one which they exhume is so fragile that it turns to dust almost before their eyes.

Though these explorers initially decide to keep the gold and their secret, one of them reports the find to the professor with whom he studied at the university in Pretoria. Because of this, the gold objects are retrieved from the members of the group, the government of South Africa purchases the site and the archeologists begin their studies.

The findings have been exciting, revealing, maddening. For example, the top of the hill, according to one scientist, has a soil cover weighing at least ten thousand tons, but most of this "has every appearance of having been artificially transported from the surrounding countryside!"[20] Another scholar discovered a large burial ground and in it fragments of twenty-three skeletons and many objects of gold and other metals. One of the skeletons had seventy ounces of gold on or near it; another had legs "wreathed in over a hundred bangles constructed of coiled wire. Several pieces of beautifully worked gold plating were also found, as well as about twelve thousand gold beads." Obviously the bodies buried here were those of royalty, not peasants. The cemetery was the first ancient royal burial ground to be found intact in South Africa.

Since the original discovery of Mapungubwe—the name of this site—at least twenty other places have been found where similar pottery and artifacts are major features. So far, the scientists have deduced that these people lived in the area from

Stone Age times. Radio-carbon dating tells us that some of the burials were made about a thousand years ago, perhaps much earlier. (One interesting note is the remains of cattle buried ceremonially as in prehistoric parts of ancient Egypt.) Conquered by a more advanced people from the north, these people then began to use iron and grow crops. Also, for protection, they moved to the top of Mapungubwe.

Here, able to exist with considerable self-sufficiency, these people developed a culture that traded with, and was perhaps an adjunct of, Zimbabwe and the Monomotapas. Mapungubwe pottery has been found throughout the southern Monomotapa areas, to mention one bit of evidence. And ironwork has been found at Mapungubwe and surrounding sites, so it is clear that these people had entered the Iron Age, though at this point the date of that event is unclear. One other note of significance: The Portuguese never reached either Zimbabwe or Mapungubwe and lived to tell about it. The reports in Portuguese records are all second-hand or the retelling of local native legends and myths, interpreted by the Europeans as they saw fit—witness da Gama's logbook entry that the coastal people told him of Prester John's capital a short distance inland. From every indication, da Gama was responding to native descriptions of Great Zimbabwe.

Much remains to be discovered about Mapungubwe, Zimbabwe and their interrelationship. But one fact stands out: These two are but the most spectacular of an incredible wealth of archeological sites from the border of the Congo through northern and southern Rhodesia, south of the Zambezi through Mozambique, the Transvaal, into Swaziland. In this broad expanse of many thousands of square miles there are innumerable places dating back from four hundred years to a millennium or more. These include stone fortified spots, dry wells, storepits, hut walls and intricate, elaborate, finely-executed hill terracing for growing grains. There are also a vast number of mine shafts and digs for minerals, not to mention smelting and metalworking sites. Dams, water conduits, roads and roadway grading through hillsides are also in evidence. Much of the most elaborate and skilled construction dates back to the period when the empires of the Western Sudan were climbing to greatness under the leadership of Sunni Ali Ber and his successors.

THE LAND OF ZANJ

The settling of the east coast of Africa was beyond men's memories two millennia ago. Even the written records tell us that, in legend and in fact, men settled, traded, fought, loved and worshipped along hundreds of miles of this Indian Ocean coastline before human history was grown to adolescence.

Zanj—the Arabic term for dark-skinned Africans—is first mentioned in a Persian record dated 293 B.C. In it, the Persian king, Narseh, is reported to have had relations with *Zhand Afrik Shah*, a black king of Africa. But as the term is usually used, it refers to a land with undefined boundaries in antiquity.

To some writers it stretched from the Horn at the Gulf of Aden down the east African seaboard to the border of what today is Mozambique. To others it was the coast of modern Mozambique, Tanzania and Kenya, plus Madagascar and the lesser islands. Even today the term Zanj survives in Zanzibar, meaning the coast of the Zanj. But generally, all the peoples of Africa's east coast were, in olden times, called the people of Zanj, blacks who lived beyond Ethiopia.

The land of Zanj is one long reported in myth and is often misrepresented. Who is not familiar with Zanj from the exploits of Sinbad the Sailor? It was along the coast of Zanj that Sinbad sailed, from city to city, "port to port, and from island to island, selling and bartering our goods, and haggling with merchants and officials wherever we cast anchor." Legendary though Sinbad's exploits were, there was nothing unreal about the chain of ports, cities and trading stations strung along the vast East African coast of Zanj.

Somewhat less enticing is the earliest written mention of Zanj in the Arab records available to us. In this note by Ibn Hordadbeh in the year 886 A.D. we find "whoever goes to the land of the Zanj, surely catches the itch."[21] Most of those who went to Zanj, however, had an incurable itch before they started their journey—an itch for riches, for profits to be made from the thriving trade in gold, ivory and iron.

About 60 A.D., a Greek in Alexandria wrote the first detailed record describing the cities and products of the African coast down as far as Tanzania (Zanj). A huge book that directs sailors and merchants to their harbors, it tells about routes, ports, about the political situation in the port cities and, most important of all, the products prized by the people as imports and exports. The book is called the *Periplus of the Erythraean Sea*, but it would be more accurate to call it an atlas-encyclopedia, for it fills seventy-five hundred pages.

The Greeks limited their African coastal trading to the Indian Ocean ports above Mozambique and concentrated on the Tanzania-Kenya coastal area they called Azania. The goods they gathered in Azania included ivory (used as inlay in their statues), rhinocerous horn, palm oil and tortoise shell. Each market town, the *Periplus* noted, "is ruled by a separate chief."

But the Greeks had much competition for the Azanian or Zanj trade. The Indians from Gujerat, Cutch and Cathawar were regular traders, bringing to African markets rice and other grains and foodstuffs, cotton cloth and clothing and, in early times, iron weapons and tools. The host of traders from Arabia also brought iron goods to the African shore—daggers, axes, tools; and they traded beads and glass as well. Later, traders came from China, as the vast quantities of porcelain show, and from Indonesia or Malaysia, bringing goods, settlers who colonized Madagascar, the revolutionary foodstuffs sweet potato, banana and taro root and, it appears, the outrigger canoe.

Lest we think of these trading missions as small in scope and limited in scale, remember that Arabic records tell of Javanese ships carrying up to two hundred people, that the Chinese perfected their sailing vessels to the point that they were using ships of two thousand tons or more, with four to seven masts, at a time when Europeans were having difficulty with two-masted vessels (this was in the fourteenth century). Furthermore, there is a record of one fleet of ships that carried more than twenty-seven thousand Chinese to the East African shore! With this facility in seafaring, it remains unclear today what policy decision caused the Chinese about 1500 A.D. to shut down their ship-yards, destroy their ships and go out of the sea trade altogether. This move left the seas to the Arabs and the Portuguese, who battled for the Zanj trade. Somewhere in Chinese records may be answers to many questions about Africa and Zanj before 1500, but few Western scholars have had the interest or opportunity to review such materials. With the current Chinese Communist regime in power, the possibility of such research is, unfortunately, extremely remote.

Zanj in the Tenth Century

Our best information about the Zanj comes from some Arab reports. One of these, by Abdul Hassan ibn Hussein ibn Ali al Mas'udi is a classic. He was born near the end of the ninth century to an Arabian family living in Baghdad. By the time he died in mid-tenth century at Fostat (modern Cairo), Al Mas'udi was one of the Marco Polos of his day and had written one of the best sellers: *Meadows of Gold and Mines of Gems*. We have, to date, only a partial translation of this travel record and in French it runs to nine volumes. Here are some of his observations of the Zanj of one millennium ago:

The sea of the Zanj reaches down to the country of Sofala and of the
   Wak-Wak which produces gold in abundance and other marvels; its climate is warm and its soil fertile. It is there that the
   Zanj built their capital; then they elected a king whom they
   called Waklimi. The Waklimi has under him all the other
   Zanj kings and commands three hundred thousand men . . .
   [Waklimi] means supreme lord; they give this title to their
   sovereign because he has been chosen to govern them with
   equity. But once he becomes tyrannical and departs from the
   rules of justice, they cause him to die and exclude his posterity
   from succession to the throne, for they claim that in thus
   conducting himself he ceases to be the son of the Master, that
   is to say, of the king of heaven and earth. They call God by
   the name of Maklandjalu, which means supreme Master. . . .
   These peoples have no code of religion; their kings follow
   custom, and conform in their government to a few political
   rules. . . .

   The Zanj use the ox as a beast of burden, for their country
has no horses or mules or camels. . . . Snow and hail are

unknown to them. . . . Some of their tribes have sharpened teeth and are cannibals. The territory of the Zanj begins at the canal which flows from the upper Nile and goes down as far as the country of Sofala and the Wak-Wak. Their settlements extend over an area of about seven hundred parasangs in length [about twenty-five hundred miles] and breadth; this country is divided by valleys, mountains and stony deserts; it abounds in wild elephants but there is not so much as a single tame elephant. . . . Although constantly employed in hunting elephants and gathering ivory, the Zanj make no use of ivory for their own domestic purposes. They wear iron instead of gold and silver . . . [tusks from Zanj] go generally to Oman, and from there are sent on to China and India. . . . In China the kings and their military and civilian officers used carrying chairs of ivory; no official or person of rank would dare to visit the king in an iron chair, and ivory alone is used for this purpose. . . .

The Zanj eat bananas . . . but the basis of their food is a plant called *kalari* which they take from the ground like a truffle, and the *elecampane* root. . . . They also have honey and meat. . . . Each worships what he pleases, a plant, an animal, a mineral. They possess a great number of islands where the coconut grows, a fruit that is eaten by all the peoples of the Zanj. . . .[22]

This fascination with ivory was characteristic of the African-Indian trade and it has continued to the present day. Basically this is because the African elephant tusks are softer and larger than the Indian and are therefore more easily worked and made into bigger pieces of jewelry. Ivory bangle bracelets are extremely important in India, because Hindus use them in their marriage ceremonies. They are given to the wife and she is the only person ever to wear them; when she dies these are cremated with her. Thus there is a continuous and expanding demand for ivory from Zanj for Indian brides.

One of the major trade items developed over the centuries was iron. The beginnings of the Iron Age in Zanj stretch back more than a thousand years, as revealed in the dig at Kalambo Falls below Lake Tanganyika. Here, the evidence shows, iron-working was under way in Christ's time. Stone Age settlements stretching back thirty-six thousand years were also found. But the development of iron mining, smelting, and tool-making changed the Zanj culture and gave its ports a commodity that was in great demand. By Al Mas'udi's time trade in iron mined in Zanj was just beginning.

By the time of Al Edrisi, who wrote a description of Africa for a Sicilian king two hundred years later, new and prosperous cities had sprung up, owing their very existence to the iron trade. One such was Malindi, which did not even exist in Al Mas'udi's time. Al Edrisi reports to his king that "there are a great number of iron mines in the mountains of Sofala. The people of the Zanedj Islands [thought to be the Maldive Islands off the Indian coast] and other neighboring islands come here for iron which they carry to the continent and islands of India, where they sell it at a good price, for it is a material of great trade and consumption in India. . . . "

Large profits from this trade were made by the people of Malindi and Mombasa, says Al Edrisi. The Indians prized African iron, he reports, because it was superior to the iron of their own land—it was plentiful, easily worked and of high quality. The iron was mined in Africa, forged into weapons in India and finished into world-famous swords in Damascus—weapons discovered by the Crusaders to be superior to their European blades.

This flourishing trade caused the growth of coastal settlements and the development of cosmopolitan communities. One researcher has identified sixty-three pre-European towns along the Tanzania coast alone, and expects to date them back as early as the second century B.C. Among the better-known trading centers along the Zanj were Mombasa, Malindi, Kilwa, Sofala and Zanzibar. One Moslem traveler visited the African coast in 1331 and described it this way:

We arrived at Mombasa, a large island two days' travel from the land of the Swahili. On the island, bananas, lemons and oranges grow. The people also eat a fruit they call *jammun* which looks like an olive but has a very sweet taste. Mombasa's natives do not farm, but import grain from the mainland, but the mainstays of their diet are bananas and fish. They are devout Moslems of the Shafi'i rite, and are chaste and virtuous.

In Mombasa the Mosques are built sturdily of wood. Near the door of each mosque are wells a foot-and-a-half to three feet deep. From these they draw water with a wooden bucket attached to the end of a thin stick about a yard long. The earth around the mosque and the well is stamped flat . . . .

After a night on Mombasa we set sail for Kilwa, the principal town on the coast. Most of Kilwa's inhabitants are Zanj of very black complexion. Their faces are decorated with scars for beauty. Sofala is fifteen days' march from Kilwa and from that city to Youfi, in the country of the Limiin, is an additional month's march. Youfi is a center for gold dust, which is then brought to Sofala for trading.

Kilwa is one of the most beautiful and well-built towns in

the world. All of it is elegantly constructed. The roofs of the buildings are made of mangrove poles. There is much rain. Kilwa's people are devoted and pious Moslems of the Shafi'i rite and are carrying on holy war [*jihad*] against the pagan people of Zanj.[23]

The coastal trade was complex and tightly supervised before the Portuguese smashed it by taking the trading towns one by one. An idea of the way the trade was conducted and the riches it gave the ruler of Kilwa is available from another Portuguese report. Before the Europeans sacked and slaughtered their way to dominance of Kilwa, this is the way the business was run:

Any merchant who wished to enter the city paid for every five hundred pieces of cloth, no matter what the quality, one gold *mitqal* as entrance duty. After this, the king took two-thirds of all the merchandise, leaving the trader one-third. From this—which was not to be taken from the city—a revaluation was made and the merchant was assessed an additional thirty *mitqals* for every one thousand *mitqals* of value. Then the trader could leave with his goods for Sofala. But, upon arriving there, he had to pay an additional duty amounting to one piece of cloth for every seven he brought with him. And everyone returning from Sofala was obliged to stop at Kilwa. There he had to pay the king fifty *mitqals* of gold for every thousand gold *mitqals* he carried with him. Having done this, he could stop at Mombasa without further payment. However, if he skipped Kilwa he was expected to stop at Mombasa. If he did not have with him a clearance proving that he had paid at Kilwa, the authorities would confiscate fifty *mitqals* of every thousand and return this levy to the king of Kilwa.[24]

With tariffs such as these, it was no wonder that the king of Kilwa was wealthy; the wonder is that the merchants were able to make any profit at all. Such traffic in goods and exchange made it necessary to issue coins for trade. Kilwa did so from the thirteenth century on, minting in copper, with no dates on the coins.

The Swahili people referred to are the settlers, traders, merchants and townspeople of these coastal settlements. They are predominantly blacks, with a mixture of Semitic blood from the Arab voyagers who came to the coast back in the time of Sheba and Solomon and all times thereafter. In this area there developed a language and a culture. The name given it by the Arabs was *Swahili:* "of the coast." Both the language and culture are, as one authority emphasizes, "not an Africanized Arab product but an Arabized African product: Its basis and most of its elements are African—Bantu-speaking African—but with a strong Arab infusion. . . . "[25] As early as 1150, and probably much earlier, the poets and troubadors of this Swahili culture were writing *Mashairi*, their lyric songs, and *tendi*, epic poems. They continue to write them even today and have consistently recorded them in Swahili, using an Arabic script for their purpose. There is a school of Swahili poets north of Mombasa and they have created a national literature.

For three hundred years Kilwa was the queen of the Swahili city-states. It was located off the coast of Tanzania on a small island. Wealthy and powerful, Kilwa's traders controlled the gold flow from Zanj and were the central depot for overseas merchandise coming into a vast region. There are contemporary chronicles of Kilwa and also observations by travelers which give us a reasonably accurate picture of the luxurious affluence of this city.

The Flourishing Coastal Trade

One of the most illuminating reports on the Swahili places of Zanj was written by a Portuguese trader in 1518. At Sofala, he tells us, traders came in small vessels called *zambucos* from the kingdoms of Kilwa, Mombasa and Malindi, bringing much cotton cloth in bright colors and vivid patterns. All of these came from north India in great ships. For these wares the "Moors" from Malindi and Mombasa paid in gold at such a price that the merchants "departed well pleased."

The merchants of Sofala sold these goods to the heathen of the kingdom of Benametapa (Monomotapa), who brought gold and exchanged it without weighing it for the cloth. These traders also collected great quantities of ivory which they found near Sofala. They sold this in northwest India at five or six *cruzados* per hundredweight. They also sold some ambergris, which was brought to them by ocean traders and it was apparently exceedingly good.

Most of these Moors were black, the report says, but some of them were tawny; some of them spoke Arabic but most used Swahili. They clothed themselves from the waist down with cotton and silk cloths, and over their shoulders wore capes and turbans on their heads. Some of them wore small caps dyed in checked patterns and woolen clothes in many tints; also expensive Angora or camel-hair satins and silks. They ate millet, rice, meat and fish. Near Sofala were many huge wild elephants, lions, deer and other wild beasts. It was a land of plains and hills with many streams of sweet water.

The Portuguese tells us that in Sofala they made white cloth but did not know how to dye it. They took the Indian cloth and unraveled it and used the thread with their own white goods to make colored cloth which they sold for gold.

Journeying from Sofala forty leagues more or less toward Mozambique, this report continued, there was a very great river which they called Cuama (Zambezi), which led into the interior kingdom of the Benametapa more than a hundred and seventy leagues. In the mouth of the river was a town whose king was called Mangalo. Another river went to a town called Angoya, and there the Moors used goats to carry cloth and other merchandise and to bring gold and ivory to Angoya. This town was 140 leagues further along the coast. It was a great trading center also and had many merchants who dealt in gold, ivory, silk and cotton cloth and Indian beads. The Moors of Sofala, Mombasa, Malindi and Kilwa carried there merchandise in very small boats concealed from the Portuguese ships and in this way transported great quantities of provender, millet, rice and meat.

Along the coast from Mozambique was the island of Kilwa. It was a Moorish town with houses of stone and mortar, with windows after the Portuguese fashion. It had well-arranged streets, and the houses had flat roofs. Their doors were of carved wood, well-crafted. Around the city were streams, orchards and fruit gardens with many streams of good water. It had a Moorish king and they traded with Sofala for gold which they, in turn, traded with merchants from all over *Arabia Felix*, the Indian Ocean seacoast villages and towns.

Before the king of Portugal sent out his expedition to discover India, the Moors of Sofala, Cuama, Angoya and Mozambique were all subject to the king of Kilwa, who was the mightiest of them. Kilwa was rich, as no ships passed toward Sofala without first coming to this island. Of the Moors there were "some fair and some black." They dressed beautifully in rich garments of gold, silk and cotton. Also, they wore gold and silver chains and bracelets on their legs and arms, and jeweled earrings in their ears. These Moors spoke Arabic and followed the creed of the Koran.

Because Kilwa's king was so "arrogant" as to refuse to obey the Portuguese king, the town was taken by force. Many prisoners were captured and the king fled from the island.

Further on was Mombasa, the report went on. It was a handsome place, with lofty stone and mortar buildings, well aligned in streets after the fashion of Kilwa. Here also the wood construction was excellently done. Mombasa had its own king, a Moor, and was a land where food was plentiful. They had fine sheep with "round tails," cows and other cattle in great plenty, and exceedingly fat fowl. There was much millet, rice, sweet and bitter oranges, lemons, pomegranates, Indian figs, sundry vegetables and sweet water. The men were seldom at peace with the mainland, though they traded with them for honey, wax and ivory.

The king of Mombasa also refused to obey the commands of the king of Portugal and because of this "arrogance" the Portuguese also took this island by force. The king fled and the invaders slew many of his people and took hundreds of captives. But the conquerors burned the city, looted and plundered it. Great booty in gold and silver was taken, bangles, bracelets, earrings and gold beads—plus a great store of copper and heaps of other rich goods—and the town was left in ruins.[26]

Evidently the situation at Malindi was quite different. Perhaps these folk, seeing the futility of opposing the superior strength and ferocity of the Portuguese, decided to cooperate rather than fight.

Malindi was on the mainland along the coast. It had many stone and mortar houses several stories high with windows and flat roofs after the Portuguese fashion. Its streets were well laid out. It also had traders who dealt in cloth, gold, ivory and other goods, both with the Moors and the heathen of the great kingdom of Cambay (India). To Malindi came every year many ships with gold, ivory and wax. In this traffic the Cambay merchants made great profits. Malindi also had plenty of food— rice, millet and wheat imported from Cambay, plus many kinds of fruit from the local orchards and gardens. Also plentiful were the round-tailed sheep, cows, hens and fowl. The Portuguese were welcome in Malindi and there their ships put in for supplies.[27]

Perhaps it is unnecessary to point out that the attitude of the Portuguese toward the people and the way of life they observed in these coastal city-states was not one of contempt for an "inferior" people, but admiration and awe of the towns, the dress of the people, the goods being exchanged, the foodstuffs available and the mouth-watering worth of the trade. The point is that the standard of living on the coast was on a par with or superior to what the Europeans were familiar with back home.

Evidence of wealth and a highly-developed society did not save these cities, however. On the contrary, they seemed to inspire the merciless rapacity of the Portuguese. The fate of Kilwa, like that of many of the flourishing African coastal cities was sealed by the Europeans. Here is the report on d'Almeida's expedition which took Kilwa in 1505. The description is attributed to Hans Mayr, a German on the Grand-Captain's flagship, *San Rafael:*

In Kilwa there are many strong houses several stories high. They are built of stone and mortar and plastered with various designs. As soon as the town had been taken without opposition, the

Vicar-General and some of the Franciscan fathers came ashore
carrying two crosses in procession and singing the *Te Deum*.
They went to the palace, and there the cross was put down
and the Grand-Captain prayed. Then everyone started to
plunder the town of all its merchandise and provisions.
[d'Almeida put the city to the torch after the looting was
ended, two days later. The greater part of the city was
destroyed.][28]

There is an epitaph for the great days of Kilwa, a benediction
that applies to the other city-states and their greatness, crushed
by the Portuguese. This is a poem in the Swahili literary tradition, written more than 150 years ago:

> *How many rich men have you seen*
> *who shone like the sun*
> *who had control of the weapons of war*
> *and stored up silver and gold?*
>
> *All the world paid them homage*
> *and their world was straight ahead of them*
> *they walked with heads held disdainfully*
> *and eyes closed in scorn.*
>
> *Swinging their arms and arching their necks*
> *while behind and in front crowds accompanied them*
> *everywhere they lived there were seats of honor*
> *and troops of soldiers attended them.*
>
> *Their lighted houses were aglow*
> *with lamps of crystal and brass*
> *the nights were as the day*
> *beauty and honor surrounded them.*

They decorated [their houses] with choice porcelain
and every goblet was engraved
and in the midst they put crystal pitchers
amongst the decorations that glittered . . .

Now they lie in a town on finger's span
with no fine curtains nor cushions
and their bodies are destroyed
for the constraint of the grave has come upon them . . .

Their lighted mansions are uninhabited
the young of bats cling up above
you hear no whisperings nor shoutings
spiders crawl over the beds.

The wall-niches for porcelain in the houses
are now the resting-place for nestlings;
owls hoot within the house . . .[29]

THE INLAND STORY

While the coastal cities basked in the attention of eager merchants from many lands for the centuries until their destruction at the hands of the Portuguese, there were inland metropolises of considerable size which exploration and history passed by. Gradually, but all too slowly, some of these are being discovered and investigated.

▷ *Engaruka* Engaruka is one of these. It first came to the attention of the outside modern world in 1935 when a district officer in Tanganyika told of a city in ruins located more than three hundred miles from the coast on the Kenya-Tanganyika border. An anthropologist specializing in African peoples went to have a look. It was not an easy hike: The ruins were located on a cliff bordering the Rift Valley near Lake Natron. Climbing the escarpment was difficult and hazardous—the base of the cliff was rock, stone and loose pebbles that shifted and slid underfoot and were accented by thornbushes.

The anthropologist expected little from his trip, inasmuch as the area was peppered with stone huts and terraces that had been reported by a German specialist as far back as 1913. But when he managed to reach the ruins of Engaruka, the scientist walked into something considerably different. It was a city that had, he estimated, "sixty-three hundred houses in the main city of the scree slopes . . . and . . . about five hundred houses in the valley ruins, where burials are far commoner than houses." In this nearly inaccessible place a city of some thirty thousand to forty thousand souls had lived, he announced, with the footnote, "I think this may be an underestimate."[30]

Engaruka was not a haphazard cluster of dwellings. The houses rested on stone walls; there were terraces for paths and huts; in the valley there were intricate stone constructions that must have been some irrigation-agricultural complex. There were no skeletons, no inscriptions or records. Yet from the available evidence it seemed that the city was less than three hundred years old. Others scientists estimated that to feed this population would have required harvests from eight thousand acres of grain. And that was that—for the moment.

Another scientist has suggested that the villages of the Sonjo, not many miles away, are similar in construction. Did these people simply move out of Engaruka for unknown reasons, generations ago? Why was the city deserted? The direct evidence is not yet available. However, invasions from the north became frequent in East Africa beginning with the fourteenth century.

One specialist theorizes that there was an advanced civilization called the Azanian, flourishing in the Horn of Africa (modern-day Somalia) in the first seven hundred years A.D. But then, he believes, this culture, which had borrowed freely from Nubia, the Axumites, Sabaens and Middle Egypt, was smashed by Moslem invasions. The Azanians fled southward before the thrust of the Islamic Arabs and finally settled beyond their range in Kenya and southward, perhaps in the fourteenth and fifteenth centuries.

They took with them their skills in metalworking, construction and agriculture. When overwhelmed by the invaders, the artisans, smiths, farmers, masons, roadbuilders, terracing and irrigation specialists became the serfs of the conquerors and as growth was stifled, decline set in.

Parallel with this, the Portuguese disrupted the coastal trade and dried up the demand for products from the hinterland, giving the "Azanian civilization" another body blow. Only the groups in the south were able to carry on the Iron Age, as we have noted at Zimbabwe, Mapungubwe and at such sites as Khami, Dhlo-Dhlo, Penhalonga, Inyanga and Van Niekerk. All of these are ruins of sizable settlements in an arc running from present-day Bulawayo in Southern Rhodesia, eastward and north in the mountains between that country and Mozambique.

Incomplete as the information about Engaruka is, it is far more than we have about most of the inland places. Our knowledge of these interior cities and nations is growing, but really requires a systematic, coordinated effort to bring to light the facts about peoples who flourished in the past but are today gone and forgotten. Here is a quick summary of what we know about a few of these peoples:

▷ *Khami*   Khami is a complex of forts and stone settlements, probably dating back to about 1600. From the ruins it appears that the people had a rough-and-ready culture, lacking the luxuries and art and artifacts of a highly-developed civilization.

One major system of stone buildings is some thirteen miles west of Bulawayo in Southern Rhodesia. Only a few of the people lived on the stone-walled platforms; far more lived in huts on the hillsides. Judging from the implements found, the way of life in the two types of dwellings was very similar. In the elaborate ruins, imported china, ceremonial pottery, and gold ornaments have been found in the places on the upper hill. None of these items have come to light in the other huts. The theory developed from these facts is that the ruins on the hill were the quarters of the ruling chief, his court and family members. The common folk probably lived outside the walls.

Though the people of Khami remain a mystery, we do know a bit about the fate of the town. In 1834 a chieftain called Zwangendaba crossed the Limpopo River with an army of marauding troops and destroyed Khami, leaving its stone dwellings and walls to crumble, its fields to go wild and its terraces to run dry.

▷ *Penhalonga and Niekerk* Hillside terracing of a very sophisticated type was used by these peoples of the southeastern Rhodesian highlands. The ruins of Penhalonga are thought to have been inhabited from 900 to 1700 A.D. and perhaps even earlier. The combined area of Penhalonga, Niekerk and Inyanga includes nearly three thousand square miles, ranging from hillside terraces to forts, houses, pits and storage buildings built on steep cliffsides.

All of the circular stone, rock-lined buildings seem almost identical in age and design. One theory is that these people brought their building styles from some other place and the possibility of the Kenya highlands, with its ruins of similar hut circles, has been suggested.

We know little about the fate of the Penhalonga people except that Tschangana bands from Mozambique overwhelmed the forts.

The Niekerk settlements were on the hillsides rising from the coastal plain, climbing all the way to the great central plateau in Rhodesia. Their forts and arrangement of their huts indicate that their settlements were defensive complexes for self-protection. The Portuguese were in contact with these people and located "factories" (primarily trading stations) among them.

One observer in 1905 estimated that Niekerk had some fifty square miles of terracing that closely resembled the terraces in Ethiopia and the Sudan. It was almost impossible to walk a dozen paces, he said, without stumbling on a wall, a building or some stonework. These people were master engineers and their dams changed the courses of mountain streams, bringing water to their hillside terraces. These terraces and dams were constructed without cement, using natural stones and including many boulders weighing up to a ton. One expert estimated that as much work had gone into these terraces as into the pyramids of Egypt! Another admired their water conduits which ran for several miles, commenting that the gradients were superior to the work of modern (c. 1905) engineers.[31]

It is noteworthy that under the dwellings of Niekerk are traces of two earlier cultures that date back to about 500 A.D. The latest, or "third-stage" group, is believed to have flourished between 1400–1750.

▷ *Bigo* The largest system of fortifications in all of Africa—perhaps in the whole world—is at a site called Bigo in western Uganda. Discovered only in 1909, these forts presumably flourished about 1350–1500 A.D., the time that ancient Zimbabwe was at its height.

There is evidence of a great deal of mining and smelting of metal ore by the ruling Bachwezi tribe. And, like Mapung-ubwe, Bigo is located near a river ford; like Zimbabwe it is egg-shape in outline and some beads and pots found at Bigo are reminiscent of Zimbabwe. The construction, however, was fun-damentally different: At Zimbabwe the material was stone; at Bigo it was packed earth and trenches, extending over many acres to enclose royal herds of cattle as well as to protect against intruders. From this center the Bachwezi ruled a vast area—all of southern Uganda—around 1400 A.D.

From this sampling, limited though it is, it should be obvious that there are many exciting locations where black African people have demonstrated extraordinary skills in build-ing and organizing; in agriculture, engineering, fortification, commerce, art and the manifold manifestations of civilized men. Limitations of space do not permit us to consider the many other cultures equally deserving of attention and examination. It is to be hoped that the reader will be stimulated to do this on his own, and it is suggested that the bibliography and chapter notes be used as references for further reading and research.

NOTES

1. Bernard E. B. Fagg, "A Life-Sized Terracotta Head from Nok" in *Man 95*, 1956. (He excavated in Nok in 1956 and was responsible for carbon-dating the sculpture.)
2. ———"Archeological Field Work Since 1953," Conference on African History, II, London University.
3. John E. Flint, *Nigeria and Ghana*. (Englewood Cliffs, N.J.: Prentice-Hall, 1966),p. 39.
4. Frank Willett, "Ife and its Archeology," *Journal of African History*, 2, 1960.

5. Muhammad Bello, *Infaq al-Maysar;* trans. by E. J. Arnett in *The Rise of the Sakoto Fulani*, (Kano, 1929.)
6. Samuel Johnson, *History of the Yorubas*, 1897.
7. Dr. S. O. Biobaku, lectures, Lagos, 1955, quoted in Basil Davidson, *Lost Cities of Africa*, (Boston: Atlantic, Little Brown, 1959).
8. Chief Jacob U. Egharevba, *Short History of Benin*, 1953.
9. Ruy de Pina, Chronicle written for King John of Portugal, c. 1486.
10. Richard Eden.
11. Roland Oliver and J. D. Fage, *A Short History of Africa*, (Baltimore: Penguin Books, 1966), p. 106.
12. O. Equiano, *The Interesting Narrative of the Life of Olaudah Equiano or Gustavus Vassa the African*, 1793.
13. *Ibid.*
14. J. D. Fage, *An Introduction to the History of West Africa*, Cambridge, 1962.
15. R. H. Bacon, *Benin, the City of Blood*, 1897.
16. D. P. Abraham, "Maramuca: History of Mwanamutapa Empire," *Journal of African History*, 1961, #2.
17. Diego de Alcancova, 1506.
18. Joao Dos Santos, a Portuguese Dominican priest.
19. *Ibid.*
20. C. J. van Riet Lowe, "Mapungubwe," *Antiquity*, Sept. 1936.
21. Ibn Hordadbeh, quoted in Basil Davidson, *Lost Cities of Africa*, (Boston: Atlantic, Little, Brown, 1959).
22. Al Mas'udi (Abdul Hassan ibn Hussein ibn Ali), trans by Aloys Sprenger, in *Meadows of Gold and Mines of Gems*, (London: Oriental Translation Fund, 1841).
23. Ibn Battuta, *Travels in Asia and Africa, 1325-1354*. (Translated by H.A.R. Gibb, 1929).
24. Alcanova. *op. cit.*
25. Davidson, *op cit.*, p. 178.
26. Duarte Barbosa, *The Book of Duarte Barbosa*, Hakluyt Society, 1918.
27. *Ibid.*
28. Hans Mayr, quoted in Basil Davidson, *A History of East and Central Africa*, (Garden City: Doubleday Anchor, 1969).
29. Abdulla ben Nasir, "Utendi wa Inkishafi," in *Swahili Poetry*, (translated by Harries, Lyndon, Oxford, 1962).
30. L.S.B.Leakey, "Preliminary Report on the Engaruka Ruins," *Tanganyika Notes and Records*, 1936.
31. D.R. MacIver, *Medieval Rhodesia*. 1906.

When vision was short
And knowledge scant,
Men called me Dark Africa

Dark Africa?
I, who raised the regal pyramids
and held the fortunes of Conquering Caesars
In my tempting grasp.

Dark Africa?
Who nursed the doubtful child
Of civilization
On the wand'ring banks
of the life-giving Nile,
And gave to the teeming nations
Of the West a Grecian gift.

MY AFRICA[1]
by Michael Dei-Anang

◁▷ ◁▷ ◁▷ ◁▷ ◁▷ ◁▷ ◁▷ ◁▷ ◁▷ ◁▷ ◁▷ ◁▷

NORTH AFRICA

◁▷ ◁▷ ◁▷ ◁▷ ◁▷ ◁▷ ◁▷ ◁▷ ◁▷ ◁▷ ◁▷ ◁▷

X

LITERALLY AND GEOGRAPHICALLY, NORTH
Africa is that divot of green that rests on the northernmost
"top" of the continent. It is that strip along the Mediterranean
shore from the mouth of Suez on the east, stretching to the horn
on the west where Ceuta and Tangier rise opposite Gibraltar to
form the "Pillars of Hercules." This strip extends past Tangier,
however, down the Atlantic coast to the region about Ifni,
opposite the Canary Islands. In depth, reaching inland, this

area is bounded by the Sahara and varies from a few miles to scores of miles and encompasses the Atlas Mountains in Morocco, continues east across Algeria, Tunisia and the northernmost coast of Libya and Egypt.

In point of fact, North Africa played a primary role in the continent's "modern" history—that is, after the decline of ancient Egypt. To this strand the Minoans sent their ships as did the Greeks of Homer's time. About 600 B.C. the Greeks established the city of Cyrene on the Libyan coast.

Figure 64

Legend tells of Queen Dido, fleeing from Asia Minor in 822 B.C., who led her Phoenician sailors to the site of Carthage where they struggled to start a settlement on the alien shore. Then, as Virgil relates in the *Aeneïd*, the last remnants of Troy's survivors, led by Prince Aeneas, found their way to the place. The widowed Queen Dido welcomed the refugees and fell in love with their leader. When Aeneas moved on to Italy after a sojourn at Carthage, the lovesick queen threw herself in despair into a funeral pyre.

The Phoenicians were vastly energetic sailors and merchants whose trading posts brought them great wealth from the eighth century B.C. on, and made Carthage mighty. However, the records of the city were destroyed, and all we have are the records of the Greeks and Romans with whom they traded and battled, so our knowledge of their culture is incomplete at best. We know that the Carthaginians were notorious for human sacrifices in their worship of the god Baal which they brought with them from the Lebanon shore. The government was in the hands of a group of wealthy merchants and the army was recruited from the Berbers, the tribes who lived in the area. Carthage grew rich and powerful and reached out, controlling the North African coast and Spain, founding new colonies, even

on Corsica, Sardinia and Sicily, until the fateful conflict with
Rome. It is indicative of our lack of knowledge about Carthage   *Figure 63*
that of all her thousands of citizens the names of only a handful
are known today—Hannibal and Hamilcar Barca being the
most famous.

A Province of Rome

In 146 B.C., Scipio Africanus the Younger defeated Carthage,
and Rome vented her wrath on the city. Every Carthaginian
was enslaved and the city was systematically destroyed, piece   *Figure 65*
by piece and, according to legend, its fields were sown with
salt to prevent its rebirth.

 The Romans later took Cyrene and then Egypt. North
Africa was a rich province of Rome, indeed the "granary" of
the Empire, for from this land above the Sahara came the
wheat that fed and oil that lighted the capital. Roman engineers,
using the native Berber population as serfs, pushed back the
desert with roads, irrigation projects, reservoirs, dams and aque-
ducts, turning marginal land into rich agricultural plains. The
Romans also held Morocco, even along the Atlantic shore as far
south as modern Rabat, and organized tuna fishing west of the
Straits of Gibraltar.

 Order was maintained by the Third Augustan Legion,
consisting of about five thousand soldiers. Originally they were
all Europeans, but because there was no racial discrimination,
the Legion became almost totally African in two or three generations. Soldiers married African women and their sons became
Legionnaries with Roman citizenship, retirement rights and
small grants of land.

 Even before Roman times, North Africa had been dotted

with trading centers. The Romans vastly expanded this, shipping wood (fuel for those indispensable Roman baths), ivory, fruit, marble and other building stone, horses and wild animals for the gladiators and circuses, in addition to the basic commodities: wheat, oil and wine. They greedily pursued the elephant for his ivory until he was extinct in North Africa. Their insatiable lust for the bloody circuses extinguished above the Sahara the lions, hyenas, bears, ostriches, antelopes and almost all the leopards and boars (a pitiful few of these latter survive today).

The Romans made North Africa a place of unprecedented prosperity—for the rulers. The laborers were the poor native

Figure 66   Berbers who did the work and lived outside the cities and towns in their hovels—uneducated, landless, dispossessed and disenfranchised. Some of them who managed by birth or marriage to work their way into the ruling class, however, shared in the benefits of this wealthy society. One of these was Septimius Severus, born at Leptis Magna in Tripolitania in 146 A.D.

A soldier in the Roman Legion, Severus had been well educated, became a civil magistrate and military commander, in which capacity he went to Rome. In 193 A.D., through army politicking, he became Emperor. Africa suddenly was the focus of attention for Rome, and the Emperor showered buildings and improvements on his boyhood homeland. He even promoted the breeding of camels, understanding their importance in freight, transportation and military strategy. Severus also pushed the area of Roman land-holding to its ultimate, driving the Berbers into the desert where they, in turn, drove away the black natives of the oases, pushing them into the Western Sudan toward the Niger River. The Berbers, then set about plaguing the Roman outposts and settlements, raiding and pillaging beyond the ability of the Legionnaires to subdue them.

There were other famous Africans in Roman times. Tertullian, a contemporary of Septimius Severus, was a brilliant writer, an upper-class pagan Roman who became a Christian and campaigned against the moral decadence of the times. There were the Christians St. Perpetua, a slave, and St. Felicitas, a noble lady of (resurrected) Roman Carthage and, about 258 A.D., St. Cyprian, bishop of Carthage. There was no shortage of Christian martyrs in North Africa. They were anonymous, with few exceptions, and numerous.

Perhaps the most famous African of Roman times was the "architect of the Catholic church," St. Augustine. Born into a well-to-do provincial upper-class family, he led the easy, self-indulgent life of his fellows, to the dismay of his devoutly Christian mother. In his *Confessions* he describes this life, his education and his conversion in Milan. Sent back to Africa, he was made bishop of Hippo, an important See in his home district.

By the beginning of the fifth century Rome was crumbling at home and abroad. The Berber tribesmen raided and looted even the cities. And in 364 A.D. they were able to attack the great cities of Tripoli unchecked.

It was another force which struck in 429—the Vandal invasion under Genseric. Driven out of Spain, the Vandals crossed at the Straits of Gibraltar with an estimated fifteen thousand fighting men and a total strength of some eighty thousand. Eastward along the coast they went, consuming all in their path, leaving a trail of murder, rape, looting and ashes. They were all but unopposed, and their conquest of Roman Africa was officially recognized by Rome in 435. Genseric's strong fleet and audacity carried him to Italy itself twenty years later, when he led an expedition that sacked the capital city. He returned to Africa burdened with priceless booty, including the sacred vessels from Solomon's Temple at Jerusalem.

The Vandals took over the Roman structure in North Africa and, as Arians, persecuted the Roman Catholics. Thus they turned against them the most vital intellectual and educated elements of the society, the very elements that might have provided leadership to help them. As it was, the Vandals enjoyed the luxuries and the vices of the Roman cities, gradually declined in militancy and ability (though they continued to raid and plunder by sea) and were defeated by Emperor Justinian's Byzantine armies, sent from Constantinople in 533 A.D. The Vandal kingdom collapsed and all of Roman North Africa now became a province of Byzantium. Actually, it was little more than a military occupation. Meanwhile the marauding Berber tribesmen had become so bold, skillful and successful that they kept the Byzantine forces continually in the field. Under rapacious Byzantine generals and military administrators, the peasants were ground under still more.

Moslem North Africa

It was at this time that the great Prophet Mohammed was born in Arabia—the year was 571. In 640, eight years after his death, a Moslem army crossed Suez and defeated the Byzantines in Egypt. In the next sixty years Islam conquered all of North Africa, in a victory of incalculable importance. During this span of two generations the North changed its religion, its language, its culture and its laws. Many tenets of Islam have broad appeal: Polygamy is one; egalitarianism is another of great strength. All Moslems are equal in the eyes of God; slavery or freedom, wealth or poverty are merely accidents, thus all Moslems are "brothers" and there is no aristocracy. "Unbelievers" are fair game for Moslems, since tolerance is theoretically impossible, therefore the Sons of the Prophet are encouraged to band together to war against the infidels and, if the loot is at hand, help themselves. What could have been more appealing to the oppressed peasants of North Africa? The peasants, the Berber tribes, the city dwellers and even the remaining clergy converted to Islam.

The impact of Islam on Ifriqiya, as the Arabs called Africa, was, as we have noted, profound. One of the first acts of the conquerors was to dispatch an expedition to Nubia in 651. The Moslems quickly learned the deadliness of the Nubian archers and gladly entered a treaty that insured Nubia its independence. The agreement called for freedom of religion and movement by Arab traders and for the Moslems to supply needed steeds, fabrics and foods. It also required Nubia to send 360 slaves a year to the Moslem ruler of Egypt.

Over a period of 150 years the Moslem "empire" in North Africa broke down into factions which became independent of the central rule of the Abbasid dynasty in far away Baghdad. Egypt broke away, so did Tunisia and Morocco. And within even Tunisia, Tripoli and Morocco, Berber groups formed small independent communities of their own—at Sijilmasa, the historic caravan terminus, for one, and the Idrisid state which established its capital at Fez, for another.

It should be noted that as time went on the Moslems learned from and adopted the advantages of the Mediterranean civilization that they had conquered, modifying and adding to their own Arabian culture. Thus the great centers of learning that grew at Rabat, Tlemcen, Marrakech, Cordoba, Granada, Fez, etc., had an important effect in changing and improving the way of life and broadening the cultural outreach of the

Arabs and Berbers, giving them a glorious Golden Age in which their arts, science, government and philosophy flourished in contrast with the Dark Ages in Europe.

Also, it should be remembered that this condition changed drastically in 1061. Then the ruling Moslems in Egypt, troubled by the independent kingdoms of the Mahgreb (the Arab "west," referring to North Africa beyond Egypt) sent against them the pesky Bedouin tribes who had bedevilled them in Egypt. These were the Beni Halil and the Beni Soleim: illiterate, primitive desert tribesmen, carrying their few belongings and moving as a mass of families migrating into a "promised land." They swept across North Africa like "a swarm of locusts destroying all in their path," as one great Moslem historian put it. Among the things destroyed were the small states and petty kingdoms whose people fled to desert or mountain strongholds or were submerged by the Bedouin tribes.

Reconnoitering parties of Arabs had been sent into the lands of the blacks west of the Sahara and there had been some contacts even down into the Sudan, to Ghana and Kanem. But the numbers of Arabs were few and their attention was directed not so much south as north to Spain and the sea and east to the center of the Moslem world.

Now, as the empire of Ghana expanded on the south and the primitive Bedouins pushed from the north, the Berber and Tuaregs were squeezed in the middle. Thus they were ripe for leadership and at this critical time a leader emerged. With the blind zeal of the puritanical reformer, a Moslem divine named Ibn Yasin, originally from Sijilmasa, led a *jihad* of the dispossessed and discontented that swept over the western Moslem lands. Called the Almoravids (after the Moslem monastery where Ibn Yasin had trained his followers), they whirled out of the desert. One group thrust south against Ghana. The larger body drove north, overrunning Morocco and the Mahgreb. A call for help from the Moslems in Spain who were being hard-pressed by Christian Europeans brought a quick response and the Almoravids crossed the Straits and took over, completing their Iberian "reconquista" in 1103.

A century and a half later another group of Moslem reformers, calling themselves the Almohades (monotheists), repeated the process. Over the next 250 years central control deteriorated under the pressure of the various ethnic and dynastic groups until there were ultimately three general divisions in the North African Mahgreb—Morocco on the west, Algeria in the middle and Tunisia on the east.

THE ECONOMIC BACKGROUND

The prosperity of these northern coastal areas was dependent on agriculture, but even more on trade with Europe north beyond the Mediterranean Sea and with the Sudan, south beyond the Saharan sand sea. The backbone of the cross-Sahara trade was gold and ivory coming north from the Sudan and salt going south. True, there were many other commodities involved: European and Asian goods, from cooking pots to swords, copper and fabrics, luxury items, jewelry and trinkets. From the south came civet, kola nuts, hides, ivory and lesser items. Slaves were traded in both directions from the very earliest times, though they were in greater demand in the north than in the south.

To serve this trade, little markets first were established at convenient points many centuries ago. As the traffic on these desert routes increased, the markets grew into villages and towns with the growing specialization that urban life promotes. They had craftsmen who made shoes, clothing and equipment for the caravans. They had scribes and accountants, tax men and governors, police and other officials. Inns and entertainment were geared to the travelers and the trade. Some of these villages developed into cities and became famous and powerful: Timbuktu, Jenne, Gao. Others had transient power or glory and disappeared into the sands when the ships of Europe replaced the ships of the desert in the trade: Audaghost and Sijilmasa, Kumbi Saleh and Tekrur.

The routes across the desert were not many. On the west, there was the path that led from Fez through Marrakech in the north, paralleled the African coast until it reached the Senegal River, then turned inland to the gold area about Walata, some five hundred miles from the Atlantic. A second route went from Fez south through Sijilmasa, jumped off into the desert and made "port" at the bleak salt center and oasis town of Taghaza, then continued south to the town of Walata and beyond to the Niger, following it east to Jenne, Timbuktu and Gao.

A third major route began at Tripoli and went almost due west to Ghadames and Tuat in the desert, then on southwest to Walata or Timbuktu. The fourth important road began at Cairo, followed the coast of the Mediterranean west to Tripoli and then on as just described, or cut west-southwest across the Libyan desert to the oasis towns of Murzuk and Ghat, then on to Gao. Another route of lesser importance was the salt traffic from the Lake Chad area both east to the Nile and west to the Niger. Another salt source and oasis of significance was Agades, in the southern Sahara, more than four hundred miles north of Lake Chad.

The hazards of the traffic across the desert were enormous: the natural afflictions of the sand, the blinding, searing sun, the heat—highest temperatures recorded on earth: 176° F—and chilling nights were bad enough. The additional complications often included sandstorms, disease and accidents which might cripple or kill, plus the always-present possibility of bandits. The taxes imposed at each stopping place were high and—when there was weak central control of the region—might be exacted by so many hands as to make the journey profitless. The profits of the successful traders, however, were enormous. They had to be, to warrant such risks.

The camel was the basic unit in the freight train. Each of these could carry three hundred to five hundred pounds, travel a minimum of three days without water, and step along at a rate of twenty-five miles a day. As the most important link in the trade chain, the camels deserved and received favored treatment. A great portion of the freight on each such journey consisted of food and water for the beasts.

The harrowing desert crossing has been described many times. Perhaps one of the best and earliest descriptions is that of the peripatetic Ibn Battuta who went along the western route from Sijilmasa and Taghaza to Walata in 1352, crossing "a desert haunted by demons." Here is a sample of his report:

... [At Taghaza, the salt mining center] we passed ten days of discomfort because the water there is bitter and the place is plagued with flies. And there ... water supplies are laid on ... for the crossing of the desert ... which is a ten nights' journey with no water on the way except on rare occasions.

We indeed had the good fortune to find water in plenty, in pools left by the rain. ... One day we found a pool of fresh

water between two rocky hills. We quenched our thirst at it
and washed our clothes.

At that time we used to go ahead of the caravan and when
we found a place suitable for pasturage we would graze our
beasts. We went on doing this until one of our party was lost
in the desert; after that I neither went ahead nor lagged
behind. We passed a caravan on the way and they told us
that some of their party had become separated from them.
We found one of them dead under a shrub, of the sort that
grows in the sand, with his clothes on and a whip in his
hand . . . .[2]

Two months after leaving Sijilmasa, Ibn Battuta arrived in
Walata, to his great relief, having endured the 140° heat and
20° chill, the parched throat and the gritty feeling from head to
foot, the primitive food and makeshift shelters and the alternate
walking and riding and above all the pervasive, gnawing uncer-
tainty about whether he would or would not survive.

The Sahara, after all, was as big as a continent, extending
thirty-two hundred miles east-west and fourteen hundred miles
north-south. Caravans of literally thousands of camels assembled
to make the crossing. There are reports of some caravans with
seventeen thousand camels! Some stretches of desert between
oases were often hundreds of miles. It sometimes happened that
the oasis the caravan depended upon for life itself had gone dry
or had been covered by a sandstorm. Frequently the bones—
both animal and human—of the last to arrive at the dry hole
greeted a thirsty caravan.

Profit was the spur and gold was the magnet that pulled
men across this ocean of sand at all costs. With their cheap
baubles, cloth and necessities such as salt and weapons, the
traders of the north braved the mirages and greater dangers of

the desert for the yellow metal. For until the discovery of the Americas, the Sudan was *the* source for the Western world's gold. Only with the wealth of the Americas did Europe's dependence on Sudanese gold supplies dwindle in importance. And this could happen only because in the fifteenth century the technology of shipbuilding and navigation leaped ahead. The voyages of Columbus, de Gama and the Portuguese, Dutch and French were spectacular examples of this. Thus North Africa—and the interior and Guinea coast—were hit by a technological revolution beyond their control: the impact of the new, large ocean vessels. With these advances the ships of the sea became more important to Europe than the ships of the desert. North Africa diminished in relative importance in European trade. There was a tremendous upsurge of interest and exploitation in the Western Hemisphere and in the direct contacts with West Africa via the caravels which easily circumvented Morocco and the North African lands. And, as the gold trade experienced competition from a new quarter, the Europeans turned to a new, even more lucrative trade: the bitter traffic in black slaves.

The effects on Africa were overwhelming.

NOTES

1. Michael Dei-Anang, *My Africa*, in *Poems from Black Africa*, Langston Hughes, (ed.), (Bloomington, Indiana: Indiana University Press, 1963), p. 74. Reprinted by permission of Indiana University Press.
2. Ibn Battuta, *Travels in Asia and Africa 1325–1354*, (trans. by H. A. R. Gibb), (New York: R. M. McBride & Co., 1929).

◁▷ ◁▷ ◁▷ ◁▷ ◁▷ ◁▷ ◁▷ ◁▷ ◁▷ ◁▷ ◁▷ ◁▷ ◁▷ ◁▷ ◁▷ ◁▷ ◁▷

APPENDIX: CHRONOLOGY

◁▷ ◁▷ ◁▷ ◁▷ ◁▷ ◁▷ ◁▷ ◁▷ ◁▷ ◁▷ ◁▷ ◁▷ ◁▷ ◁▷ ◁▷ ◁▷ ◁▷

DATE BC	EVENTS IN AFRICA	DATE BC	ASIA	EUROPE	DATE BC	AMERICAS
40,000,000	Numerous large apes in area of Egypt.					
25,000,000	Pro-Consul, ancestor of man; Lake Victoria.					
2,000,000	Early humans in East Africa.					
1,750,000	Pre-Zinjanthropus—homo habilis (vegetarian)—in Tanzania area.					
800,000	Australopithecus Africanus man (meat eater) in South Africa.	800,000	Java man.			
		400,000	Peking man.	Heidelberg man.		
5000	New Stone Age (Neolithic era) Some six hundred different languages of Africa begin to develop.					
4000	Stone and copper age: Settlement of the Nile Valley. Tribal settlements in Sahara area.					
3200	King Menes unites the kingdoms of the Delta and the Nile (Upper and Lower Egypt). I Dynasty. Egypt invades Nubia.	3200	Cities of Sumer established.			
		2870		First settlement at Troy.		
2700	King Zoser; Imhotep and Step Pyramid at Sakkara. III Dynasty.					
2600	Khufu (Cheops) and Great Pyramid at Giza. IV Dynasty.					
2500	Egypt sends expeditions to land of Punt and into Sahara area.	2500	Cities of Harappa and Mohenjo Daro in Indus Valley.			
2280	Old Kingdom ends; First Intermediate Period in Egypt.	2400		Minoan civilization develops; cities on Crete.		
2100	Middle Kingdom begins; Mentuhotep establishes XI Dynasty at Thebes. Egypt expands southward into Nubia.	2100	Ziggurat of Ur.			

2000 Babylon established.
1800 Phoenicians invent alphabet.

1760 Shang Dynasty in China.
1700 Code of Hammurabi.

1600 Hittites conquer Babylon; Kassites and Mitanni emerge.

Stonehenge in Britain.
Minoan culture at peak.
Greek city-states develop.

1500

Minoan culture ends abruptly.

1350 Mitanni conquered by Hittites.

Assyrian kingdom on the rise.

1300

Troy VII.
Mycenean (Greek) kingdom flowers.

Mycenean citadels destroyed.

Etruscans invade central Italy.
Trojan War.
Colonization in Mediterranean.
Time of Phoenician traders.
Dorians invade Greece.

1100 First cities established in South America.

900 Olmec cities built.

2000 Amenemhet I, founder of XII Dynasty.

1780 Second Intermediate Period; Egypt has fifty rulers in slightly over a century.
Civil war erupts.

1660 Asiatic invaders (Hyksos) conquer Lower and Middle Egypt.

1557 Ahmose I drives Hyksos out of Egypt; establishes XVIII Dynasty.
New Kingdom begins.

1511 Thutmose I reconquers Nubia; Egypt expands into Asia and Kush area.
Queen Hatshepsut sends expedition to Punt.
Sahara becomes desert.

1400 Amenophis III.
Queen Tiy.

1360 Amarna Period in Egypt; Akhnaten, the heretic Pharaoh.

1340 Pharaoh Tutankhamen.

1300 Time of Moses.
First horses in Africa.

1230 Exodus of Israelites from Egypt.

1200 Invasion by sea peoples. Hittite kingdom destroyed.

1150 Assyrians conquer Babylon.
1100 Chou Dynasty in China.

1000 David succeeds Saul as king of Israel.
King Solomon.

1000 Makeda of Axum (Queen of Sheba) visits Solomon.

950 Kush breaks away from Egypt.

900 Nok culture flowers.

850 Queen Dido, leading Phoenicians, establishes Carthage.

800 Etruscan civilization.
Homer.

DATE BC	EVENTS IN AFRICA	DATE BC	ASIA	EUROPE	DATE BC	AMERICAS
		753		Rome established.		
751	Kush, under King Kashta, conquers Upper Egypt, establishing XXV Dynasty. Piankhi conquers all of Egypt.					
		700	Sennacherib. Isaiah.			
690	Pharaoh Taharqa.					
650	Assyrians under Assurbanipal conquer Egypt. Capital of Kush moved to Meroe.					
600	Greeks establish colony at Cyrene.	600	Founding of Japan by legendary Emperor Jimmu.	Athens: Solon's constitution.		
		600	Persia becomes world power.			
		563	Gautama Buddha born. Croesus reigns as king of Lydia. Mesopotamia becomes a Persian province.			
		551	Confucius born.			
		550	Babylon rebuilt by Nebuchadnezzar. Israelites captive in Babylon.	Greek civilization flowers. Etruscan kingdom collapses.		
525	Persians, under Cambyses, conquer Egypt.	521	Darius I becomes king of Persia.	Persians invade Greece.		
500	Axum begins to develop.	486	Xerxes I becomes king of Persia.			
		480	Persian wars.	Battle of Thermopylae.		
		460		In Greece, the Age of Pericles.		
450	Herodotus visits Egypt and Kush. Earliest construction at Zimbabwe.	431		Peloponnesian War.	450	First pyramids.
		399		Socrates condemned to death.		
		356		Alexander the Great born.		
332	Alexander the Great conquers Egypt.	335		Alexander the Great conquers Greece.		
304	Ptolemy I establishes dynasty.	326	Alexander the Great conquers to the Indus Valley.		300	Mayan calendar invented.

290 Rome begins rise to power.

250 Asoka empire in India.

214 Great Wall of China built.

200 Han Dynasty in China.
    Rome expands into Middle East.
    Parthian Empire.

150 Cities of Zanj established.

146 Carthage conquered and razed by Rome.

146 Rome conquers and subjugates Greece.

130 Teotihuacan reigns.
    Tiahuanaco culture begins.

100 Julius Caesar born.

46 Cleopatra becomes mistress to Augustus Caesar.

44 Julius Caesar assassinated.

42 Cleopatra wins love of Marc Antony.

31 Augustus Caesar conquers Egypt.
   Antony and Cleopatra commit suicide.

27 Augustus Caesar founds Roman Empire.

AD

1 Jesus Christ born.

30 Lion Temple built in Kush.

60 Rome conquers Mesopotamia.

67 *Periplus of Erythraen Sea* written.
   St. Paul and St. Peter martyred.

97 Chinese expedition to Persian Gulf.

146 Septimus Severus born at Leptis Magna; becomes Roman emperor, 193.

200 Nok culture fades away; Ghana begins.

250 Nasca culture.

300 Mississippi Valley mound builders.

306 Constantine the Great ascends throne.

313 Christianity becomes state religion of Rome.

320 Gupta Dynasty in India.

326 Constantinople founded; Roman Empire split.

DATE AD	EVENTS IN AFRICA	DATE AD	ASIA	EUROPE	DATE AD	AMERICAS
333	King Ezana of Axum becomes a Christian.					
350	Axum supersedes Kush.					
354	St. Augustine born at Carthage.					
429	Vandals invade North Africa.					
450	Zimbabwe construction begins(?).	455		Vandals sack Rome.		
500	Rise of Ghana. Van Niekerk inhabited.					
525	Ellesbaas becomes king of Ethiopia.	527		Justinian becomes emperor of Byzantium.		
534	Justinian's Byzantine expedition conquers North Africa.					
571	Yoruba migrations from Upper Egypt begin(?).	571	Mohammed born.			
600	Greeks establish Cyrene.	600	China united under Siu Dynasty.	Mongols invade Europe.		
		618	T'ang Dynasty in China.			
		622	Hegira; start of the Moslem era.			
700	So tribes settle Kanem (Lake Chad). Bantu peoples spread out.					
702	Axumite expedition sacks Jedda, port of Mecca; Arabs retaliate, occupy Red Sea Coast, smash Azanian culture.	711		Moslems from North Africa conquer Spain.	731	Mayan Empire at peak.
		732		Moslem invaders defeated at Tours.	750	Toltec Empire.
800	Kanem develops.	800		Charlemagne crowned.		
		850	First book printed in China.			
		866	Fujiwara era begins in Japan.			
870	Eldad the Danite writes.	871		Alfred the Great rules in England.		
900	First dynasty established in Benin.; Mapungubwe site in use. Penhalonga culture at Penhalonga, Niekerk and Inyanga. Ghana at its peak.	900	Al Masudi writing.			

950 Kilwa established. University of Cairo founded.

960 Sung Dynasty in China.

975 Falashas, under Judith the Fire, ravage Ethiopia.

987 Mayan Empire declines.

1000 Leif Ericson discovers North America (?).

1016 King Canute begins reign.

1050 Baghdad University founded.
Chichen Itza built. Inca civilization flourishes.

1054 Almoravid Moslems invade Ghana.

1061 Beni Halil Moslems invade North Africa.

1066 Norman invasion of England.

1076 Almoravids capture Ghana's capital.

1096 Crusades begin. Angkor Wat begun.
First Crusade.

1146 Second Crusade.

1150 Ethiopian stone churches; Lalibala.
Al Idrisi writing.
Mixtecs at zenith.

1161 Gunpowder used in China.

1165 Prester John's "letter" delivered. Universities in Spain.

1189 Third Crusade.

1200 Ife terra cottas produced.
Mongol Empire; Genghis Khan.
Fourth Crusade.

1203 Sosso king, Sumanguru, captures Kumbi Saleh. Kanem reaches peak; Mai Dunama.

1215 Magna Carta.

1216 Fifth Crusade.

1235 Mandinke chief Sundiata defeats Sumanguru.

1260 Kubla Khan rules China.

1265 Dante born.

1270 Literary flowering in Ethiopia.
Eighth and last Crusade.
Aztecs at height of power.

1290 Ottoman Dynasty in Turkey.

1295 Marco Polo returns to Venice.

1300 Mansa Kankan Musa rules Mali.

1304 Ibn Battuta born.

1324 Mansa Musa's hajj to Mecca.

1325 Gao captured by Mali; Mali at zenith.

1337 Mansa Musa dies.

1338 Hundred Years' War begins.

1341 Sunni Ali Kolon takes Gao.

DATE AD	EVENTS IN AFRICA	DATE AD	ASIA	EUROPE	DATE AD	AMERICAS
1350	Black plague in North Africa.	1348	Black plague strikes.	Black plague strikes.		
		1368	Ming Dynasty in China.			
1400	Rise of Monomotapa.	1394		Prince Henry the Navigator born.	1400	Hiawatha.
		1431		Joan of Arc burned at stake.		
1450	Rise of Bornu. D'Aveiro of Benin.	1453	Turks take Byzantium.	Hundred Years' War ends.		
		1456		Gutenberg prints first Bible.		
1464	Sunni Ali Ber becomes Songhay king. Leo Africanus sees Timbuktu.					
1487	Portuguese missions to Ethiopia.					
1488	Diaz rounds Cape of Good Hope.					
1492	Sunni Ali Ber drowns.	1492		Moors and Jews driven from Spain. Columbus sails from Spain.		
1493	Askia Muhammed seizes Songhay throne.	1497	Vasco de Gama's voyage to India.		1497	Cabot discovers North America.
1505	Portuguese sack, loot and destroy cities of Zanj.					
1506	Changamire challenges Monomotapa.				1510	Period of Spanish Conquistadores.
1508	Lebna Dengel becomes king of Ethiopia. Slave trade begins.	1517		Martin Luther demands reforms.	1519	Cortes invades Mexico.
1520	Father Alvarez reports on Ethiopia.	1520	Suleiman I, the Magnificent. Turkish power at zenith.			
1526	Leo Africanus' book on Africa written.	1526	Mogul Dynasty in India.			
1527	Ethiopia attacked in Moslem holy war.					
1528	Songhay at zenith. Askia Muhammed deposed.	1529		Turks besiege Vienna.		
1541	Portuguese expedition helps Ethiopia defeat Moslem invaders.				1531	Pizzaro conquers Incas.

Year	Africa	World	Americas / Europe
1558		Elizabeth I of England ascends throne.	
1564		Shakespeare born.	
1570	Changamires oust Portuguese and Monomotapas.		
1588		Spanish Armada defeated.	
1591	Sultan Mulay Ahmed's expedition defeats Songhay armies.		
1600	Forts built at Khami.	Tokugawa Ieyasu establishes Shogunate in Japan.	Slavery introduced into Americas. English arrive in New England.
1616		Galileo faces Inquisition.	
1617	Kanem-Bornu at zenith; Mai Idris Alooma killed in battle.		
1618	Sultan Mulay-Zidan recalls Moroccan expeditionary forces from Sudan.		
1644		Manchu Dynasty in China.	
1645		Cromwell and Puritans rule England.	
1650	Dhlo-Dhlo culture active. Khami culture flourishing.		
1656			Witchcraft trials in Salem, Massachusetts. Spain and Portugal in Latin America; Dutch, French and British in North and Central America.
1683		Turks invade Vienna.	
1697			Spanish governor destroys Itza capital.
1700	Engaruka culture active. Penhalonga culture declines.		Century of the slave trade.
1712			Slave revolt, New York.
1750	Latest evidence of Zimbabwe construction. Van Niekerk declines.		
1776			American colonies declare independence.
1794			Whitney invents cotton gin; slave trade accelerates.

◁▷ ◁▷ ◁▷ ◁▷ ◁▷ ◁▷ ◁▷ ◁▷ ◁▷ ◁▷ ◁▷

BIBLIOGRAPHY

◁▷ ◁▷ ◁▷ ◁▷ ◁▷ ◁▷ ◁▷ ◁▷ ◁▷ ◁▷ ◁▷

ADAMS, WM. Y.
  "Post-Pharaonic Nubia, II." *Journal of Egyptian Archeology,*
  1965.
ALDRED, CYRIL.
  Egypt to the End of the Old Kingdom. New York: McGraw-Hill,
  1965.
——*The Development of Ancient Egyptian Art.* London: Alec
  Tiranti, 1952.
——*Middle Kingdom Art in Ancient Egypt.* London: Alec Tiranti,
  1956.

——*New Kingdom Art in Ancient Egypt*. London: Alec Tiranti, 1951.

——*Akhnaten*. London: Thames & Hudson, 1968.

ARKELL, A. J.
   A History of the Sudan, 2nd edition. London: The Athlone Press, 1961.

BARBOSA, DUARTE.
   The Book of Duarte Barbosa (translated by M. L. Dames). London: Hakluyt Society, 1918.

BLYDEN, DR. E. W.
   Christianity, Islam and the Negro Race. London: W. B. Whittingham & Co., 1888.

BEKRI, AL (ABD ALLAH IBN ABD AL-AZIZ).
   Description de l'Afrique Septentrionale (translated by Slane). Paris: Impr. Impériale, 1859.

BATTUTA, IBN (MOHAMMED IBN ABD ALLAH).
   Travels in Asia and Africa, 1325–1354 (translated by H. A. R. Gibb). New York: R. M. McBride & Co., 1929.

BARTH, HENRY.
   Travels and Discoveries in North and Central Africa, 1849–1855. New York: D. Appleton & Co., 1857.

BACON, R. H. S.
   Benin, the City of Blood. London: E. Arnold, 1897.

BOHANNAN, PAUL.
   Africa and Africans. Garden City, New York: Natural History Press, 1964.

BOVILL, E.W.
   Golden Trade of the Moors, 2nd edition. New York: Oxford University Press, 1958.

BUXTON, DAVID.
   Travels in Ethiopia. New York: Praeger, 1967.

CAILLIAND, FREDERIC.
   Voyage á Meroe, 4 vols. Paris: Impr. Royale, 1826–27.

CASSON, LIONEL.
    Ancient Egypt. New York: Time-Life Books, 1965.
CASTANHOSA.
    Portuguese Expedition to Abyssinia in 1541–1543 (translated by
    Whiteway). London: Hakluyt Society, 1902.
CATON-THOMPSON, G.
    The Zimbabwe Culture: Ruins and Reactions. 1931.
COLE, SONIA.
    The Prehistory of East Africa. New York: MacMillan Co., 1963.
COTTREL, LEONARD.
    The Lost Pharaohs. New York: Holt, Rinehart & Winston, 1961.

DAVIDSON, BASIL.
    The African Past. Boston: Atlantic-Little, Brown, 1964.
    ———*A History of West Africa.* Garden City, New York: Anchor
    Books, Doubleday & Co., 1966.
    ———*The Lost Cities of Africa.* Boston: Little, Brown & Co., 1959.
DAVIS, W. Y.
    "Post Pharaonic Nubia in the Light of Archeology, I." *Journal
    of Egyptian Archeology,* 1964, 103–120.
DE GRAFT-JOHNSON, J. C.
    African Glory. New York: Walker & Co., 1954.
DIXON, D. M.
    "The Origins of the Kings of Kush." *Journal of Egyptian Arche-
    ology,* 1964, 121ff.
DORESSE, J.
    L'Empire du Prêtre Jean, Paris: Plon, 1957.

EDRISI, AL (ABU ABDALLAH MOHAMMED BEN MOHAMMED).
    An Abridgement of his Geography (Geograph Nubiensa). (n.p.)
    Rome, 1592.
    ———*Description de l'Afrique et de l'Espagne* (translated by R. Dozy
    and M. J. de Goeje). Leyde(n): E. J. Brill, 1866.
EQUIANO, OLAUDAH.
    *The Interesting Narrative of the Life of Olaudah Equiano, or
    Gustavus Vassa, the African.* (n.p.), London, 1789.

EQUIANO, OLAUDAH.
The Interesting Narrative of the Life of Olaudah Equiano, or Gustavus Vassa, the African. (n.p.), London, 1789.

FAGE, J. D.
An Introducton to the History of West Africa, 3rd edition. Cambridge, England: University Press, 1962.

FAGG, WILLIAM.
The Sculpture of Africa. New York: Praeger, 1958.

FAIRSERVIS, WALTER A.
The Ancient Kingdoms of the Nile. New York: Thomas Y. Crowell, 1962.

FLINT, JOHN E.
Nigeria and Ghana. Englewood Cliffs, New Jersey: Prentice-Hall, 1966.

FROBENIUS, L.
Histoire de la Civilisation Africaine. Paris, 1952.

HAMILTON, R. A., ED.
History and Archeology in Africa. (Report of a conference held in July, 1953 at the School of Oriental and African Studies, London University). London, 1955.

HANSBERRY, WM. L.
"Ancient Kush, Old Aethiopia and the Balad Es Sudan." *Journal of Human Relations,* 1960, vol. viii, no. 3,4.

HEEREN, ARNOLD H.
Historical Researches into the Politics, Intercourse and Trade of the Carthaginians, Ethiopians and Egyptians, 2nd edition. Oxford: D. A. Talboys, 1838.

HINTZE, FRITZ AND URSULA.
Civilizations of the Old Sudan. Amsterdam: Edition Leipzig, 1968.

HOSKINS, G. A.
Travels in Ethiopia Above the Second Cataract of the Nile. (n.p.), London, 1835.

HOWE, RUSSELL, W.
   Black Africa. New York: Walker & Co., 1966.
HURRY, JAMIESON B.
   Imhotep, the Vizier and Physician of King Zoser. London: Oxford University Press, 1928.

INGHAM, KENNETH
   A History of East Africa (revised edition). New York: Praeger, 1965.

JONES, A. H. M. AND ELIZABETH MONROE.
   A History of Abyssinia. Oxford: University Press, 1935.

KÂTI, MAHMOÛD.
   Tarikh el-Fettach (translated by Houdas and Delafosse). Paris: Leroux, 1913.
KEATING, REX.
   Nubian Twilight. New York: Harcourt, Brace & World, 1963.
KHALDOUN, IBN (ABD AL-RAHMAN IBN MUHAMMAD).
   Histoire des Berberes et des Dynasties Musulmanes de l'Afrique Septentrionale (translated by de Slane). Paris: P. Geunthner, 1925.

LEO AFRICANUS (HASSAN IBN MOHAMMED EL WAZZAN EL ZAYYATI).
   History and Description of Africa (translated by Pory, 1600). London: Hakluyt Society, 1896.
LIPSKY, GEORGE A.
   Ethiopia. New Haven: Hraf Press, 1962.

MAS'UDI, AL (ABDUL HASSAN IBN HUSSEIN IBN ALI).
   Meadows of Gold and Mines of Gems (translated by A. Sprenger). London: Oriental Translation Fund, 1841.
MERTZ, BARBARA.
   Temples, Tombs and Hieroglyphs. New York: Coward-McCann, 1964.

MURDOCK, GEORGE P.
> *Africa, Its Peoples and Their Culture History.* New York: McGraw-Hill, 1959.

NICKERSON, JANE S.
> *A Short History of North Africa.* New York: Devin-Adair Co., 1961.

OLIVER, ROLAND.
> *The Dawn of African History.* London: Oxford University Press, 1961.

OLIVER, ROLAND AND J.D. FAGE.
> *A Short History of Africa.* Baltimore, Md.: Penguin Books, 1962.

POSENER, GEORGES.
> *Dictionary of Egyptian Civilization.* New York: Tudor Publishing Co., 1959.

SCHOFF, W. H. (TRANSLATOR).
> *Periplus of the Erythraen Sea.* Leipzig: W. Druglin, 1913.

SHINNIE, MARGARET.
> *Ancient African Kingdoms.* New York: St. Martin's Press, 1965.

SHINNIE, P. L.
> *Meroe.* New York: Praeger, 1967.

ULLENDORFF, EDWARD.
> *The Ethiopians.* London: Oxford University Press, 1960.

WELCH, GALBRAITH.
> *Africa Before They Came.* New York: Wm. Morrow & Co., 1965.

WELLARD, JAMES.
> *Lost Worlds of Africa.* New York: E. P. Dutton & Co., 1967.

WILLIAMS, JOHN A.
> *Africa, Her History, Lands and People,* 2nd edition revised. New York: Cooper Square Publishers, 1965.

◁▷ ◁▷ ◁▷ ◁▷ ◁▷ ◁▷

INDEX

◁▷ ◁▷ ◁▷ ◁▷ ◁▷ ◁▷

Note: entries recorded in boldface indicate figure numbers.

916   B79   108-72

Brooks
GREAT CIVILIZATIONS OF ANCIENT
AFRICA

916   B79   108-72

Brooks
GREAT CIVILIZATIONS OF
ANCIENT AFRICA

DATE DUE	BORROWER'S NAME
OC 2 '71	Joan Countryman
MR 24 '72	Sara P Scattergood 4/3
DEC 6 1973	S.P.S.
	KIRK STEVENS